THE FLEXIBILITY PARADIGM

THE FLEXIBILITY PARADIGM

Humanizing the Workplace for Productivity, Profitability, and Possibility

Manar Sweillam Morales

Georgetown University Press
Washington, DC

The publisher is not responsible for third-party websites or their content. URL links were active at time of publication.

Library of Congress Cataloging-in-Publication Data

Names: Morales, Manar, author.
Title: The flexibility paradigm : humanizing the workplace for productivity, profitability, and possibility / Manar Morales.
Description: Washington, DC : Georgetown University Press, 2025. | Includes bibliographical references and index.
Identifiers: LCCN 2024011624 (print) | LCCN 2024011625 (ebook) | ISBN 9781647125301 (hardcover) | ISBN 9781647125318 (ebook)
Subjects: LCSH: Flexible work arrangements. | Work environment. | Corporate culture.
Classification: LCC HD5109 .M673 2025 (print) | LCC HD5109 (ebook) | DDC 331.25/72—dc23/eng/20240730
LC record available at https://lccn.loc.gov/2024011624
LC ebook record available at https://lccn.loc.gov/2024011625

♾ This paper meets the requirements of ANSI/NISO Z39.48-1992 (Permanence of Paper).

28 27 26 25   9 8 7 6 5 4 3 2   First printing

Printed in the United States of America

Cover design by Elisha Zepeda, Faceout Studio
Interior design by Robert Kern, TIPS Publishing Services, Carrboro, NC

This book is dedicated to my dad and in memoriam of my mom. Without your love, guidance, and unwavering support throughout my life, none of this would have been possible. You taught me that anything is possible when we put our minds to it. You instilled in me the belief that dreams are worth pursuing and that the journey is as important as the destination.

CONTENTS

ACKNOWLEDGMENTS

I would like to express my heartfelt gratitude to my family, especially my husband, David Morales, and our boys, Jacob, Joseph, and James, for being the unwavering pillars of support in my life. Your love, humor, and encouragement have been my greatest motivators, reminding me to stay positive and providing the fuel that propels me forward each day. I am blessed to have you as my biggest cheering squad.

To my father, Dr. Attia Sweillam, who has always taught me to do my best and believe that everything is possible with faith and courage, I owe an immense debt of gratitude. Your unconditional love, support, and unwavering belief in me have carried me through every phase of my life. Your wisdom and guidance have been a guiding light on my journey.

I extend my sincere appreciation to the incredible Diversity & Flexibility Alliance team. There is no better group to work with, and your dedication to the mission of creating human-centered workplaces is truly inspiring. To our Alliance members, who continually strive to be the best they can be and unite as a community committed to fostering human-centric cultures that promote belonging, flexibility, and organizational well-being—your collective efforts are changing the world for the better.

I am deeply grateful to the leaders who generously shared their stories, experiences, and wisdom for this book. Your contributions will undoubtedly serve as a source of inspiration for others, creating a ripple effect of positive change in the world.

Thank you to Hilary Claggett, who believed in this project from the very beginning and encouraged me to bring it to print. I want to offer a special thanks to Emma Simpkins, whose meticulous attention to detail significantly improved this book. Your dedication to perfection is greatly appreciated. To Amanda Rooker,

I am grateful for your invaluable assistance in organizing my myriad thoughts and ideas.

Lastly, but certainly not least, I owe a debt of gratitude to Tami Booth Corwin. Your tireless efforts and determination were instrumental in bringing this book to fruition, making it better with each passing day. Your commitment to this project did not go unnoticed, and I am deeply thankful for your support.

Thank you all for being a part of this incredible journey. Your contributions have made this book a reality, and I am forever indebted to each and every one of you.

INTRODUCTION

The Best of All Worlds

Imagine if there was one culture shift that would inspire your employees to be more engaged, efficient, and committed. Imagine if this key shift also allowed you to attract, retain, and develop top talent, as well as increase performance and productivity while reducing costs.

Imagine if you could build on your strengths as an organization and create the best of all worlds, where your people's highest potential was unleashed regardless of where, when, or how long they worked!

You don't have to imagine it. Many great organizations have already transformed their cultures and reaped the benefits by adopting this key culture shift—the shift to a human-centered culture with flexibility at its core.

Flexibility in the workplace is not a new concept; it's been around for decades. But it became both a fixture and a flashpoint because of COVID-19. It was hotly debated in the headlines as companies grappled with the transition from a reliance on virtual work to the return to office, sometimes flip-flopping on their policies when they didn't get the results they hoped for. The challenges organizations faced as they tried to implement flexible work policies often resulted from organizations defining flexibility through a narrow lens, focusing solely on how often their employees should work in or out of the office.

But true flexibility is much broader and more impactful. It's a culture change, not a policy. The proven positive benefits of holistic flexibility—*when effectively implemented*—have been consistently confirmed.

Flexibility is here to stay. A recent survey from The Conference Board showed that among US workers, 65 percent said that having workplace flexibility was the most important non-salary compensation element of all—above bonuses, generous time off, and so on. The survey suggests that flexibility is not only good for people, but also for business. According to Rita Meyerson, EdD, principal researcher at The Conference Board, flexibility "opens new avenues in the competition for talent. Unlike salaries, bonuses, health care or retirement plans, workplace flexibility is the rare employee benefit that can save—rather than drain—financial resources, giving an advantage to companies that plan proactively."[1]

I've seen these results in my decades of work helping clients transform their organizational culture into one that benefits people as well as productivity and profit. Along with my team at the organization I founded, the Diversity & Flexibility Alliance, I've helped organizations focus on flexibility, diversity, inclusion, and well-being to help them be the best they can be. My work with clients, helping them attract and retain great talent and creating more diverse and inclusive workplaces, kept leading me to the same conclusion: that flexibility had to be at the core of a culture to produce these results. Since I came to this conclusion years ago, I've helped countless organizations develop practices and policies to incorporate this into their cultures with great success.

I didn't set out to become a flexibility expert; in fact, I started my career as an attorney specializing in labor law. But through a series of events, flexibility transformed my life in ways that I never imagined possible

In 2001, I was an employment litigator, representing clients on labor relations and employment law cases. I dedicated long hours to a profession I was passionate about. I was also married with a new baby, my firstborn son Jacob.

Initially, I was certain that I would continue working as an attorney, as it was an integral part of my identity. However, like many new parents, you can't truly anticipate your emotions until you are immersed in parenthood. I distinctly remember growing increasingly anxious about our childcare situation—calling home during my workday to check on Jacob or reassure myself that he was safe. As a litigator, I occasionally had to travel on short notice, which added to my conflicted feelings. I soon realized that change was necessary.

The prevailing advice at the time was to transition from litigation to more advisory work. The challenge was that I genuinely enjoyed being a litigator and did not want to give up my passion. I was determined to continue litigating but on a reduced hours schedule that did not involve travel. While it may have seemed impossible, I was resolute in finding a position that allowed me to align my career aspirations and personal life. With adjustments both at home and in the office, as well as support from others, I believed I could maintain a fulfilling career while nurturing my personal life.

I eventually secured a position that allowed me to continue litigating on a reduced hours basis without the need for travel. Importantly, reduced hours did not mean reduced commitment—I continued to provide my clients with 100 percent dedication, albeit I had fewer clients. Eventually, I started working from home and going to the office when necessary and began teaching as an adjunct faculty member at Georgetown University. My family expanded to three boys, Jacob, Joseph, and James, and I was able to actively participate in life outside of work.

It dawned on me that I was building a robust career and personal life by seeking out work that offered autonomy, enabling me to decide when and where to work while also spending time with my family. As I created a more flexible career path for myself, women who had left their careers often expressed to me, "If I was given the flexibility afforded to you, I would not have left the workforce." I would often ponder why we couldn't create work environments where flexibility was accessible to everyone, rather than being a privilege for only a select few.

It wasn't just a few who felt the push and pull between work and family; it was a topic that was simmering in workplaces everywhere and exploded in the media when *New York Times* journalist Lisa Belkin coined the term "opt-out revolution" to describe the trend of highly qualified women leaving their careers.[2] A heated debate erupted around this topic—were women leaving because the pull of family was greater than the pull of work, or were they pushed out of rigid, inflexible workplaces?

In an article in *Harvard Business Review*, Sylvia Ann Hewlett and Carolyn Buck Luce did a deep dive into the existing data and they explained the many factors that were driving this trend. Yes, women were leaving at rates much higher than men, and it was a mix of contributing factors: for many, it was to care for children, but for others it was to care for elderly parents or other family members. Another trend exacerbated this one: the traditional division of labor at home put the onus on women to carry more of the workload of home and family. Importantly, there were push factors that were as powerful, including a lack of flexibility in the workplace. Flexible work policies were not the norm, but the need for flexibility was clear.[3]

So in 2006, I began to look more closely at the intersection of diversity and flexibility and work with organizations to address these issues. In 2012, I started the Diversity & Flexibility Alliance, a membership organization and consultancy dedicated to creating human-centric workplaces that advance belonging, flexibility, and workplace well-being.

Since that pivotal time, I have conducted research, studied trends, interviewed experts, and counseled hundreds of leaders from myriad organizations. For over seventeen years I have personally seen what works and what doesn't when it comes to workplace flexibility. I've seen the proven benefits for organizations and individuals including increased productivity, talent retention, greater diversity and profitability, and higher engagement and job satisfaction, to name a few. I've come to understand the shift in mindset that needs to take place for organizations to embrace and adopt flexible work policies and practices that *really work* for both the business and the employee.

MAKING THE SHIFT

Before the COVID-19 pandemic, I spent most of my time convincing leaders that flexibility was good for business. I worked with one chair of a law firm who asked the question many leaders were asking at the time: "Flexibility may be good for the individual, but what's it going to do for the firm?" This candid question revealed a concern that flexibility may not be good for business.

Some hesitated to accept this new way of thinking because of personal bias—it was not how they had it as they came up in their firms, so why should future generations have it easier? They recalled the long hours they worked in the office as a prerequisite for being promoted, so it was hard to accept that younger generations might not have to do it the same way. Still others had misperceptions about productivity or collaboration—such as, you have to be in the office to be productive or to collaborate, don't you?

Some were simply used to working in the office. They had been successful working this way in the past, so why change? Baxter Credit Union (BCU), among the top 5 percent of credit unions in the United States, successfully implemented flexibility into their culture, but its chief executive officer (CEO), Mike Valentine, was initially reluctant. He explained, "I never thought when COVID-19 hit, that within two to three weeks, we would have deployed 98 percent of our employees to their homes. I would have said you're nuts because we're a financial institution and financial institutions require people onsite to run the business. Before that, I remember when people asked if they could work from home, I'd say, no, no, no, you've got to come to the office!"

Where does Valentine land on flexibility today? In his words: "I was wrong. Because this is the world we're in and it's real—and it's working." (I'll share much more about Valentine and BCU's evolution in chapter 9.)[4]

Trust me, many people are hesitant at first, but even the most skeptical, work-should-be-done-in-the-office executives come around when they understand the business case for flexibility. My first step when working with an organization is to help leadership understand the true nature and value of flexibility—which often includes clearing up myths and misperceptions first so that they can reset their mindset and reframe the conversation. Then I help them create their own unique business case for flexibility. Once executives understand the impact that flexibility has on the bottom line, they support it wholeheartedly.

I remember working with a client—an American Lawyer (AmLaw) 100 firm—that wanted to create a promotion process for people working on a reduced hours schedule, but in their entire history, they had never promoted an associate to partner who worked on a reduced hours schedule. How many talented attorneys quit in frustration because of that? I worked with the firm to reframe the prevailing misperceptions they had. I explained that if an associate reduces their hours to 70 percent, it doesn't mean they are now only 70 percent committed to each client. They are still 100 percent committed to their clients; they just have fewer of them. This shift in thinking really resonated with them and opened the door for change.

Another prevalent misperception was that flexibility is simply a policy. But when organizations only invest in creating a policy without first articulating the why behind the policy, and without focusing on successfully putting it into practice, it just doesn't work. Flexibility is not a policy; it's an organization-wide culture change. I witnessed many organizations create flexible work policies that collected dust in human resources manuals. In those organizations, the policy was hastily rolled out without support and effective communication, and the success of the entire initiative was compromised. The unconscious and conscious biases and stigma against flexibility in these organizations were palpable. As a result, employees were afraid to utilize the policies for fear of negatively impacting their careers or losing the best project assignments.

Alternatively, I witnessed successful launches of flexibility initiatives that had the backing of management and included communication and support from all organizational leaders. Those leaders who were willing to initiate the cultural changes needed to support a flexibility policy were able to transform their workforce from a group of tired, underengaged individuals on the verge of walking out the door to an enthusiastic, balanced, supportive, and efficient team.

THE COVID-19 TIPPING POINT

By 2019, more and more companies were talking about flexibility and taking steps toward changing their workplaces for the better. In fact, the number of companies offering flexible work options was increasing (from 52 percent in 2015 to 57 percent in 2019 according to one study).[5] At the same time, many of those companies hadn't quite gotten it right, and other companies had not invested in it yet.

Then, in 2020, the pandemic hit and accelerated the evolution of the workplace at a dizzying speed.

COVID-19 didn't just change where we work. Working at home wasn't new. What was new was the scale at which it happened. Never before had so many people worked virtually at once.

COVID-19 also prompted what some called the *great reflection.* Workers took a step back to reevaluate how work fit into their lives; their values and priorities changed. Organizations had to respond to the new demands of their workforce. They had to change how they led to meet the evolving needs of the workforce they had, not the workforce they used to have.

COVID-19 not only changed the workplace; to some extent, it changed everything. It changed *us.*

This global crisis resulted in a global opportunity.

THE BEST OF ALL WORLDS

Since the COVID-19 pandemic, organizations in every industry have continued to experiment with and roll out new ways of working that support business objectives and provide employees with opportunities for autonomy, growth, and improved well-being.

This COVID-19-driven group experiment resulted in incredible learning and innovative ideas about how to reimagine the future of work.

But it isn't just COVID-19 driving these changes. The workplace has been rapidly evolving due to shifting demographics that have changed the complexion of the workforce. The majority of US workers today are Millennials and Gen Z. These generations are digital-first and have very different values. They don't want jobs that lead to high levels of stress. They want time and space for their personal lives. They want professional growth. They want leaders who have empathy and workplaces where they belong.

It's not just younger workers who feel this way. The majority of workers want—or expect—more flexible workplaces that are responsive to their needs.[6] But there is a growing disparity between what workers want and what employers want to give. A recent Ernst & Young Global Limited (EY) survey showed that 47 percent of companies want employees in the office at least two or three days per week, but 84 percent of workers want to come in one day per week or less.[7]

We're also seeing enormous changes driven by technology, which touches every aspect of work either directly or indirectly. Because of the acceleration of technology, like artificial intelligence and automation, the most valuable job skills will shift away from those a machine can do to those that require what humans do best. According to World Economic Forum, the core skills that companies find most important include analytical thinking, creative thinking, resilience, flexibility, and agility.[8] Developing and nurturing a workforce with these skills is essential for organizations to meet their business goals. Bringing out the best in talent requires organizations to focus on people first.

To build and manage future-ready organizations, to meet the needs of the current and future workforce, leaders must intentionally cultivate a shift to human-centered culture.

So how do we build this new future?

We have to work from where we are today, and that looks different for every company. Some are embracing flexibility and thriving; some know they want flexible work but don't know how to implement it. Many companies are still struggling with the concept of flexibility, even flip-flopping from full flexibility to return-to-office mandates as they try to figure out what will work for their organizations. Some are coming out against flexibility because when they tried to implement it, their efforts fell short. Some leaders say they lost culture when employees worked virtually, others felt they couldn't collaborate well, and still others felt their employees couldn't be trusted to work virtually.

The problem isn't flexibility. The problem is the way flexibility is being positioned and implemented. The organizations struggling are those that issued flex policies without building infrastructure or changing their cultures to support them.

If you're a leader of a law firm, accounting firm, or other professional services organization, I know you have concerns about workplace flexibility that are specific to your industry. Many workplace flexibility strategies and resources from large consultancies don't quite fit the client-focused, billable-hour, partnership-based culture. Client service excellence and mentorship are key priorities, and many leaders I've talked with aren't yet convinced flexible work options can fulfill these priorities as effectively as working in the office with a set schedule. These leaders fear that they will lose important aspects of their culture if their employees work from home.

If you're a leader in industries that rely on creativity or innovation, you might be concerned that flexibility can lead to a loss of collaboration. Or if you're in an industry that requires most employees to work on-site—healthcare, retail, education, manufacturing—you might see the need to address issues like burnout and talent retention, but you might believe that flexibility is not an option for you. As you'll read throughout the book, flexibility is not a one-size-fits-all approach.

Flexibility does not only mean working virtually—there are also many other ways to apply it regardless of industry.

While many leaders view flexibility in terms of what they will lose, they actually have a lot to gain. As we'll cover in chapter 2, flexibility has a strong business case: it drives productivity, talent, diversity, engagement, sustainability, business continuity, and ultimately profitability. But flexibility has a lot more to offer than a strong business case. It also allows you to unlock the full potential of your people. It offers increased *purpose* and *possibility*, and it allows employees an opportunity to better live their whole work and personal lives in alignment. As Accenture's 2021 Future of Work Report stated, "Work is not so much about place . . . as it is about helping people to reach their full potential."[9] Organizations can help their workers reach that potential through cultures of flexibility.

To receive all the benefits of flexibility, you need more than a policy. I often tell leaders, "Policies won't bring people back; experiences will." To create the *return on experience* (ROE) required to make flexibility work, you need a *shift in perspective* to see flexibility as a way to strengthen your organization, and you need *an organization-wide culture change* to support this shift. For that, you need a framework.

The Flexibility Paradigm: Humanizing the Workplace for Productivity, Profitability, and Possibility offers you the paradigm shift, strategy, and framework organizations across industries need to create an entire culture that allows their organization to build on their strengths and lead the future of work.

In chapters 1–3, we'll cover the basics of what we call *holistic flexibility*, defining what it is and what it isn't, its history, and its business case. We'll also preview the foundations of the Flex Success® Framework.

In chapters 4–8, we'll cover the Flex Success Framework in detail, developed from hundreds of conversations with organizations, as well as the Alliance's own research analyzing workplace flexibility, inclusivity, and diversity trends over the past ten-plus years. It's helped organizations successfully transition to flexible work in a way that works for all, and it can help yours, too.

The Flex Success Framework includes the five Rs:

1. *Reflect*: Establish a Compelling Purpose
2. *Reimagine*: Create a Shared Vision
3. *Redesign*: Design the Initiative
4. *Reintegrate*: Integrate Flexibility into the Culture
5. *Reinforce*: Measure the Impact

In chapter 9, we'll illustrate how the framework is implemented, step-by-step, by presenting in-depth case studies drawn from the legal and financial industries. Finally, in chapter 10, we'll look at the future of flexibility, and its place in human-centered culture at the intersection of flexibility, inclusion, and well-being.

Since 2006, I have been dedicated to helping organizations humanize the workplace through flexible work options. I want to help you to do the same.

Through real-life examples and the step-by-step Flex Success Framework, *The Flexibility Paradigm* will show you how to build a more effective and more efficient workforce for the future. You'll be equipped to maintain and even increase your market share and transform disengaged employees into inspired and engaged team members. You'll learn how to bridge the gap between policy and practice, so that your organization gains the benefits of flexibility while avoiding the pitfalls, and your employees will know that flexibility is genuinely supported and encouraged by all in leadership. You'll also receive tips on how to support your workforce with technology, systems, tracking programs, and management incentives. While I will draw from my experience in the professional services industry in the United States, I include examples from across industries, many of which have global workforces. The concepts are widely transferrable because flexibility is fundamentally about human-centered values, and that applies everywhere.

I am passionate about flexibility and hope you will be, too. Flexibility is not just a lifestyle perk or a post-COVID-19 pandemic trend. It is an effective tool that can transform your workforce and impact your bottom line. If implemented correctly, flexibility has very few downsides. If you want your organization to be competitive and recruit the very best employees, if you want to keep your employees engaged and performing to their full potential, it's time to implement a successful flexibility initiative today.

You may be thinking, *I don't have time for a full organizational culture change right now.* I deliberately designed this book to provide you with all the relevant data, information, and step-by-step framework to develop a successful culture of flexibility within your organization. Every chapter has real-life examples from leaders just like you who have found the value of holistic flexibility, and end-of-chapter reflection questions that help guide you on your organization's unique path. After reading this book, you will know exactly what you need to do and how you will avoid the mistakes of others. The longer you wait, the more quality people you're going to lose and the more profits you're going to sacrifice. Simply put, you can't afford to wait.

Once you have read this book and understand the five critical steps to ensure that your flexibility initiative is implemented correctly and effectively, outlined in the Flex Success Framework, you will not only be able to develop and implement a successful flexible work initiative, but you will also be on the leading edge of your industry, ready to thrive as technologies and work environments continue to change.

Holistic flexibility is here to stay, and our learning curve has just begun.

That's the promise of holistic flexibility.

If that's a vision you can embrace, let's dive in.

REFLECTION QUESTIONS

Before you get started, consider your own views on flexibility in the workplace. Have you ever lost an employee because of rigid expectations about the workplace? Have you had a colleague quit because they were burned out? Do you have preconceived views on flexibility, pro or con? Note these answers. Then, come back to them again after reading the book to assess whether they've deepened or evolved.

1

THE EVOLUTION
OF FLEXIBILITY

After COVID-19 forced a sudden move to virtual work for most companies, the number one question company leaders asked me was, "Is this really going to stick?" Meaning—"How much longer do we have to put up with this online [insert expletive here]?" They wanted to roll the clocks back and walk back into the office, no questions asked, just like they'd always done before.

Yes, there are still plenty of companies that feel that way.

But now that the pandemic stage of COVID-19 has passed, questions have shifted from *whether* companies should offer flexible workplaces to *how* companies can create flexible workplaces that work—for their employees *and* their businesses. Leaders ask me, "If we're too flexible, will we lose productivity?" and "If we're not flexible enough, will we lose people?" They embrace the idea of flexibility but don't always know how to put it into practice, leading to mixed results and uncertainty about how to move forward.

One thing is clear to me after decades of studying this question—flexibility is here to stay. How 9/11 forever changed how we travel, COVID-19 forever changed how we work.

A BRIEF HISTORY OF FLEXIBILITY

Flexibility is not new; it has evolved throughout history, driven by economic crises, geopolitical disruptions, labor market changes, shifting societal norms and values, global competition, and a pandemic.

In the United States, companies first offered flexibility options during the Great Depression. Job sharing was introduced in the 1930s to avoid layoffs, stabilize wages, and keep people working. As the economy recovered, companies phased out these options. In an article published in 1984, social science advisor

1

Martin Nemirow observed that the history of job sharing might help explain the resistance many still felt toward it at the time of his writing—resistance still felt today.[1]

Also, in the 1930s, the W. K. Kellogg Company was the first large corporation in the United States to offer a flexible schedule, changing their schedule from the usual three shifts of eight hours to four shifts of six hours. That initiative lasted only until the beginning of World War II when President Franklin D. Roosevelt required all companies to operate at full capacity to support the war effort.[2]

The gas crisis and growing environmental awareness of the 1970s prompted a new interest in flexible work options. National Aeronautic and Space Administration (NASA) engineer Jack Nilles coined the term "telecommuting" in 1972, and his book *The Telecommunications–Transportation Tradeoff* (1973), considered the founding document of telecommuting, suggests working from home could be a solution to air pollution and long hours spent in traffic.[3]

Interestingly, from the beginning, Nilles believed the widespread adoption of telecommuting would not be based on technology alone, but "organizational—and management—cultural changes were far more important."[4]

In 1979, Frank W. Schiff, vice president and chief economist of the Committee for Economic Development, wrote an article published in the *Washington Post* entitled "Working at Home Can Save Gasoline." In the article, he suggests that if professionals telecommute just a day or two a week, the savings in gas, time spent in traffic, and mental stress could be significant.

Schiff could have made the same arguments for telecommuting today. He points out that the norm of working away from home was established during the Industrial Revolution only because specific working conditions demanded it; service and information-related positions were on the rise, which didn't necessarily require in-person work; and advanced technologies were making working at home more productive.

He also countered common objections we still hear today: "If people are working at home, how can one tell how well they are doing or whether they are working at all?" Schiff's answer: Performance should be measured by results, not hours spent, and those results can usually be measured whether one is working at home or in the office.

To those worried that working from home would leave workers feeling disconnected from coworkers, Schiff responded that (in 1979) most professionals communicated by telephone even in the same office. But even for those who required face-to-face time to feel connected, Schiff recommended telecommuting one or two days per week so they could still communicate in person while working in the office the remainder of the week.

And to those concerned about being overly distracted at home, Schiff responded that the opposite was often true. Distractions abound in the office, and when on a tight deadline, many professionals were already choosing to complete their work at home with fewer interruptions.[5]

As technology advanced, telecommuting became more popular among professional services organizations. Today, we would call telecommuting *working from home*, *virtual work*, *online work*, or *remote work*. The latest buzzword is *hybrid work*, a type of flexibility that combines working at the office and online work, much like Schiff recommended nearly forty years ago.

(You'll note throughout the book that I avoid using the word "remote" whenever possible because it conveys a sense of disconnection, even isolation—two pitfalls of virtual work when it isn't well supported. I prefer the term "virtual" which has a more general and neutral feeling. I also steer clear from the often-used "return-to-work" because it suggests that employees weren't working at home. "Return-to-office" is more appropriate. Words matter, so I suggest taking care with the words you use.)

Over the second half of the twentieth century, the significant rise in women in the labor market created a fundamental shift that made flexibility even more relevant. The percentage of women participating in the workforce increased from 34 percent in 1950 to 60 percent in 2000.[6] More women in the workforce meant more parents and caretakers juggling work and home responsibilities and more dual-career households feeling squeezed for time.

Women still carried more household and parenting responsibilities, and though it has fluctuated, the uneven chore divide remains today.

According to the Pew Research Center, in a survey conducted in January 2023, even as financial contributions became more equal in opposite-sex marriages, the way people divide their time between work and home life remains unbalanced. Data show that in 29 percent of marriages, spouses earn about the same amount. But in these so-called equal marriages, women spend more time on household chores than their spouses (4.6 vs. 2 hours per week) and more time on caregiving responsibilities (6.9 vs. 5 hours per week). In contrast, men spend more time on work (44.2 vs. 41.1 hours per week) and leisure (socializing or relaxing) than their wives (25.2 vs. 21.6 hours per week).[7]

Work-life conflict wasn't the only factor pressuring workers in the latter half of the century. Overworking became a norm during this time, and burnout became a common complaint in the workforce. The topic of burnout or chronic work-related stress was noted starting in the 1970s; its prevalence increased throughout the 80s, 90s, and 2000s; and its effect is still felt today.

In "Beyond Burned Out," a 2021 article in the *Harvard Business Review,* journalist and workplace expert Jennifer Moss describes the proliferation of workplace burnout before COVID-19, citing "overworked, underpaid teachers, nurses and physicians working shifts of 16 hours or more, and the technology sector where overwork is celebrated."[8]

Bill Gates, co-founder and chief executive officer (CEO) at Microsoft, was the poster child of a work-obsessed tech CEO who admitted to going as far as memorizing license plates and scanning parking lots on weekends to see who was working.[9] In a 2011 *Vanity Fair* interview, his co-founder Paul Allen said, "Microsoft was a high-stress environment because Bill drove others as hard as he drove himself."[10] This kind of overwork had a high cost. Around that time, the associated physical and psychological problems of workplace stress were estimated at $125–$190 billion per year in healthcare costs in the United States alone.[11]

Fortunately, in recent years, Gates has been trying to encourage the next generation to avoid making the same mistakes that he did. He suggested that providing flexible work options was the solution to combat burnout and attract the best talent.[12]

In May of 2023, Gates reemphasized this in a commencement address at Northern Arizona University, telling graduates, "You're not a slacker if you cut yourself some slack." Gates said when he was their age, he "pushed everyone around him to work very long hours" and said if he had to do it all over again, he would not prioritize work above all else.[13]

As for Microsoft, the company is now known as one of the best places to work, with one of the highest reviews on Glassdoor.com, one of the world's largest job and recruiting websites known in part for its transparent employee reviews of their employers.

By 2006, when I began researching this concept, many professional services organizations offered what they called *flexible work arrangements*, which included a variety of options such as telecommuting (flexibility in *where* you worked), compressed work weeks (*when* you worked), and reduced hours and job sharing (*how long* you worked).

Although these flexibility policies were technically more widely available, they were highly stigmatized.

Genhi Givings Bailey, chief diversity and inclusion officer at law firm Perkins Coie (one of *Fortune's* "100 Best Places to Work" for 2023), has been a champion in promoting and destigmatizing flexibility and a long-time member of the Diversity & Flexibility Alliance.[14] "I would characterize the early days, especially in the legal industry, as being more rigid regarding flexibility of any kind," Bailey states. "Whether it was flexibility of schedule, of location, or of when the work got done, it was an exception to the rule. There was a stigma around it. Because of this, a lot of people were reticent to talk about a flexible schedule or a schedule that was different from the regular schedule."[15]

That doesn't mean there weren't those who used these policies—and benefitted from them. Eve Howard, partner at Hogan Lovells, says flexibility saved her career and then launched it.

> *Twenty-two years ago, when I had three small boys at home, I was considering whether I could really do the job [as partner] anymore. This was against the backdrop of having lost most of my friends early on to the decision to quit. But I decided that, after having invested fifteen years into the career, I ought to give reduced time a try. I spent the following fifteen years on a reduced schedule, which would have been roughly 80 percent. Flexibility, in my case, meant working less hours overall but not necessarily less in a day. That's how I've always counseled colleagues who consider reduced time in the corporate transactional space—it is not ever a space where you can just say, I don't work Fridays, I don't work evenings. If a client is hiring us for a deal, that just doesn't work. But you can do less deals and take time off between deals in a way that balances it all out.*

And here's how it accelerated her career:

> *I was a partner already. So when my kids got a little older, I had the energy to pursue leadership within my firm. Having had that time of flexibility, I was able to do more and be more impactful in my career than I believe I could have been because otherwise I would have been burned out. Also, there was a myth—or maybe a reality—that reduced time was just a steppingstone to retirement. There weren't role models who had done corporate transactional work this way. So I had to bust the myth that I was on my way out and I was still committed.[16]*

Around that time, Deloitte consultants Cathy Benko and Anne Weisberg also introduced the idea of *mass career customization* (MCC), where the *corporate lattice* is an alternative to the corporate ladder and engagement with work ebbs and flows over time.[17] This idea was notable because it suggested an essential shift in thinking about flexibility. It incorporated flexibility into an organization's core strategy rather than viewing it as an exception or accommodation.

As of today, flexible work options have expanded for the better. "From my first formal introduction to the concept of flexibility in the workplace, to where the legal industry is now, I've seen a positive evolution," said Genhi Givings Bailey.

> *Today it is much more a part of the mainstream. It is not unusual to have someone request a flexible schedule, and organizations have systems in place to help make it easier, such as resources on who you talk to and what options exist in your work environment. I also think the lexicon around flexibility is more integrated into how people talk about work. People are more likely to say, "Here are the ways that I prefer to be communicated with," or "It's easiest to reach me in this way." And that's really refreshing to see.*[18]

THE COVID-19 TIPPING POINT

One undeniable factor in this positive evolution was the COVID-19 pandemic. Companies had to adjust quickly to virtual work to continue operating. The most effective, adaptable leaders figured out new ways of communicating with clients and teams and moved quickly to ensure employee support at home. Many of these companies saw that productivity remained high, and employees appreciated their autonomy to work when they were most efficient while still attending to responsibilities at home.

Bailey recalls that

> *pre-pandemic, we were on track in terms of normalizing the notion of flexibility. The pandemic sort of shot us out of the cannon. And there is no going back. You can use whatever metaphor you want to describe the rapid evolution: we can't slow that train down; we can't put the toothpaste back in the tube. There is no turning back. Flexible work is here to stay. To the extent there were any silver*

linings around the horrible experience of the pandemic, one is that we are embracing flexibility at an even more rapid pace.[19]

McKinsey's inaugural report, *The State of Organizations 2023*, showed that of 2,500 organizations surveyed, 90 percent had embraced some form of hybrid work model for some or most of the time.[20] My research from the Diversity & Flexibility Alliance's *2022 Law Firm Flexibility Benchmarking Study* reflects this shift from pre- to post-pandemic. Of the 68 major law firms surveyed, most offer hybrid or virtual work options, demonstrating a tremendous increase in this type of workplace flexibility (80.9 percent this year vs. 61.1 percent in our *2019 Law Firm Flexibility Benchmarking Study*).[21]

COVID-19 not only moved the needle quickly on adopting flexible work policies but also shone a brighter light on critical issues affecting work. One of the most pressing was the mental health crisis.

In the earlier-referenced *Harvard Business Review* article on burnout, survey results showed that almost a year into the COVID-19 pandemic, 85 percent of respondents experienced a decline in well-being, 56 percent said their job demands increased, and 55 percent said they couldn't balance home and work life. The author suggests that one of the reasons for this was because "we didn't give people control and flexibility" as they juggled home, childcare (including homeschooling), and work.[22]

Some companies that shifted to fully virtual workplaces decided they would rather have their employees return to the office. In many cases, they found that their employees didn't want to return and even ignored the request outright. This tug-of-war between leadership and employees played out dramatically in some cases, laying bare the issues at the heart of the conversation.

Disney was one very public case in point. CEO Bob Iger mandated in January 2023 that all employees return to the office at least four days a week, saying that working together in person would benefit Disney's creativity, culture, and the employees' careers. After Disney issued the mandate, over 2,300 employees signed a petition asking the CEO to reconsider. A *Washington Post* article described this as "another high profile clash over flexible work." It said that "The new mandate, employees argued in the petition, will lead to 'forced resignations among some of our most hard-to-replace talent and vulnerable communities' while 'dramatically reducing productivity, output, and efficiency.'"[23]

A similar debate erupted when JP Morgan's CEO Jamie Dimon made it clear in multiple quotes and conversations that virtual work was not working for him. After trying but failing to get employees back in the office in 2021, the company asked again in 2023 using more assertive language, asking half of its employees to return to the office five days a week and another 40 percent a few days a week. The memo described in *Fortune* also said that a failure to come to the office would result in "appropriate performance management steps."[24]

Many employees reacted negatively, calling the company's mandate "tone-deaf" and "divisive," according to a Reuters report, complaining "about a 'Zoom culture' in which staffers were stuck on virtual conference calls even when present in the office. They also grumbled about the challenges posed by long commutes and family caretaking responsibilities."[25]

CEOs from Goldman Sachs and other Wall Street institutions seemed to be in sync with Dimon,[26] but there were influential executives from the financial world sharing opposing viewpoints just as vocally, notably Sallie Krawcheck, co-founder and CEO of Ellevest and former chief financial officer (CFO) at Citi. She didn't mince words when she commented, telling CNBC, "They were saying we have to get back to the way it was." The problem with that thinking, Krawcheck said, is that the pre-pandemic work environment "worked for white men, not everyone, and certainly not women and underrepresented groups." The most progressive leaders are not looking to return to pre-pandemic ways, Krawcheck said, but instead strive to offer arrangements that work for all employees. She pushed back against the idea that culture can exist only when people are in the office or that full-time in-office attendance is required to get ahead.[27]

At the time of this writing, the state of workplace flexibility is still very much in flux as organizations refine their strategies and practices. This evolution will continue as organizations learn from their individual experiences, ideally iterating as they learn so that flexibility becomes more and more beneficial.

A VUCA FUTURE

As we look ahead, we can assume the one thing that will not change is change itself. We live and work in a *VUCA* world—volatile, uncertain, complex, and ambiguous. This acronym was widely used in the US Army War College's curriculum for strategic leadership to help train leaders to lead successfully under unpredictable conditions. This curriculum was based in part on the writings of leadership guru Warren Bennis, who served in the Army himself as one of the youngest lieutenants in Europe during World War II and who went on to become a pioneering thinker, scholar, and teacher of modern leadership.[28]

Bennis wrote and spoke often about the importance of preparing for and accepting change. In a 2007 paper, he implored leaders to change their thoughts to keep up with a changing world. He said, "Never before has American business faced so many challenges. . . . Uncertainties and complexities abound. The only thing truly predictable is unpredictability."[29]

He also said, "In life, change is inevitable. In business, change is vital."[30]

Those words are just as valid today. Consider the complexity and uncertainty surrounding the economy, the labor market, geopolitics, a racial reckoning, environmental, social, and governance risk factors, a complex global marketplace, and the accelerating technological changes. This VUCA world requires us to move the conversation away from how we respond to COVID-19 changes in the workplace and toward the bigger question of whether we are effectively creating adaptive leaders within our organizations who can proactively manage the changes that will continue to impact us. If we don't have adaptive leaders able to shift the way that they operate, how can organizations possibly deal with all the other challenges and opportunities that are coming their way?

We can't afford to resist change. Jack Welch, former CEO of General Electric, said, "When the rate of change inside an institution becomes slower than the rate of change outside, the end is in sight. The only question is when."[31]

Agile, flexible leadership is a must for future-ready organizations. There will be many factors coming at us that we can't predict, but here are some that we can:

Technology Acceleration

According to Eric (Astro) Teller, CEO of Google X, technology is accelerating faster than humans can keep up with.[32] It leaves leaders with constant challenges, opportunities, and questions. Take artificial intelligence. For many, the topic seemed to come out of nowhere, but it took just two months for ChatGPT to reach 100 million users.[33]

Technology won't only disrupt in negative ways; it will produce opportunities and advancements that will make working virtually even more effective and engaging. Think augmented reality, meeting our colleagues or clients in the metaverse. The most competitive companies will quickly assess and adopt new, effective technologies that allow their employees to communicate, collaborate, and build community in more productive—and less draining—ways.

Generational Shifts in the Workforce

For the first time ever, five generations of talent are in the workforce. Since leaders at the top of many companies are still baby boomers, born before computers, the internet, and mobile apps were even invented, and the workforce they manage is quickly becoming digital-first, this is an essential shift for leaders to grasp. By

2030, 74 percent of the workforce will include Millennials and Gen Z.[34] You may have grown up connecting with somebody in person first. But increasingly, more of our workforce grew up connecting digitally first. So if you're in an older generation, when you hear somebody say that we can only effectively connect in person, ask yourself if that's true for everybody or if that's just true for you.

Gen Zs and Millennials are more apt to expect and readily embrace technology and have strong opinions and expectations about their employers and workplaces. Deloitte's 2023 Gen Z and Millennial Survey reported that 49 percent of Gen Zs and 62 percent of Millennials say work is central to their identity; this combined group also noted that having good work-life balance is the top trait they admire in their peers and their most important consideration when choosing a new employer. They also clearly value virtual and hybrid work. Three-quarters of respondents working in flexible roles would consider looking for a new job if their employer asked them to work full-time from the office.[35]

The Growth of the Gig Economy

Another trend causing a massive shift in the workplace is the increase in the number of freelancers, collectively called the gig economy. Recent data from the World Bank show that almost half of the global workforce works independently.[36] Freelancers will grow from 73.3 million in 2023 to over 90 million in 2028, according to Statista.[37] That is roughly half of all workers. In a 2022 survey from McKinsey & Company, in the United States alone, 36 percent of employed respondents were independent workers, which equates to 58 million Americans.[38]

According to Upwork's most recent Freelance Forward survey, "Americans have responded to the shifting trends toward independent work and have embraced the flexibility, job satisfaction and earning potential that freelancing provides." The study conducted online between September 21 and October 7, 2022, surveyed 1,164 freelance and 1,836 non-freelance workers and found the majority of freelancers reported they are more satisfied with all areas of work—like work-life balance, control of work conditions, and freedom to do work that suits them— than their non-freelancing counterparts.[39]

Speaking to *Forbes*, Upwork's vice president of talent solutions, Margaret Lilani, addressed the move toward freelance work. "We are watching this major shift happen in the workforce where highly skilled professionals are finally questioning aspects of the old, traditional ways of work," said Lilani. "It's as if people are looking at freelancers, who have more flexibility and control, and asking, 'Why can't my work be like that too?'"[40]

Even if companies require employees to work 100 percent in the office, many will still have to work with freelancers as a growing percentage of their teams, creating a different version of a distributed workforce. Companies will also compete with self-employment when hiring full-time talent in-house.

The Competition for Talent

Talent competition will continue to be a driver of flexibility more broadly. Firms need to meet talent where they are or lose out to firms that do. The Thomson Reuters Institute's *2022 Report on the State of the Legal Market* compared firms with low turnover (*Stay Firms*) to those with high turnover (*Go Firms*) and found that money alone is not stopping talent from leaving. Despite attorney compensation being up 11 percent overall in the survey (15 percent at the most profitable law firms), firms also saw record turnover (23 percent of associates had left in the past year). The report indicates that Stay Firms are focusing on "culture, not cash" with flexible work cited in the top 5 reasons attorneys are satisfied where they are.[41]

The drive for more diversity will also require more flexibility. Companies need a broader pool in a competitive labor market, making hiring from anywhere and allowing virtual or flexible work even more critical. As we will note in chapter 2, not only is our workforce becoming more diverse, but the business case for diversity continues to be proven.

We're clearly poised to create a future of work that works for all. The question is how we will create a future workplace that supports the organization and all its people.

HOLISTIC FLEXIBILITY

The answer is *holistic flexibility*. At the Alliance, we define holistic flexibility as a complete and integrated approach to working that meets organizational and employee needs in a way that produces a healthy culture, employee loyalty and productivity, and a profitable bottom line.

Holistic flexibility includes not only *where* you work but also *when* and *how long* you work. It's a form of deparented, degendered, and destigmatized flexibility. In other words, it's an approach that creates a judgment- and bias-free culture that no longer assumes every mother wants to work from home, every baby boomer wants to work in person, or everyone is always most productive at the office. It's work that is humanized.

As mentioned earlier, another term we hear often is *hybrid work*. Hybrid work is not a synonym of holistic flexibility but a subset that specifically relates to *where* you work. The Alliance defines hybrid work as bringing together the best of who we are in person and the best of who we are online to equal the best of who we'll be in the future.

For us, the term *holistic* conveys that one size does not fit all. With holistic flexibility, an organization empowers people to work in a way that meets their unique needs and unleashes their full potential. Holistic flexibility is giving management and employees the tools and training they need to manage teams or their careers and workdays.

Holistic flexibility is flexibility for all of us.

WHY HOLISTIC FLEXIBILITY IS HERE TO STAY

Earlier I mentioned that just as 9/11 forever changed the way we travel, COVID-19 forever changed the way we work.

If flexibility has historically been used with varying effectiveness and often surrounded by stigma, why is this time different?

Because never before have so many people worked from home simultaneously. As a result, we were all forced to experience flexibility at scale and find a way to make it work.

Now that we know it's possible to make it work, there's no going back.

Here are five specific reasons why flexibility—and specifically holistic flexibility—is here to stay:

- Status quo is no longer a barrier. Historically, very few people used flexibility options, even when they were available. Most people worked full-time in an office, the primary working model since the Industrial Revolution. When speaking to leaders about flexibility before the pandemic, I often heard a lot of resistance, usually in the form of "But this is how we've always done it." The status quo was solid, clear, and longstanding.

  Today, that is no longer the case. COVID-19 forced us all—organizations and individuals—to reimagine how to run meetings, how to mentor, how to hire, and how to collaborate, all while working from home. We could no longer rely on "the way we had always done it" because it was no longer an option.

As a result, in 2022, 58 percent of job holders in the United States have the option to work at home at least one day per week— and 87 percent of them take it. Estimates of growth rates vary, but according to McKinsey, flexible work has grown from one-third to ten times since the pandemic.[42] A new status quo has been created, and it's likely to stick because flexibility works.

COVID-19 showed us that flexible work options *increased* productivity and access to talent, and they improved nearly every benchmark that matters. In chapter 2, we'll discuss the business case for flexibility in more detail. Thanks to the pandemic, we all found we could be profitable *and* flexible in ways we had never thought possible.

- Its stigma is reduced. According to another survey before the pandemic, 93 percent of law firms had some form of flexibility policy in place, but usage rates were 8.8 percent.[43] Low usage in law firms was typically due to the characteristically large gap between policy and practice and the stigma associated with using those policies. The irony is that while stigma resulted in low usage rates, low usage resulted in more significant stigma, as people made assumptions about flexibility that weren't necessarily accurate, resulting in a vicious cycle.

  This stigma existed across industries: many believed if you weren't working at an office, you wouldn't be as productive, you'd be distracted, or you wouldn't be as available to coworkers or clients. As Schiff pointed out in "Working at Home Can Save Gasoline," these objections were common in the 1970s and weren't even true then. In 1973 and 2023, professionals can focus, be productive, and be available when working at different locations than their coworkers or clients or at times other than the typical 9–5 workday. People assumed otherwise simply because they hadn't experienced it.

  When COVID-19 forced nearly everyone to work at home, those assumptions changed. The leaders who had said they could *never possibly* work from home suddenly were. Our shared experience at scale naturally reduced the stigma.

- It has become a necessary skill. Before the pandemic, nearly all business was conducted in person, so tools for online work were largely optional. Online work was not considered as effective, as it was seen as difficult to build trust and rapport. For this reason, many top-level leaders could get away with preferring not to do video calls.

However, when in-person options disappeared, we were forced to conduct business and build trust and rapport with online tools. The companies that could make this shift succeeded. Those that couldn't were more likely to struggle or fail.

Today, online work skills are not just business as usual; they're crucial to every business's continuity plan. Now that we know we can effectively conduct business online, employees *and* clients will expect this option from now on. Online work is no longer a choice; it's a necessary skill.

As previously mentioned, the rate of change is growing exponentially,[44] so we need to keep adapting to change. Clients will only be requesting more virtual meetings, and soon, we'll all have no choice but to navigate online, in-person, and hybrid meetings regularly if we want to stay competitive.

- Many employees do not want to be forced to return to the office. Historically, there has been a clear boundary between work and personal life. Allowing relationship or parenting issues to seep into your work life was unprofessional. No matter what was falling apart at home, we needed to show up at work as if nothing was happening.

During the COVID-19 pandemic, people experienced an alignment between their personal lives and work in ways that never happened before. The personal issues that were previously hidden were communal and impossible to hide. When we saw our accountant's four-year-old burst into the room during a virtual meeting, we understood what she was going through at a deeper level. And we couldn't unsee it. At the same time, our accountant found creative ways to parent a preschooler and effectively contribute to the company at the same time. And she doesn't want that sense of alignment to end.

A Gartner study shows you're likely to lose up to 39 percent of your workforce if you force everybody to return to the office full-time.[45] People want the autonomy to decide how to work so they can continue experiencing that alignment between their work and personal lives.

- Working at home has become increasingly convenient. During the pandemic, people were forced to invest in technology to work effectively from home, which increased its convenience. That convenience also isn't going away, so if your people are going to work in an office, there must be a clear return on experience (ROE) for them. We'll discuss creating this ROE for your people in the Flex Success Framework.

As Massachusetts Institute of Technology (MIT) lecturer and Presencing Institute co-founder Otto Scharmer said, "As systems collapse, people rise."[46] That's precisely what happened in our organizations: our systems at home and work collapsed, and our employees rose to the occasion to work and allow our businesses to continue. Now that we know we can work effectively in various ways beyond being together at the office at the same time, it's nearly impossible to go back. And most don't want to.

In all the years I've been looking at flexibility, though it has had ebbs and flows, on the whole, it has never gone backward. It's not a question of *if* you move toward it as an organization. It's a question of *when* and *how*.

REFLECTION QUESTIONS

Think about your organization's and your personal experience of living and working through the COVID-19 pandemic. How have you seen attitudes, priorities, or values change? How have yours changed? Aside from the aftermath of the pandemic, reflect on what else is driving change in your organization now and into the future.

2

THE BUSINESS CASE
FOR FLEXIBILITY

Kim Koopersmith, the chair of Akin, an American Lawyer (AmLaw) 50 firm that employs 900 lawyers around the globe, names flexibility as the secret to her success:

> *If I had not been given the opportunity to have some flexibility in my work life when I first had children, I wouldn't have stayed at the firm. I didn't know that going into being a parent. But I learned quickly that I felt a strong, compelling desire to continue to work and a strong, compelling desire to spend time with my kids. If I had not had that ability to have that room, I would have done something else that allowed me to be more flexible.*[1]

Koopersmith worked reduced hours for six years, slowly increasing her time at work as her kids increased their time in school.

As Koopersmith advanced within the firm, she freely used her influence to share her path with a broader array of people, including senior leaders. Her message: "It was a positive for me, but it was also a positive for you in that I stayed with the firm, and you received the benefit of my contributions. You had the benefit of me being able to grow and learn and ultimately return in a fulltime capacity."

After those six years, in the early 2000s, the firm chair asked Koopersmith to draft Akin's flexibility policy. "The chair said, 'You seem to be someone who has made this work.' We hadn't really invested in flexible work options previously. Women who worked on a reduced workload basis were basically off track. They were helping others succeed, but they weren't on a path where they themselves were able to progress at the firm."

Since then, Koopersmith says,

> We've had more than 150 people take advantage of that program, who have found they can be fulfilled in their work lives and in the rest of their lives.
>
> Before the pandemic, we had baked in flexibility as something we believed in. Without us making a point of it, we were early adopters. We invested in making it easier for all of our lawyers to work at home. We said, "Here, you can press a button on our portal, and you can have a full home office tomorrow." So we had more and more people saying, "You know, I could use some more flexibility. It would be helpful if I could take some time to make dinner or help with homework and then go back online later, after dinner or after my kids are asleep."
>
> The pandemic was a propulsion force in thinking about how much flexibility can be part of the working model. While other firms were scrambling to figure out how to do this, large numbers of our people were already set up at home and had some sense of how you get work done, and how you combine your obligations at home. We're living in a world where people want to take their parents to a doctor's appointment, participate in school activities with their kids, or just have the ability to choose to work at home to think and be undisturbed. That's all part of flexibility. To our people, we say, "We need you here. We need you to learn, and we need to create a sense of community, but we also need to be flexible and recognize that work can be done in different places, and it can be done well."

Kim Koopersmith's story is an example of flexibility positively impacting the organization and the individual. Koopersmith's leadership in the area of flexibility positioned Akin not only to survive a global pandemic but also to serve as a model for success far into the future.

Decades of research and compelling experience show a strong business case for flexibility as a driver of *talent, productivity, diversity, engagement, profitability, sustainability,* and *business continuity*. Too many leaders think of flexibility as doing their employees a favor, a "nice to have," or a pandemic-era accommodation. Flexibility is neither just a benefit nor an entitlement. It's a business imperative that quantifiably impacts your bottom line.

In the following sections, I've included studies, statistics, and examples that show that holistic flexibility makes good business sense across a broad set of metrics. Remember flexibility means more than just flextime, hybrid, or virtual work; holistic flexibility encompasses flexibility in when, where, and how long you work and can manifest in many ways depending on each organization's unique needs and goals.

A DRIVER OF TALENT

Decades of research have consistently shown that offering workers flexibility in when, where, and how they complete their work is a highly desirable benefit that attracts and retains a diverse, talented workforce.[2]

Although the pandemic did not create the demand for flexible work, it further enhanced it; for example, according to a 2022 Future Forum survey, 68 percent of knowledge workers prefer hybrid work arrangements, 78 percent want location flexibility, and 95 percent want schedule flexibility, demonstrating an increasing demand of workplace flexibility.[3]

In a 2023 Zoom Morning Consult survey about workplace preferences, knowledge workers of every generation listed flexibility—defined broadly as having control over how you spend your time—as the most important. Of the population, 43 percent said flexibility is a basic expectation, not a perk.[4]

In a 2021 study in *Harvard Business Review*, 59 percent indicated that flexibility was more important than salary or benefits and mentioned that they would not work for a company requiring them to be full-time onsite.[5]

In addition to recruiting new talent, flexibility helps organizations keep their talent; conversely, a lack of flexibility drives attrition.

According to Thomson West, turnover is costly, nearly $1 billion a year in the legal industry.[6] Of the lawyer population, 44 percent feel so strongly about having an opportunity for hybrid and virtual work options that they would leave their place of employment to work more flexibly elsewhere, according to a report issued by the American Bar Association's *2022 Practice Forward Report: Where Does the Legal Profession Go from Here?* Younger lawyers, women, and lawyers of color felt even more strongly.[7]

One reason for this is stress and burnout. As mentioned in the previous chapter, burnout heavily affects individuals' mental and physical health and costs businesses in turnover and lower productivity. According to the *US Surgeon General's Framework for Workplace Mental Health and Well-Being*, chronic stress in the workplace—arising from heavy workloads, long commutes, unpredictable schedules, limited autonomy, and long hours, among other things—affects overall health and leads to higher risk of disease and mental health issues. It states that "workplace well-being affects productivity and organizational performance. When people feel anxious or depressed, the quality, pace, and performance of their work tends to decline." The report also stated that 76 percent of respondents reported at least one symptom of a mental health condition, an increase of 17 percentage points between 2020 and 2022.[8]

A Deloitte survey of US professionals found that 77 percent have experienced burnout at their current job. Of these professionals, 91 percent said stress and frustration negatively impact their work quality, and 64 percent said they are frequently stressed. Almost 70 percent said their employers aren't doing enough to help alleviate or lower workplace stress. And 42 percent of all respondents, and nearly half of all millennials, have left a job because they felt burned out.[9] It is critical to pay attention to the potential cost of burnout.

Another factor driving the need for workplace flexibility has been the tremendous growth in the number of workers balancing work and family obligations simultaneously.[10] In the legal field, for example, women make up over half of those enrolled in law school and half awarded Juris Doctorates (JDs).[11] A lack of workforce flexibility often determines whether workers will remain in their jobs. Despite equal representation of women receiving JDs, women are vastly underrepresented at the partner level[12] and much more likely to leave private practice than men, citing a lack of work flexibility as a primary reason.[13]

Many organizations are seeing similar "regrettable losses" (lost talent that an organization would have wanted to keep) due to resisting flexibility. As many as two million working women in the United States and Canada were considering taking a leave of absence or leaving the workforce in 2022, mainly due to a lack of flexibility at work.[14]

Some leaders accept the loss of talent as inevitable, especially in industries like the legal or professional services industries. I hear leaders say they work on an "attrition" model. They say that not everyone will make partnership, and that's okay. But it is very costly when valuable talent walks out the door. That's when humanizing the workplace with flexibility and acknowledging the employee's needs comes in.

Organizations that effectively implement a culture of flexibility can hold on to their employees or recruit from organizations that don't. In the report above from the American Bar Association, two-thirds of women and lawyers of color cite better work-life balance as the number one factor that would cause them to leave their jobs. And 39 percent of all women and 24 percent of men said they would quit their jobs for the opportunity to work a reduced workload elsewhere.[15]

Law firm Gibson, Dunn & Crutcher is a strong proponent of offering reduced-work-hour arrangements to retain and recruit talent. Gibson has been a member of the Diversity & Flexibility Alliance for over a decade, and I've had the opportunity to both observe and help facilitate their successful evolution toward greater flexibility. Zakiyyah Salim-Williams, chief diversity officer and partner, has been working with management to increase the number of women partners and retention overall. "Flexibility became a huge part of that conversation," she explained, "To keep our lawyers at the firm, we had to create a path for more of them to make partner on a flexible work schedule."

"When I came out of law school, I was told you couldn't have kids and be a partner," Salim-Williams told me.

> *I remember those days as well. Some women waited until they made partner to get pregnant, and others didn't take a maternity leave at all. Though this may still be true in places, I'm happy to see more firms have changed their cultures to support the career path of all their people. And it's not just women who want reduced hours at some point in their careers; Millennials, Gen Z, and more and more men wish to have time to honor and experience other parts of their lives.*

The commitment to flexibility has paid off, as Salim-Williams explains:

> *Our attrition rate of women is lower. . . [and] the promotion rate is higher. Engagement is higher. It's truly a success story. I don't think we would be here if we didn't figure out the flexibility piece. [When I was told I could not have kids and make partner] I immediately knew it was not something I wanted to pursue. Fast forward, I work for a firm that is led by a woman who has had kids throughout her entire career. And I later became a partner while working as the firm's chief diversity officer.[16]*

Salim-Williams's experience, that of Kim Koopersmith, and many others, shows the positive power of the reduced hours flexibility model for both the employee and the organization.

An important note on the reduced hours option—reduced hours can make it more possible to meet both work and family obligations because of its flexibility. Still, reduced hours do not automatically mean one can achieve what some people call work-life balance. I don't think balance exists; I think of it as alignment, where your professional and personal lives can coexist flexibly to allow you to live your life fully. But people still work lots of hours in these scenarios. There's a reason many people became burned out during the COVID-19 pandemic. To make reduced hours and other flexible options work, organizations must design their flexibility initiatives to consider boundaries, support for mental health, and more. If they do, as in the case of Kim Koopersmith, these initiatives can help organizations and people thrive.

The Surgeon General report makes the same point, saying that workplaces can be "engines of mental health and well-being. . . . When people thrive at work, they are more likely to feel physically and mentally healthy overall, and to contribute positively to their workplace." The report goes on to offer a framework for addressing these issues, which includes "providing more autonomy over how work is done, making schedules as flexible and predictable as possible, increasing access to paid leave, and respecting boundaries between work and nonwork time" (which we will address throughout the book).[17]

To recruit and retain the best talent, flexible work options *work*.

A DRIVER OF PRODUCTIVITY

Flexibility makes it possible for employees to get work done when and where they are most efficient and available, and it drives well-being, motivation, engagement, and other related factors—making it a strong driver of productivity as well.

A 2021 Global Workplace Analytics study looked at one form of flexible work—working virtually—and it showed substantial productivity gains and mental health benefits, such that 83 percent report similar or higher productivity, 55 percent report more hours worked, and 74 percent reported better mental health with virtual work.[18]

Similarly, the 2022 American Bar Association *Practice Forward* report shows that 70 percent of lawyers are working either entirely remotely (30 percent) or on a hybrid schedule (40 percent), most reporting that working remotely or on a hybrid basis did not adversely impact the quality of work, productivity, or billable hours. Of the population, 56 percent said it had no impact on productivity, 31 percent said it increased productivity, and around the same percentages applied to number of hours worked.[19]

However, despite the statistics, there are still concerns about flexibility and productivity in the legal industry.

Genhi Givings Bailey, chief diversity and inclusion officer at Perkins Coie, notes, "There is almost no resistance to the notion that flexible work can help organizations retain and advance talent. The tension today, though, is how do law firms balance the strong business case for flexibility with the need for more billable hours?"[20]

It's not just the legal industry. According to a 2023 Future Forum Pulse Survey, executives across industries rated reduced productivity as their second highest "serious" flexibility-related concern.[21] Many leaders perceive flexibility and productivity as opposites that must be balanced in a zero-sum game.

Despite widespread perceptions, the data show that flexibility does not detract from productivity. It is a productivity driver, according to objective and self-reported employee benchmarks.

The earlier mentioned Thomson Reuters Institute's *2022 Report on the State of the Legal Market* that compared firms with low turnover (*Stay Firms*) to those with high turnover (*Go Firms*) also showed that Stay Firms that retained talent by offering flexibility and other features that contribute to strong cultures outperformed on productivity too, showing a gain in productivity (0.2 percent) between 2019 and 2021 while Go Firms' productivity declined by 0.8 percent.[22]

The same Future Forum Pulse Survey that reported high concerns about productivity from executives found that "flexible work continues to be associated with higher productivity, not less." Those with full schedule flexibility report 39 percent higher productivity and a 64 percent increased focus ability than those without schedule flexibility.[23]

Much like the data on talent, these findings are familiar.

In a *Harvard Business Review* article, Harvard Business School professor Raj Choudhury said,

> *Research has shown performance benefits. A 2015 study by Nicholas Bloom and coauthors found that when employees opted into WFH [work from home] policies, their productivity increased by 13 percent. When, nine months later, the same workers were given a choice between remaining at home and returning to the office, those who chose the former saw even further improvements: They were 22 percent more productive than before the experiment. This suggests that people should probably determine for themselves the situation (home or office) that fits them best.*[24]

Choudhury calls this scenario "work from anywhere."

One of the first studies to look at the correlation between flexibility and innovation among knowledge workers, published in the journal *Frontiers in Psychology* in 2023, concluded that flexible work arrangements drive innovation behaviors. They defined flexibility generally as having choice and flexibility in where and when to work and explain that the resulting autonomy and well-being stimulate innovation.[25]

A related finding resulted from Project Aristotle, an often-cited research project at Google, that showed the number one thing that high-performing teams have in common is psychological safety, where individuals feel safe speaking up about their own needs or sharing thoughts with others.[26] Amy Edmondson, organizational scientist and professor at Harvard Business School, introduced this concept. With psychological safety, team members can speak up about when and how they work best—supporting the autonomy that drives well-being and innovation.[27]

Nurturing a healthy, human-centered culture gives organizations an edge over those that don't. In fact, according to an article in *Fortune*, the companies that made up the Fortune 100 Best Companies to Work For in 2023, revenue per employee, an important productivity metric, was 7 percent higher than the prior year. Discretionary effort, another productivity-related metric that measures employees' willingness to do extra work, was 70 percent higher than a typical US company.[28]

The good news is that organizations don't have to choose between flexibility and productivity or even balance the two. When done right, flexibility *drives* productivity. Or as the previously referenced *Fortune* article summed it up, "Productivity and performance are not at odds with supporting your people."[29]

A DRIVER OF DIVERSITY

Workplace flexibility promotes a more diverse workforce in terms of typical demographics such as age, race and ethnicity, gender, and ability. It not only retains older employees who want to remain employed with increased flexibility but it also retains diverse workers who have varying nonwork commitments and require flexibility to meet these obligations.[30] According to research from Deloitte, providing flexibility to embrace differences in when, where, and how individuals get work done can help foster a sense of inclusion, which studies show has a positive impact on retention.[31]

Further, people of color and women have a slightly stronger preference for location and time flexibility.[32] According to data from Future Forum, the following percentages of racial and ethnic groups surveyed preferred location flexibility:

- 86 percent of Asian people/Asian Americans,
- 81 percent of Black people,
- 80 percent of Hispanic/Latinx people, and
- 79 percent of white people.[33]

The following percentages of racial/ethnic groups surveyed preferred schedule flexibility:

- 71 percent of Asian people/Asian Americans,
- 68 percent of Black people,
- 66 percent of Hispanic/Latinx people, and
- 64 percent of white people.[34]

There is also a difference among gender lines: a Future Forum report states that 52 percent of women prefer working "at least mostly remotely," versus 46 percent of men.[35]

The deltas are not large, but the differences are measurable and consistent. And the impact is clear. Earlier, we mentioned the "regrettable losses" of women due to a lack of flexibility options. According to the 2022 McKinsey & Company Women in the Workplace report, "49 percent of women leaders say flexibility is one of the top three things they consider when deciding whether to join or stay with a company, compared to 34 percent of men leaders."[36]

Flexibility also helps in recruiting more diverse talent. One reason is that if you allow employees to work from home some or all the time, you open a much broader geographic opportunity to find talent. You can cast a wider net. If a job candidate lives ninety minutes away but only must come into the office twice a week, they will be much more open to the opportunity than if they had to commute that distance five days a week.

Zakiyyah Salim-Williams discovered this recruiting advantage as an unintended consequence of COVID-19. In their case, Zoom became an invaluable tool. During a panel discussion on diversity at the Diversity and Flexibility Alliance's 2022 Annual Conference, Salim-Williams described how virtual gatherings helped to strengthen the community for Black lawyers, which in turn helped to make recruiting Black talent a lot easier:

> *At the time, in 2019, we had a small number of Black lawyers and Black partners. We got together and said we want to change the face of the firm. Then when we worked to build a community through over 60 Zoom gatherings virtually, it was the best thing that could have happened to allow us to recruit better and integrate lawyers into the firm. We made a pact that all Black lawyers would be a part of the recruiting across the firm. We would no longer recruit for one office. We did this across 10 of our offices. We were easily able to get people to join us by Zoom. There are really great things that you can do to integrate people in a virtual environment too.*

The efforts worked—Gibson, Dunn & Crutcher had a 100 percent increase in Black lawyers and a 60 percent increase in Black partners between 2020 and 2022.[37]

However, Vernā Myers, diversity and inclusion strategist and thought leader, cautions against assuming flexibility alone will create equitable environments. "Anytime you have shaped a system to favor a certain group of people, or anytime you create a system where you've centered and normed one group of people, you are going to be less likely to have diversity," said Myers.

> *You've set it up to echo the status quo. If the status quo wasn't diverse, then it's not going to become diverse unless you remove some of those barriers that allow exclusivity to reign. So on some very basic level, you should not expect to see women, people of color, et cetera growing in their representation if nothing has changed about how you work, what kind of systems you have in place, how you reward people, and how you hire people.[38]*

We can only expect diversity to increase if we change the system that draws a homogenous group of people in the first place.

Myers also reflects on why underrepresented groups might prefer flexibility.

> *Part of it is that your lived experience is a little more demanding, in the sense that you may have obligations that are different from*

those in the mainstream. That's a big generalization. But if you add in the correlation between socioeconomic class and race, for example, people in the workplace are also responsible for taking care of the elderly and the children. They might be the sole bread-winners, which adds a whole other level of obligation. All of it makes it harder for them to be in the office all day or all night, and not have flexibility.

Another part relates to people's experience in the workplace: the lack of understanding, bias, microaggressions, and inequities. During the pandemic, we heard reports about how people of color and folks with disabilities were feeling so much better. They didn't want to return to the office because they didn't feel safe there. They can kind of bypass all those daggers that weren't even intentional but were still happening every day if they could work in their kitchen.

According to Myers, whether organizations prioritize flexibility depends on whether they value a diverse workforce. "[As an organization], you have to look at what is happening, what world we're living in right now, what the talent looks like, how they are thinking about things, and how you're going to be the kind of employer that attracts people. But you also have to believe that the people who you could attract if you were more flexible are just as valuable as the people whom you don't have to work so hard to get them there."[39]

In the legal industry, Genhi Givings Bailey has seen evidence of flexibility's impact on diversity. "I think the ability to destigmatize flexibility and normalize [flexibility] has supported efforts to retain and advance women of all races," Bailey said.

I've seen it firsthand, [the] support efforts to retain and advance women of color. And that's important, because we know that in the legal industry, the ability to retain and advance women of color is difficult. It's incredibly difficult because of lots of systemic barriers that exist, and so progress around flexibility is one less barrier that exists today.[40]

I've also seen more men—again, of all races—be very transparent around their need for flexibility and the types of flexible arrangements they have requested. For instance, many more men, not just younger or Millennial men, but men of all

generations are being transparent about taking paternity leave,
the amount of time they're taking, and how excited they are about
taking it, that they are able to show up and not just be better
fathers but also better parents and co-parents with their part-
ners. It's great to see that because that allyship also supports
women and women of color.[41]

The practice of working from home is very likely to result in siloes by default. To avoid those siloes and create a culture of connection, we must intentionally *design* that culture—precisely what the Flex Success Framework will show you how to do.

A DRIVER OF ENGAGEMENT

Highly engaged employees drive positive business outcomes. In fact, according to Gallup, compared to business units with disengaged employees, businesses with highly engaged employees have 23 percent better profitability, 81 percent less absenteeism, 43 percent less turnover (in low-turnover organizations), 10 percent higher customer loyalty, and 18 percent higher productivity.[42]

According to Gallup, employee engagement is "the involvement and enthusiasm of employees in their work and workplace."[43] Highly engaged employees feel closely aligned with their organization's purpose and values, feel a sense of belonging, feel respected by their managers, and are willing to go the extra mile to hit a deadline or create their best work. They're loyal to their organizations and less likely to seek a job elsewhere. They are *motivated* to contribute to their organization's success.

Where does flexibility fit with engagement? Flexibility can increase or decrease engagement based on many factors. These include autonomy (an employee's perceived control over their work) as well as respect and trust (an employee's sense that their managers care about their well-being; trust that they are professionals who can do their jobs without micromanagement; help meet their needs; and treat them with respect).

A workplace culture that offers flexibility shows employees they can be trusted to do their work in the office or elsewhere. It shows employees that they know when and where they are most productive. It also conveys support for allowing employees time for the rest of their lives.

At the heart of engagement is motivation; the most enduring form of motivation must come from within. Rewards and carrot-and-stick or command-and-control approaches are superficial in comparison. Intrinsic motivation drives engagement. According to the book *Drive* by Daniel Pink, of the factors that influence intrinsic motivation, autonomy—the need to direct your own life and work—is first. He describes it as being able to "control what you do, when you do it, and who you do it with. . . without needing to conform to strict workplace rules. By rethinking traditional ideas of control—regular office hours, dress codes, etc.—organizations can increase staff autonomy, build trust, and improve innovation and creativity."[44]

Despite how critical engagement is to performance, Gallup's *State of the Global Workplace 2023* report shows that only 23 percent of the global workforce is engaged (21 percent in the United States), 59 percent is not engaged (also called *quiet quitting*), and 18 percent are actively disengaged (or *loud quitting*). Gallup estimates that low engagement costs the global economy $8.8 trillion.[45] These statistics point to a tremendous opportunity for organizations to improve culture and engagement and humanize their workplace, which will drive better results.

One major challenge to fixing this problem is that many leaders believe flexibility *threatens* engagement. I've received many phone calls from leaders concerned that engagement has gone down since implementing their flexible location policy, and they need to "get people back in the office because we need more engagement."

The problem is that these leaders needed to define the problems accurately to solve them effectively. If leaders define engagement as in-person interaction because that's how they have experienced it, they will want to increase engagement with more in-person interaction. However, the real essence of engagement is not defined by whether an employee is physically in the office.

In fact, according to Gallup's research, engagement goes *down* if employers force people to return to the office full-time. The research shows that when a job can be performed virtually, but employees aren't allowed to work in their preferred location, they have more serious intentions of leaving, experience more burnout, have lower life evaluations, and lower employee engagement.[46]

How work flexibility benefits employees and ultimately serves organizations is relatively intuitive; individuals desire to be trusted, have job control, and receive support for their well-being. When individuals are trusted to accomplish their work regardless of when, where, or how they do it, it creates the opportunity for employees to manage the responsibilities in their lives better. This trust leads to the flexibility employees need to promote their health and well-being, sense of autonomy, and overall productivity in both their work and nonwork lives. An abundance of research has documented the many benefits of workplace flexibility to employees, including increased job performance and commitment[47] and increased job satisfaction and engagement.[48,49]

For managers who believe the answer to engagement, productivity, and culture is just being physically in the office, read on. The office itself does not provide any magic on its own, yet it can and should be a powerful place of connection, collaboration, and culture when leaders intentionally cultivate those things. Much more on that throughout the book.

A DRIVER OF PROFITABILITY

Flexibility is also a driver of *profitability*. Much of its effect on profitability is downstream of its effect on productivity, talent, diversity, and engagement, all of which can result in an organization's greater success. For example, research has shown that organizations with greater diversity reap significant profitability gains.[50]

According to the Society for Human Resource Management (SHRM), a British telecommunications company study showed that 58 percent of US companies and 61 percent of global companies adopting flexible work policies have seen increased profitability. The same study showed an 83 percent increase in productivity.[51]

Other research documents benefits such as enhanced business continuity readiness[52] and time and cost savings due to the reduction of unnecessary travel,[53] which increases profitability.[54]

Fortune's "The World's Best Workplaces" list shows that it's often workplace culture that focuses on well-being, flexibility, and equity that puts them on the list.[55] These high-trust, human-centered workplaces, in turn, drive bottom-line results. According to research from Financial Times Stock Exchange (FTSE) Russell, companies that make this list outperform the market by a factor of 3.36. According to research from Alex Edmans of the London Business School of Economics, companies on the list outperformed the stock market by 2 percent to 3 percent per year between 1984 and 2009.[56]

Workplace flexibility also reduces absenteeism by an estimated 12 percent to 20 percent,[57] which saves organizations significant resources. Economic researchers estimate that the cost to an organization for each absence is 1.28 times the absent employee's daily wage. This cost increases as finding a replacement worker becomes more difficult, as is often the case with professional, complex positions.[58]

Organizations that offer hybrid and virtual work policies save additional costs in real estate by reducing their office footprint. Organizations that have implemented hoteling have found ways to reduce their office space needs.

All of this points to the fact that flexibility impacts many of the drivers of profitability both on the cost side (like cost savings from lower turnover) and on the revenue side (like increased productivity and profit).

A DRIVER OF SUSTAINABILITY

Flexibility is a driver of *sustainability*, reducing commuting time, travel, and the corporate real estate footprint.[59] In this era of increasing scrutiny and urgency around environmental issues, this becomes more of a factor.

As far back as 2011, the existing 2.9 million US virtual workers saved an estimated 390 million gallons of gasoline, preventing the release of 3.6 million tons of greenhouse gases annually. Virtual work policies allow organizations to demonstrate their social responsibility to shareholders and other stakeholders who demand organizations not only boost the bottom line but also help address some of the country's most challenging problems, including those concerning economic development and the environment.[60]

Global Workplace Analytics states, "Eliminating or reducing commuter travel is the easiest and most effective way for an organization or individual to reduce their carbon footprint. Based on our estimates, if those with a work-from-home compatible job and a desire to work remotely did so just half the time, the greenhouse gas reduction would be the equivalent to taking the entire New York State workforce off the road. These estimates assume a 75 percent reduction in driving on telework days."[61]

A DRIVER OF BUSINESS CONTINUITY

Before COVID-19, most organizations did not consider flexibility as a driver of business continuity. Therefore many executives did not actively invest in flexibility and *work anywhere* infrastructure and systems to increase readiness in the case of unplanned business disruptions. The pandemic revealed a global lack of sufficient business continuity planning overall. Preparing for another pandemic-sized disruption should now be part of planning for any business, and a vital piece of this is ensuring you have a flexible workforce set up to work effectively from anywhere without skipping a beat. CEOs around the world agree. According to a PwC survey that asked CEOs to prioritize which business models needed adapting after the COVID-19 pandemic, the top three included digitizing core operations, adding digital products to operate virtually, and increasing the share of remote or contingent workers who are flexible.[62]

This makes sense when you tally up the cost of disruptions to business. In one example, SHRM stated that according to the Mobile Work Exchange, "if all federal employees could telework in the event of a disaster, the average agency could save $60 million in just one day."[63]

It isn't just disasters that cause business disruptions; being set up for flexible work reduces missed workdays due to other unforeseen events that are more localized, like weather or transportation-related disruptions. Flexibility will help organizations be more resilient in many scenarios, increasing productivity and saving money.

This data means that flexibility—implemented well—can be a key to building a culture that's as good for employees as it is for the bottom line.

That leads us to the Flex Success Framework.

REFLECTION QUESTIONS

Flexibility is cited by more and more people as a top priority. How important is flexibility for you personally? How has flexibility, or a lack of flexibility, affected you in your own life?

3

THE FLEX SUCCESS FRAMEWORK

Barri Rafferty, former global president and chief executive officer (CEO) at Ketchum Public Relations and the Alliance's 2020 Flex Leader Honoree, led her firm through a company-wide transformation to a flexible workplace well before COVID-19—a rare step for a public relations (PR) firm at the time. She stated, "I have always felt that if we trust people to do their jobs it doesn't matter where they work or what time of day. Flexibility allows [everyone] to be successful in the workplace, as parents, as friends, and helps with better self-care. We all win."[1]

Taking the step to pause and consider where they were and where they wanted to go was a crucial step in laying the foundation for an effective program. Over time, the firm took a comprehensive, consistent approach, training their managers, seeking feedback, measuring, and iterating.

The commitment and structured approach paid off. The firm could track measurable results and watch them over time through quarterly surveys and company timesheets. Rafferty shared the impact of flexibility: "At no cost to a company, flexibility can be the highest value perk you can offer to employees. When employees have control of their schedules to plan work-life integration, you increase their productivity, engagement, and their work product. Flexibility became both a recruiting and retention tool for us."[2]

As Ketchum's process illustrates, successfully implementing a flexibility initiative must be done by *design* versus by *default*. This is where the Flex Success Framework comes in.

The Flex Success Framework takes everything we've learned about what works in healthy, productive, and flexible workplaces and breaks it down into actionable steps. This chapter will introduce this framework to create your holistic flexibility initiative.

33

ESSENTIAL REFRAMES FOR FLEX SUCCESS

All lasting change begins with mindset—and for organizations, the mindset of leaders is crucial. To develop a flexibility initiative that works for employees *and* employers, start with clarity around what flexibility means (and what it doesn't).

There are still plenty of myths and misperceptions surrounding flexibility that need clearing up. Leaders need to reframe their thinking to make these essential mindset shifts to achieve true flex success (more detail on key messages in these shifts throughout the book).

From Policy to a Positive Culture Change

When leaders start developing a flexibility initiative, many dive right into deciding what forms of flexibility they will offer—how many days people should work in the office, what percentage of days each month they are allowed to work from home, what the parameters should be around reduced hours programs, who is eligible. They're defining flexibility narrowly. They're seeing flexibility as a policy only.

But instituting flexibility in the workplace is much more akin to a culture change. When done right, creating a flexible, human-centered culture affects your business and your people more than just adopting a policy alone.

Successfully implementing a flexibility initiative that captures every benefit flexibility offers requires a change in your culture, your business systems and infrastructure, and the mindset and practices of leaders throughout the organization. It requires leaders to embrace it, embody it, and support it.

If you drop a flex policy into your current work environment without developing the infrastructure, team, and practices to make it work, it will fail. And it won't be a failure of flexibility; it will be a failure of execution.

If you embrace flexibility as an essential cultural component of a resilient, future-ready organization, it will drive employee engagement, productivity, retention, and more. It will strengthen the fabric of your organization's culture.

Flexibility Starts with Purpose, Not Policy

This important reframe asks you to stand back and think about the purpose behind the policy before you develop it—starting with the *why* instead of the *what*. A successful policy is built on a foundation of purpose.

Starting with purpose means identifying the cultural values you want to express. Where does flexibility fit with your organization's values? It could be a crucial part of how your organization conveys that you value your team's well-being or that you are a human-centered organization that values your employee's ability to enjoy time outside of work.

Defining your purpose also includes the behaviors and outcomes you want to incentivize. When a leader tells me they want their team to return to the office part of the time, I ask them, "Why?" "So that they can collaborate," they might answer. Again, I ask them, "Why?," drilling down to specifics. Perhaps it's to drive innovation through group brainstorming sessions, facilitate career growth, or increase technical expertise in a growth area through in-person mentoring.

Chicago-based law firm Neal, Gerber & Eisenberg LLP utilizes flexibility to provide a runway to partnership for people that more rigid career paths historically left behind. Marlon Lutfiyya, director of talent and diversity, explained, "We've seen people struggle with health issues, parenting issues, or other issues that affected their ability to perform. The firm customized solutions for them and lengthened their track to partnership as a way of retaining talented people—instead of forcing them into an up-or-out situation."[3]

There can be many parts to your purpose and many goals you want to achieve. When you develop policy, the more clarity you bring to your purpose, the better the result. We'll dive into this in chapter 4.

The Office Does Not Equal Culture

Particularly after the pandemic, many leaders expressed concern about their employees working virtually, saying that employees needed to work together in the office to build culture, collaboration, and engagement. This concern was the genesis of many return-to-office policies mandated by employers. They were only sometimes well received, frustrating many workers. Plenty of employees ignored the mandates, frustrating employers in return.

In many of these cases, employees not coming into the office was cited as a problem that had to be solved in and of itself. Organizations should go much deeper and look at what the real issues are. You may want employees to be more engaged, so you've required them to come into the office more, but you still need to take the other steps to lay the groundwork for that *intentionally.* Maybe when they're in the office, they just sit at their desk and do Zoom calls that they could have done at home—without the commute.

Some employees see the return-to-office policies as leaders demanding *presenteeism* for the sake of unnecessary face time. They say that when they used to go into the office, it doesn't necessarily make them feel engaged.

That's not surprising. Gallup data show that only 20 percent of employees feel connected to their company's culture regardless of how often they work in the office. As Gallup says, "The reality is that the office never equaled culture. While in-person interactions are powerful, they alone were never enough to create the magic of connectedness."[4]

In the case of hybrid workers, more of them report a higher level of connection to their company's culture (23 percent) than all employees overall, making a case for flexible workplaces. Why would hybrid workers feel more connected? Gallup posited that "the office and the remote workplace are being treated with greater intentionality. Hybrid workplaces have been forced to make in-office experiences more meaningful and substantial. In addition hybrid workers feel more supported in their well-being. They are more likely to feel that their organization cares about *them*, which makes them feel more connected to the organization's values, mission, and purpose."[5]

In other words, employees need to get some return on the experience when they go into the office. Return on experience (ROE) at an organizational level means developing your culture and creating the experiences your people and your organization need to thrive. If you're asking your people to commute to the office, you have to create experiences that cause people to *want* to come. These experiences should include more than just free food. They should consist of opportunities for connection, collaboration, and contribution, as discussed in chapter 7.

I'll give you a recent example. A managing partner at a law firm told me that he started a weekly partner meeting and mandated in-person attendance. When it started, everyone showed up. Within a short time, only about half of his team was showing up and the rest were giving him various reasons why they couldn't come. When he expressed his frustration, I asked him what the agenda of the meeting was. Essentially he was just talking at his employees for the duration of the meeting. I suggested he come up with an agenda that included their participation, that engaged them, where they were all collaborating. Six months later he told me that he revamped his agenda to make it highly participatory and this made his meetings a success. Not only did people show up in person, but the productivity, collaboration, and engagement levels soared.

Providing the right kind of flexibility also gives your employees autonomy, something that improves their stress levels, overall mental health, and engagement.

Flexibility Is Not a Trade-off for Performance

Flexibility executed well actually *increases* performance and productivity despite assumptions to the contrary. Blaming flexibility for performance problems is one of the top myths that needs busting. It's essential for leaders who make that assumption to shift their mindset about the result of a well-crafted flexibility initiative—from declining performance to a driver of performance.

Another common myth that compounds this issue is *believing vagueness equals flexibility*. Some firms say, "You're adults; you can do what you want. We're not going to set a policy." As a result, their expectations of when and where people can work aren't clear. Data from Microsoft's 2022 Work Trend Index reflects this, revealing that 38 percent of hybrid employees say their greatest challenge is knowing when and why to come to the office.[6]

Yet when I ask the leaders directly about their expectations, their expectations are typically quite clear. Leaders have a specific number of days in the office or a percentage of time in mind. They just haven't told anyone—and then hold it against them when their people can't read their minds.

Clarity is kind. Vagueness masked as flexibility is not. Tell them directly if you have a clear idea of how much time your people should be in the office to be successful. Just as managers need to provide clarity on flex policy, they also have to hold their people accountable for their output and impact, whether at home or in the office. Being flexible about an employee's location does not mean managers have to be flexible about everything—deadlines and work expectations still need to be met.

Flexibility Is Not a Work-Life Balance Tool

Flexibility is *not* a work-life balance tool, even though some think it is.

I often ask people, "Did you work longer and harder during COVID-19 than before? Did all that flexibility give you more time and less stress?" The answers, of course, are usually yes and no, respectively.

I had one partner say to me, "Somebody just put a call on my calendar for one o'clock in the morning; what am I supposed to do?" She wasn't the only one with these issues. We lost all sense of boundaries during the COVID-19 pandemic. Employees juggling childcare were working longer hours to make up the time, and employers had the feeling that employees had nowhere else to go anyway. Hence meetings and calls just kept getting earlier and later.

Research from Indeed.com bears this out. According to 2021 surveys among US workers that looked at burnout after the pandemic,

- Those who worked remotely reported more burnout than those working in the office (38 percent vs. 28 percent);
- 53 percent of employees working from home reported working longer hours than they worked in the office; and

- Of those who work from home, 38 percent said they felt pressure
from their managers to work longer hours, and 21 percent said it
was a toss-up between their managers and clients pressuring them
to work longer hours.[7]

Boundaries are an essential component in flexible work environments. But even with boundaries, many employees still work very long hours; they just work them flexibly. Implementing flexibility with boundaries must be combined with genuine support and appreciation for what employees need to facilitate their health and productivity. In other words, flexibility and boundaries must be supported by an emphasis on well-being and a healthy, human-centered culture.

Flexibility is Responsibility

To make flexibility genuinely work, organizations, leaders, and individuals must take responsibility and be intentional. Responsibility is the flip side of flexibility.

Organizations must implement structures, systems, and guidelines to foster success. These are necessary for employees to have the tools to flourish. These can include new technology; new recruiting, mentoring, training, workload allocation, and feedback programs; activating accountability to make sure leaders and employees are following policy expectations and spelling out expectations clearly; monitoring results to ensure that you're achieving desired outcomes; building support for the new environment by sharing data and trends; and periodically seeking input from colleagues through pulse polls and engagement surveys.

Leaders set the weather for the team. Employee loyalty and perceptions about their organizations are often tied to their direct supervisor. For workplace flexibility to succeed, leaders must not only accept the new work environment but shift their behaviors so that they manage and lead differently. While organizations must train leaders on these best practices, it is the responsibility of leaders to incorporate these best practices.

Employees must be intentional about their success in this new environment in order to prioritize career goals and team or organizational needs. A wait-and-see approach will not work; it is not a good approach in any environment, especially in a flexible work environment where employees must take even more ownership.

Embracing flexibility as a collective responsibility will help steer clear of pitfalls and move you toward your goals.

Flexibility is the Future

Though the trend will continue to evolve, with some forward and backward steps along the way, we will not see the trend reverse entirely. As discussed in chapter 1, we need to shift our thinking from flexible work as a COVID-19-era accommodation to an element that belongs in every future-ready organization's culture. Though flexible work was a feature of the COVID-19 era, most organizations have under-emphasized that COVID-19 changed how we work. It impacted people's expectations of work in an enduring way. We've changed; you've changed.

As organizations look to what their people want, they see that the command-and-control leadership that many leaders exhibit or tend to default to will no longer work. I've had countless conversations with leaders who've come to us with some level of frustration to say, "You know, we've set our policies, we've talked about hybrid, we've done what we thought people wanted, yet people still aren't coming back at the level that we have set." Many of you might experience that within your organizations. And that's because people are looking for the more modern *inspire and influence* form of leadership today.

Part of this is trusting your people and allowing them more autonomy and self-direction. It also means honoring an alignment between what's happening in each individual's life and their work—meeting their needs and supporting their well-being and future.

We're seeing that many organizations have tackled the future of work at a surface level. The future of work changes and impacts everything you do as an organization. The future of work will not be shaped by default. It will only be shaped by design—design within your organization, paying attention to how you can align your people with your purpose, why you do what you do, and empowering every individual to feel a sense of purpose and belonging within the organization—alignment between your principles, your policies, your practices, and your people.

THE PILLARS OF FLEXIBILITY SUCCESS

In our experience, there are three critical pillars to flexibility success: for flexibility to work, your approach must be *intentional*, *inclusive*, and *iterative*.

Intentional

First, you must be *intentional* to move from *default* to *design*. What does it mean to be intentional in a flexibility strategy?

Creating a Plan

First, it means intentionally *creating a plan* for what we will design. Many leaders I talk to have similar fears about flexibility, so much so I've started calling them the five Cs: They worry about loss of control, loss of contribution, loss of connection, loss of collaboration, and loss of culture.

The truth is, they're right to be concerned. By default, each of those five C scenarios is likely to happen. But by design, they don't have to. You can intentionally design a policy to preserve everything you're most concerned about losing.

When I ran focus groups during the pandemic for some organizations, I heard that the leaders who greatly emphasized mentorship found a way to do it because they valued it. Others said, "I used to mentor by people coming into my office. When people come back in, I'll mentor again." So they didn't mentor. That's a clear example of how, if leaders were intentional about mentoring, they continued it; if they weren't, it just went away. Unsurprisingly, you're starting to see gaps in people's knowledge and skills.

Similarly, some employees told me that when they had an issue or needed something clarified from their supervisors, they didn't want to ask through email or by phone, they preferred to wait until they saw them in person. The employees just suffered in silence, not raising the issue at all. This led to frustration or lower levels of productivity that sometimes were blamed on flexibility: "If we were all in the office, it would be easier," they told me.

These situations are not a result of flexibility. They occur when leaders and employees don't do what they need to do. Getting rid of flexibility isn't the solution in these examples. Intentional action and proactive communication are much more effective options.

A successful flexibility strategy deserves a plan. Offering options for when, where, and how long you work affects every individual and every business process. It involves your talent, your technology, your office design, and so much more.

That means you must think through what key results you want from your flexibility strategy, what you want to avoid, what kind of resources you will allocate, what scenarios are likely so you can implement it effectively, and what you will measure to know it's successful. In short, intentionality requires designing each aspect of your flexibility strategy ahead of time for your unique business situation rather than copying and pasting a policy from a top organization in your industry.

Positioning Flexibility as a Strategic Priority

Second, it means intentionally *positioning flexibility as a strategic priority*. If you integrate flexibility into your organization, how you position it is crucial to its success.

The key is to position flexibility not as a policy or an initiative but as a strategy; this is easier said than done. As we saw in chapter 1, flexibility has been historically viewed as a temporary accommodation or benefit for so long that to view it as a strategy—and position it that way consistently—requires a significant shift in how you think and talk about it.

This shift starts with purpose, as discussed earlier. What is the *why* behind the initiative? What are the goals you want to achieve?

Building on Strengths

Third, it means intentionally *building on strengths* rather than focusing on weaknesses.

As mentioned, many view flexibility policies as a necessary evil—and sometimes for good reason. Many of us are apprehensive about large change initiatives because they sometimes bring out the worst in people.

But what if they could bring out the best in people? What if they could strengthen your organization in the ways that matter most to you, your leadership, your people, your organization, your clients, and your stakeholders?

That's what we've experienced—and it's supported by research.

On an organizational level, focusing on the positive facts of our present situation and a positive vision of the future drives better outcomes than focusing on what's missing.

At the Diversity & Flexibility Alliance, we use a strength-based experiential approach to this. This is similar to Appreciative Inquiry (AI), an organizational philosophy developed by Suresh Srivastva and David Cooperrider in the 1990s that leverages the power of positive inquiry. A summary of the approach is worth quoting:

> At its heart, AI is about the search for the best in people, their organizations, and the strengths-filled, opportunity-rich world around them. AI is not so much a shift in the methods and models of organizational change but a fundamental shift in the overall perspective taken throughout the entire change process to "see" the wholeness of the human system and to "inquire" into that system's strengths, possibilities, and successes.[8]

Whether as individuals or organizations, we choose what we focus on. When we intentionally focus on our strengths, resources, and positive possibilities, even the most ambitious change initiatives can bring out the best in us and strengthen not only our organizations but ourselves, our clients, our stakeholders, our communities, our societies, and our world.

Inclusive

The second key pillar is to be *inclusive*, bringing more voices into the process to ensure that everyone has an opportunity to thrive and feels valued.

Holistic flexibility involves the entire organization and affects the whole culture, which means we need buy-in across the organization. If we take the time to ensure all voices are included at the table, we will retain all the business case benefits of flexibility we saw in chapter 2. If our people don't feel included in critical decisions or their lived experience is disadvantaged, they will leave.

For flexibility policies to work, as mentioned in chapter 1, they must be deparented, degendered, and destigmatized. One of the gifts of the pandemic was to accelerate this mindset shift for everyone. Employees experienced working from home at scale in a way they never would have otherwise, which naturally helped break down some inaccurate assumptions. We realized that flexibility works, and different people work best in different ways. That's not to say it's no longer stigmatized; we'll discuss specific strategies to face the inevitable resistance to flexibility in chapter 8.

Inclusivity doesn't happen by default. What does happen by default are *unconscious biases*—specifically proximity bias, assumed similarity bias, and confirmation bias.

When I ask audiences of employees what their biggest fear is regarding flexibility, the top answer is being in an outgroup. That fear of being in an outgroup is related to *proximity bias*, where an ingroup and outgroup are formed based on who is physically closest (i.e., who is in the office and who isn't).

In fact, according to Future Forum, proximity bias is executives' top concern regarding flexible work as well.[9]

This concern is disproportionate to women: According to the American Bar Association's 2022 Practice Forward Report in the legal industry, women are more concerned than men about "career consequences if they don't work in the office when asked." More women than men were "extremely" or "very" concerned that they would be overlooked for meaningful assignments (21 percent of women vs. 12 percent of men), receive a lower review (18 percent of women vs. 7 percent of men), and be viewed as not committed to their organization or employer (27 percent of women vs. 13 percent of men).[10]

And there's good reason: according to the Society for Human Resource Management, 67 percent of supervisors believe "remote workers are more replaceable than onsite workers," and 42 percent admit they "sometimes forget about remote workers when assigning tasks."[11]

According to the American Psychological Association's Dictionary of Psychology, *assumed similarity bias* is "the tendency for perceivers to assume that other people possess the same qualities and characteristics that they have."[12] If they prefer to work in the office and feel isolated at home, they assume others do, too.

If we want to be inclusive, we must understand that others have had different experiences than we have. As the popular quote says, "We are not all in the same boat. We are all in the same storm."[13]

I remember working with an executive committee, where someone mentioned longing for the days when somebody could just walk by their office and take them out to lunch. A Black woman on the executive committee spoke up and said, "Nobody was walking by my office. Nobody was taking me out to lunch. You have this vision of what used to happen, and you can't wait to go back to it, but that was not ever my experience."

First, we must be clear that the past wasn't great for everybody. Second, we must recognize that those serendipitous moments when people would walk by your office and take you out to lunch were often people who were right next to you and similar to you. To be inclusive, we want to intentionally choreograph connections between people who don't regularly connect.

For flexibility to work, "you have to be curious about how your life differs from others," says Vernā Myers.

> *If you're assuming you are having the same lived experience, then you are operating as if everyone is you. And you're immediately setting up a situation where only certain people can thrive. That kind of curiosity came to me during the pandemic, when I became much more aware of others' differences—where they live, whom they live with, what their obligations were. For example, someone said, "My parents live in another country, and now I can't get to that country because of the lockdown. That means I won't have seen my parents for four years."*
>
> *Before then, I would have never thought of something like that. The fact that somebody might have planned to take off for a month to see their parents, and it's during a big project, but they didn't know it was going to be a big project, so now they feel conflicted—I would have never asked, "How long has it been since*

you've seen your parents?" There wouldn't have been a judgment,
but it would be happening through my lens of what life is like. Now
I would see that person as serious and committed.[14]

Psychological safety is needed to counter common biases and create a more inclusive environment where people feel comfortable sharing their experiences.

Now that the lines between work and personal life have been blurred, individuals must disclose personal information to allow their managers to plan their team's flexible work schedule, for example. In light of biases like assumed similarity bias, the real question for psychological safety at work becomes, "Do I feel safe to talk about my life at work? Can I voice my opinion, even when I disagree?"

Says Myers,

> *When I was working in a minority-owned firm, all the partners*
> *were men. I remember getting an assignment from one of the part-*
> *ners and saying, "I just don't know how I'm going to get this done*
> *tonight." He said, "Well, just do it when you go home." And I said,*
> *"No, at home, I have a whole other job. I have to do the dishes, I*
> *have to talk with my child, bathe my child, and read him a book;*
> *I also would like to spend some time with my partner.*
>
> *He answered, "Well, when I get home, I just go in my office."*
> *"Who does all that other stuff?' I asked.*
> *"My wife," he said.*
> *"Well, I don't have one of those," I answered. And I thought*
> *to myself, You're assuming that we have the same life, and as a*
> *result, if I'm not able to get this work done, you will then judge me*
> *as not as good or capable or committed.*
>
> *That to me is one of the biggest issues we face in trying to*
> *instill both diversity and flexibility. If you can get past the judg-*
> *ment, and you can get curious, then you can get creative. Now*
> *that you know this is how other people live, you must ask yourself,*
> *"What would I do differently?" instead of just saying, "Oh, wow,*
> *that's a lot. But I'm still going to ask you to do the same thing.*
> *And if you can't, I'm going to find someone who can."*
>
> *Flexibility is not about whether you're here or whether you're*
> *not here, but it's an attitude and approach. It's about thinking,*

"Where can I flex, and what becomes possible if I view this situation as a positive—not something I have to deal with?"[15]

Confirmation bias is closely linked to both proximity bias and assumed similarity bias. If I believe that others in the office are in the ingroup and are more committed, and I think everyone prefers working in the office as I do, I will look for all the ways to make those beliefs true. If someone working from home doesn't return my phone call in a timely manner, that's proof they're not working. Due to proximity bias, if I'm in the office and more aligned with people who are also there, I may give work and opportunities to the people next to me. You can see how that fear of proximity bias is well-founded.

Proximity bias, similarity bias, and confirmation bias can be strongly present in a flexible work environment—if we're not intentionally interrupting them. For example, leaving people out who are working from home happens by default. Designing your work allocation systems and review structures to ensure people working at home are getting the same opportunities as those working in person is intentional.

We must avoid the focus group of one voice. Our flexibility strategy must include a mechanism to gain input from all voices of the organization at every stage of development and to apply flexibility to all areas of the organization.

It also means we use a leadership style of *influence and inspire*. When people are inspired by the vision of flexibility at their organization, believing they are building a positive future together, they feel a sense of ownership in both the design and the outcome—and are invested in the organization.

Jenn Flynn, head of Small Business Bank at Capital One, has played a leadership role in her organization's flexibility strategy and has seen firsthand the importance of including all voices: "Now we have multiple formats for working: how do we excel in doing it? It all comes back to trust and empathy, regardless of where people sit in the organization, and continuing to iterate on that current state while making sure that everyone has a voice in the process."[16]

When you're inclusive, everybody can learn from each other. Leaders in professional service organizations tend to focus on top-down mentoring, but we also have many opportunities to experience *reverse mentoring*, such as learning to use technology efficiently or communicating on different platforms. Including everyone's voice in shaping flexibility at your organization expands those opportunities for everyone to mentor each other.

Iterative

Finally, a flexibility strategy must be *iterative*, moving from *static* to *dynamic*.

We must intentionally build processes to measure whether our strategy is producing results we designed it to produce in the first place so we can dynamically change over time.

Iterative means continually improving and constantly tweaking our strategy so it will work even better. Having the mindset of continuous improvement is a strength. Google has called it "continuous evolution" and considers it a competitive advantage. The founders of Google also called it "uncomfortably exciting," which I think reflects the natural tension and opportunity inherent in change.[17]

Whenever we initiate significant change, it's natural to notice what isn't working as well as "the way we used to do it." From an iterative perspective, we can't expect our new policies to work perfectly. Any organization going through organizational change must expect some bumps in the road and some things that might be working better than before. The challenge is not to automatically revert to the old ways just because something isn't working.

Instead we must be iterative, meaning we need both commitment to the overall vision and benefit of flex as well as an active feedback loop that allows us to continually assess what worked, what didn't work, and what we want to adjust as a result—keeping our flexibility strategy living and dynamic.

THE FLEX SUCCESS FRAMEWORK

I built the Flex Success Framework to walk organizations step-by-step through creating an intentional, inclusive, and iterative flexibility strategy. This framework consists of five Rs:

- *Reflect*: Establish a compelling purpose. With *reflect*, you begin with why flexibility matters to *your* organization. What *positive* possibilities does it create for your people, organization, clients, and stakeholders? If you look at your data, what positive impacts have you seen? Has it been a driver of talent? A driver of diversity? Recruitment? Engagement? Has it expanded your ability to achieve your mission or vision? Why does it matter?
- *Reimagine*: Create a shared vision. Now that you know why flexibility is vital to your organization, you'll have the opportunity to reimagine your organization's values, vision, and culture to

create policies and practices that align with your highest aspirations of who you want to be.

It starts with questions like, "Who do you want to be?" "What do you want the market to say about you?" "What do you want your competitors to say about you?" "What do you want your people to say about you?" and "How can flexible work options make that vision a reality?"

Just as importantly, regardless of how the future of work changes for you as an organization, what needs to stay the same at your organization? What are your strengths? What do you want to preserve, no matter what? Many leaders want to make sure they keep their culture and maintain connection. What do you want to create, and what do you want to preserve?

- *Redesign*: Design the strategy. Designing your policy is where most organizations want to begin. But if you start with steps one and two, you can get *macro* clear, so steps three, four, and five can be *micro* easy. What options do you want to offer once you build a strong foundation with *reflect* and *reimagine*? How many days do you want your people in the office—or do you want to require a percentage of hours per week or month? What forms of flexibility do you want to include, and what kind of support structures and infrastructure will those forms require?

  Also, steps one and two are important because they give you the best chance to enroll your leaders and employees when you roll out your policies. You can explain the purpose behind your shift to flexibility in language that resonates with your cultural values. You can explain how flexibility is a business imperative for your organization, not just an accommodation or a benefit. And you can explain in detail how it will allow you to build on your strengths and fulfill your vision in measurable terms.

- *Reintegrate*: Integrate flexibility into the culture. If you stop with redesign, all you have is a policy. But for that policy to be success-ful, you need to build a culture that supports and embraces that policy. In *reintegrate*, your policy becomes an organization-wide practice. You'll return to the purpose you clarified in the first step of *reflect* so you can align your purpose, principles, policies, practices, and people.

- *Reinforce*: Measure the impact. Creating and implementing your flexibility initiative is an iterative process, meaning you must measure it. The good news is because you built your policy on a solid foundation, you know why you created this policy, and so you also know exactly what outcomes to measure. In this step, you develop a set of key performance indicators (KPIs) that align with your purpose and measure to understand what's working, what's not, and what needs to be adjusted so your policy continues to improve.

I encourage every organization to engage with the five R process as a continuous cycle so you can proactively evaluate what works best in a constantly evolving environment.

With the Flex Success Framework, you can create the best of all worlds for your people and your organization, intentionally designing a workplace where culture, collaboration, contribution, and connection thrive.

Let's get started.

REFLECTION QUESTIONS

We covered the essential reframes necessary for a successful flexibility shift. Which of these resonates most for you? Which seem important for your team or organization? Are there other reframes that you are experiencing?

4

WHAT IS FLEXIBILITY'S PURPOSE?

Countless organizations have come to me, either during the pandemic or since, to ask for help in developing their flexibility policies. Either they are formalizing a policy for the first time, or they ask me to review a current policy because it isn't working. Many of them start by asking, "How many days per week should employees be in the office? I see other organizations going from three to four days, is that what we should do?"

Instead of starting with the policy, I help them take a big step back to uncover the *why* behind the policy first. Putting purpose before policy is how you build a strong foundation that is most likely to lead to a successful flexibility initiative. This means stepping back to ask organizations why it matters to them, what benefits they expect to gain from it, why the employees value flexibility, and how it will help them reach those goals. This is the *reflect* stage, the first step in the Flex Success Framework.

I had a conversation recently with talent professionals in a law firm. They told me that some partners had asked them when they would be going back to full-time in the office. This question reflects a common roadblock in some organizations—a mindset that believes that going back to what worked in the past is the best way forward. I can't say this strongly enough: you can't build for the workforce that you used to have; that workforce is gone! You have to build for the workforce you have today and the one you want to have in the future. In other words, what got you here won't get you there! That's why the purpose piece is so important: so that when you get to the step when you are drafting your policy, it is in complete alignment with your purpose, goals, and values. That's how you build a foundation for success.

In this crucial first stage, we begin to get *macro* clear so that later, the drafting and implementation of the policy is *micro* easy—and the initiative is set up for maximum success.

Flexibility is a tool often misunderstood and undervalued by leaders but one that can optimize their most valuable resource—*their people*. Flexibility can play a significant role in unlocking human potential—something any of my clients would tell you I'm passionate about.

Creating a flexibility framework starts with defining the purpose and the business case that supports how flexibility will impact your business. To create a flexibility shift that will deliver all the business benefits discussed in chapter 2 and set you apart as an industry leader, you must begin by taking a step back to *reflect* on why flexibility is vital for your organization.

To do that, first look at how you've incorporated flexibility in the past and where you are now. This review is an essential step in building the foundation for the future. You can only get to planning and a policy once you know why you're doing this and what flexibility can do for you. So yes, organizations come into the door thinking this is all about policy, but we quickly elevate the conversation to a much more impactful place. And that conversation becomes more powerful and productive when all parties have a voice.

FORM A FLEXIBILITY WORKING GROUP

Because flexibility is an organization-wide change, you must put together a dedicated working group of influential leaders and diverse stakeholders to guide your organization through the change process. Be sure your working group has sufficient authority, credibility, and support to effectively lead the change effort and navigate any potential obstacles or resistance. Here are some recommendations.

Include Your Top Leader and Five to Seven Key Stakeholders

Ideally the organization's top leader will be a part of the working group. The most senior leaders' commitment, support, and active involvement inspire confidence and drive organizational alignment. Their involvement signals the strategic importance of the initiative and encourages others to participate and contribute to the change effort.

In addition to senior leaders in the organization, I recommend including five to seven key stakeholders from various areas within the organization, ensuring representation across talent, diversity, technology, operations, recruiting, and human resources. There should be some in the group who are in a supervisory role as they will have responsibility for rolling this out and working with their reports on the implementation. Each stakeholder brings unique expertise, perspectives, and insights essential for developing a comprehensive and inclusive flex strategy.

Include Employee Representatives

I also highly recommend including employee representatives who will be directly impacted by the flex strategy. This will offer the group valuable insights into the workforce's needs, concerns, and aspirations. Including employee representation will not only increase the effectiveness and legitimacy of the strategy but will also promote buy-in, trust, and a positive organizational culture that embraces inclusion, change, and innovation.

Map Out Your Responsibilities

The working group's primary responsibility is working through every Flex Success Framework aspect. As you'll see in the following chapters, this will include conducting comprehensive assessments, analyzing current practices, identifying gaps and opportunities, defining objectives, developing implementation plans, and monitoring progress. The group will also collaborate closely with stakeholders, gather relevant data, seek employee input, and ensure the flex strategy aligns with the organization's goals and values. Plan to regularly communicate flex strategy updates and progress to the executive committee and seek the necessary approvals.

In sum, for each of the steps in the Flex Success Framework, the flexibility working group will lead the change and implement the processes recommended in each chapter in a way that best meets the organization's needs.

BUILD A COMPELLING CASE FOR FLEXIBILITY

According to widespread research, the most effective organizational change efforts start with a *compelling purpose*. As most of us now know, thanks to author and consultant Simon Sinek, we must "start with why." According to Sinek, the most influential leaders and change agents, from the Wright Brothers to Dr. Martin Luther King Jr. to Steve Jobs, led with inspiration based on a compelling purpose, not directives.[1]

In addition to considering purpose, looking at the future with a lens of possibility is essential to set your organization up optimally for change. This positive, forward-looking view is supported by the well-researched process of Appreciative Inquiry, where the most effective change efforts begin by *reframing a problem in terms of what's possible.*

A commonly cited example is British Airways's response to customer complaints about lost baggage. Instead of starting with the question, "How do we deal with excessive baggage loss?" they asked, "How do we create outstanding arrival experiences?" Framing the purpose of the change effort in terms of positive possibilities resulted in one of the most effective change initiatives in British Airways's history.[2]

In the case of flexibility initiatives, an example of a purpose-driven reframe might be a shift from "How do we write a flexibility policy to accommodate the demands of our employees?" to "How do we create a culture that makes us an industry leader in attracting and retaining the best talent that will drive excellence in every area of our business?" We need to stand back and look at flexibility with a wide lens—as a driver of possibility in the future.

To define and articulate that vision for your organization, start the process by assessing what is going on today and what has happened in the past to begin defining your vision for the future. These current factors point to your purpose for implementing a flexibility initiative and your unique business case for flexibility.

You may know all there is to know about the general business case for flexibility, but that won't help when things get difficult later on. You must put it in your own words and on your terms from the beginning. In my experience, when leaders later question why they're going to all this effort, being able to quickly remind them of their specific business case for flexibility puts them back on track.

Without a compelling purpose, it's too easy to get caught up in the inconveniences or the challenges of a change effort and all the things we miss about the old way.

As we saw in chapter 2, flexibility has an excellent business case for companies: the data show it's a driver of talent, productivity, diversity, engagement, profitability, sustainability, and continuity.

That's why I encourage all organizations to start with a *specific business case* for their organization. Start by outlining why it makes excellent business sense for your organization based on all parties' past data and experience. That will motivate all stakeholders to invest in your long-term flexibility initiative. In this way, you're being *intentional* and *inclusive* from the start.

In this chapter, we'll follow a process designed to help you gather all relevant inputs needed to define the strategies and policies that will work for your unique organization:

- Articulate your organization's culture and values.
- Gather data on the past business impact flexibility has had on your organization.
- Gather input from surveys and focus groups, including all stake-holders, about their experiences with flexibility and their current needs and preferences.
- Assess the data and input you've gathered.
- Outline your unique business case for flexibility.

Reflecting on your compelling purpose and getting clarity on your business case for flexibility from the beginning establishes a solid foundation to build on in the following steps.

DESCRIBE YOUR ORGANIZATIONAL CULTURE

According to business theorist and Massachusetts Institute of Technology (MIT) Sloan professor Edgar Schein, organizational culture "is the pattern of basic assumptions that a given group has invented, discovered, or developed in learning to cope with its problems of external adaptation and internal integration, and that have worked well enough to be considered valid, and therefore to be taught to new members as the correct way to perceive, think, and feel in relation to those problems."[3] Put another way, culture is a collection of values, expectations, and practices that drive the daily work of the organization. Culture affects how people behave and the values and social norms that evolve. The focus is on how people act and interact rather than what is written down in vision or values statements.

Gallup has a simple way of describing culture: "how we do things around here." They also describe it as "a force multiplier for the outcomes that matter most to you—and when properly harnessed, it becomes a powerful differentiator for your organization."[4] In other words, culture matters! Organizations must understand their culture clearly; to do that, they need a more profound definition of culture.

Edgar Schein states that organizational culture can be analyzed at three different levels:

1. *Visible artifacts*, which include the visible environment, including technology, office layout, visible or audible behavior patterns, and recruiting materials;
2. *Espoused values*, which include the reasons and rationalizations people give for their behavior and can often be discovered by interviewing key members of the organization; and
3. *Underlying assumptions*, which are the unconscious beliefs that determine how group members perceive, think, and feel.[5]

Using Schein's construct, culture exists on many levels. I see too often that people don't understand culture or they look at it superficially. But culture is complex, and it runs deep. It will help to be clear on what is needed to optimize it. When it comes to flexibility, the *visible artifacts* might be your written policies; the *espoused values* might be the current flexibility practices, or how flexibility may be showing up in your organization; and the *underlying assumptions* might include things that can make you successful—like a belief that flexibility is part of well-being and well-being is a cornerstone of your culture, or it might include assumptions that negatively impact culture like unconscious biases or a stigma around employees working virtually.

I often use a simple exercise when I work with organizations to help them define their culture. I ask executives and employees to come up with three adjectives to describe their culture, and then ask them to give me examples of when they saw those attributes in action in their organization. For example, if you describe your organization as collegial, also give an example of when or how you see collegiality at its best in your organization. I ask leadership this question separately, often in an executive committee meeting, then poll the rest of the organization. It can be very illuminating to see if leadership and the workforce use the same words—or not. Do others see the organizational culture like you and the leadership team see it? Do you find that some leaders come up with an adjective but can't come up with any examples? Is there a gap between how employees describe the culture and how leadership would describe it? For example, I have seen plenty of cases where executives say they have a family-friendly culture. But employees say their company culture comprises unrelentingly long hours or a lack of autonomy and flexibility (hardly family-friendly). If there is a gap, you'll work with this in the reimagine stage.

Once you've defined your culture at a high level, you'll define your organization's values more precisely.

DEFINE YOUR ORGANIZATION'S CORE VALUES

An organization's values are closely tied to culture, but they are distinct from one another. Culture can include current beliefs, practices, and shared values, but values can act as guiding lights that help govern company operations, decision-making, strategy, ethics, and visions for the future. In companies that created purposeful values from the beginning, the values likely influenced the developing culture. In companies that did not define values upfront or went through transitions or evolutions along the way, values need to be updated or defined so that everyone in the organization is on the same page.

According to their website, PwC defines and communicates its corporate values so that every member of their 65,000-person-strong workforce knows them, understands them, and is ideally guided by them. Their values are inherent in their stated purpose: "building trust and delivering sustainable outcomes for business and society." This statement of purpose, in turn, guides their actions: "Through the actions we take and the choices we make, we aim to make a meaningful difference in the world, for our clients and for our people. . . . When we bring people, capabilities and technology together in line with these commitments, we're not only helping our clients build trust and deliver sustained outcomes, we're also bringing purpose to life." They define their values across many categories, including well-being, diversity, equity, and inclusion, all of which correlate with flexibility.[6]

In 2022, when PwC launched what they called a *reimagined people experience*, it was a clear expression of living and working their purpose; the My+ program centers around choice, flexibility, and purpose, allowing employees to personalize their careers and providing an even deeper commitment to instilling a culture of flexibility and autonomy.[7]

In the best of all worlds, your clearly defined company values drive the best and most effective policies that positively impact business outcomes. But on the flip side, a misalignment between stated values and actual practice can do significant damage.

If you do not have a list of established values, look to your mission statement or a strategic statement. Frequently, values are embedded in these statements or can be inferred.

If nothing is in writing, are there ways leadership talks about the organization that reflect core values? How does your chief executive officer (CEO) communicate the company values? How do you describe yourself on your website, your marketing materials provided to clients, or the information you provide to employee candidates?

Corporate values might include trust, integrity, diversity, equity, inclusion, transparency, creativity, innovation, excellence, client-focusedness, and human-centeredness. They might be expressed in value statements like these found on company websites: "Democracy on the web works" (Google), "Protect our home planet" (Patagonia), and "Our company values—create the future, own the outcome, raise the bar, and be genuine—represent who we are, how we show up in the world, and how we'll define our future success" (Adobe).

If you are defining your organizational values for the first time, be as creative as you like, but be sure to be explicit and ensure the values you define are particular to your organization. Importantly if your workforce sees your organization differently than leadership sees it, feel free to change how you express your values to guide your aspirations for the future—more on this in the next stage of the framework.

GATHER DATA

After you define your culture and values, you'll gather the data you'll need to form your business case for flexibility. In this step, you'll look at the effect flexibility (or lack thereof) has had on your organization, gathering quantitative and qualitative information. Begin by gathering all your current flexibility policies and guidelines. Review the requirements and who is eligible to use them. We advise leaders to look at how their teams worked together during the COVID-19 pandemic and gather data on those measures' impact on all areas of business outcomes. Additionally, look at any flexibility or hybrid measures your organization implemented before and after the pandemic to understand the impact.

Beyond COVID-19, if you've supported any flexible practices in the past, even informally or on a case-by-case basis, identify those. These past practices could include an informal understanding that allowed for one-off arrangements or flexible work periods granted to employees for special circumstances.

Rather than starting with your beliefs and impressions, begin with the data. Review available statistics that may reveal outcomes you did not personally witness. Look carefully at your hiring, attrition, and promotion data over the last three to five years to understand any correlation between flexibility and recruiting, retention, development, and advancement.

Next look at crucial work, client, and leadership experiences and whether flexible workers have as much access to them as their counterparts. Assess who in your organization has had access to important sponsor relationships, high-profile projects, critical skill development experiences, and important leadership roles.

Look at the following categories and cross-sections of data to understand trends and correlations, breaking each question down by various flexible arrangements, departments, offices, levels, genders, and demographics.

Current Usage

What trends can you identify from the usage statistics if you have current flex policies? Identify what works well and reverse engineer this information to identify specific elements contributing to that success. For example, what are the types of flexibility with the highest and lowest usage in the organization?

Identify potential markers of flexibility stigma, including the concentration of flex usage with a particular demographic (i.e., gender, race, or generation) or no use in a specific group or office (which may indicate leader sentiment impacting usage).

Recruiting Data

Look at current and past recruiting data to assess whether flexibility or lack thereof (real or perceived) plays a role in recruiting and retention. For example, what forms of flexibility are being asked about during the recruiting process? Do you include information on the organization's flex policies in recruiting material? On the website? Does it have an effect on attracting candidates?

Advancement Data

What percentage of flex employees are promoted each year? Look back ten years and identify any trends. Are flex employees promoted as often as their counterparts? Who are your most influential leaders? Who worked with them? Are there any differences between flex schedule employees and their counterparts regarding access to these leaders?

Attrition Data

Are there any discrepancies in attrition between flex employees and their counterparts? What percentage of people left due to a lack of flexibility? What trends can you identify, and what is the relationship to the availability or lack of flexibility? Has the organization experienced regrettable losses?

Client Data

What are your clients' attitudes toward flexible work? Who among your clients are champions of flexibility, either as an individual or an organization? Examine client surveys and diversity surveys. Are clients asking about flexibility in surveys?

Market Data

What are peers offering? What are the corporate trends? What kinds of flexibility are your clients offering? Review benchmarking surveys to analyze where you are in comparison to industry standards.

GATHER INPUT FROM TEAM SURVEYS AND FOCUS GROUPS

Data only tells half the story. You must understand your people's needs and experiences to build a flexible strategy. Gather input from team surveys, interviews, and focus groups to ensure your process is inclusive. This input should give you a clear picture of how your people have experienced and engaged with flexibility at your organization.

Surveys are a great way to collect information and metrics from a large workforce in an efficient manner. These responses help build a business case for the need to offer and expand flexible work arrangements. If you conduct team surveys, consider questions that look at various perspectives. For example, how important is workplace flexibility to your team? Are your managers supportive of workplace flexibility arrangements? Which workplace flexibility arrangements do you currently use on an ad hoc or informal basis?

Interviews and focus groups with employees are a great way to gain more detailed information about what's working and what's not. I recommend separate focus groups for executives, managers, and employee groups so that you can best hone in on insights important to each group and that participants feel comfortable being candid. Consider questions such as these: What has worked well with your workplace flexibility arrangement? Are there challenges or concerns with your workplace flexibility arrangement? What additional types of workplace flexibility would you like your organization to offer in the future?

Ideally your organization regularly gathers input from employees, and if so, you can draw from that input. For example, as chair of Akin, Kim Koopersmith has intentionally built an inclusive culture by gathering input from all the firm's employees throughout the year: "When I came into this role, one thing I wanted to do differently was to stay connected with everybody at the firm. I'm not just the chair of the partners. I'm the chair of the whole firm."

To stay connected, Koopersmith initiates engagement surveys and schedules town halls with all of the constituents at the firm to share firm-wide or practice-wide updates. In addition Koopersmith regularly participates in the firm's associate academies, where she learns from the associates in sessions like Chair for a Day. In these sessions individuals are divided into small groups and answer the question, "What would you do if you were chair for the day?"

That's where Koopersmith got the idea of putting together home office kits mentioned in chapter 2. "One of the Chair for a Day groups said, 'It would make my life so much easier if I could work at home more seamlessly,'" said Koopersmith. "This individual didn't have a suitable screen at home so they couldn't work as well. After the meeting, I went to the chief information officer (CIO) and asked, 'How hard would it be for people to just press a button and get what they need to each have a work setup at home?' The CIO said it wouldn't be hard at all. I would not have known that if the associates hadn't suggested it."[8]

By regularly including the voices of everyone at her organization, Koopersmith is ensuring she's not operating as a focus group of one voice, not just with flexibility, but in any strategic decision.

So whether you're gathering employee feedback regularly, as they do at Akin, or soliciting targeted feedback from surveys, focus groups, or interviews, be sure to receive input from all people as you reflect on the role of flexibility in your organization.

ASSESS OUTCOMES MADE POSSIBLE BY FLEXIBILITY

Now that you have gathered substantial data and information, it's time to connect the dots to identify trends or takeaways about how flexibility has impacted your organization so far.

- Assess how flexibility impacted or led to outcomes in the following areas. Break these results out by the type of flexible practices you employed—virtual, hybrid, reduced hours, reduced workload, and so on.
  - Talent recruitment/retention,
  - Productivity,

- ◆ Diversity,
- ◆ Innovation,
- ◆ Profitability,
- ◆ Business continuity, and
- ◆ Sustainability.
- • Why do these outcomes matter? What do they make possible?
  - ◆ For us as leaders?
  - ◆ For our team?
  - ◆ For our clients?
  - ◆ For other collaborators, vendors, and stakeholders?
  - ◆ For our organization as a whole?

For example, Susan Neely, president and CEO of the American Council of Life Insurers (ACLI), discovered that flexibility was a significant driver of talent.

"In the area of recruitment, flexibility has allowed us to recruit top-notch people," said Neely.

> When our general counsel of forty years told me she was going to retire, I had someone in mind I thought would be ideal. But when I called to tell her about the opportunity, positioning it as requiring some time in Washington, DC, she told me she wasn't interested. She lived in Columbus [Ohio], and she explained her family was flourishing, and everything was working well where she was. We continued our search, and I was still comparing every candidate to my preferred candidate. At the same time, it turned out my preferred candidate was regretting that our lack of flexibility prevented her from pursuing a leadership position. We engaged in a conversation about what might make this manageable for her and ACLI. We agreed, and it's worked perfectly. That's an example of where flexibility allowed us to get big-time talent we would never have been able to get otherwise.

In addition to recruiting new talent, flexibility has allowed ACLI to make the most of their already existing talent—allowing them to serve their members at an even higher level.

"It allowed us to hold on to those who may have otherwise retired, because that expertise is really hard to find," said Neely. "It's given us a lot more room to find the kind of highly technical expertise we need in our industry now. We're continuing to build a very capable team."[9]

When considering what flexibility made possible for her organization, Jenn Flynn, head of Small Business Bank at Capital One, saw both personal and organizational benefits.

> *Personally I love the broader connections a hybrid environment has allowed for me. I lead a team of nearly 1,000 associates dispersed geographically, and during the pandemic, I had an opportunity to interact on screen with associates I normally would not have had the opportunity to interact with in person. Moving into hybrid has allowed me to retain those connections and include those associates on our next journey.*
>
> *Also hybrid has allowed us to leverage our distributed footprint and our talent, while also having collaboration space and time for in-person problem solving. We get to have the best of both worlds without having to worry about choosing between one or the other.*[10]

CREATE YOUR BUSINESS CASE FOR FLEXIBILITY

Finally, you can combine the data, the team input, and your leadership team observations into a concise, unique business case for flexibility in your organization. This business case should clearly articulate the *why* behind the initiative, or in other words, the *purpose* that drives the policy.

As you outline your business case, here are some things to consider:

- How can flexibility benefit your clients and external collaborators? Your purpose for flex should be about more than just what it makes possible internally for your organization. The way we do our work is changing overall. For example, you will interact virtually more often with your clients and external collaborators too, and that can be to everyone's benefit. Some leaders now say, "I prefer to meet with service providers virtually for pitches first; it's more efficient therefore I'm more open to agreeing to the meeting."

  If you are on the other side of the desk in sales or business development, you will probably find that shifting to a strategy of virtual meetings increases your efficiency, as Joe Krzywicki, chief banking officer at American Community Bankers Bank (ACBB) learned firsthand. Krzywicki described this shift:

COVID definitely drove changes. I find that we are now more efficient and effective in managing client and vendor/partner relationships. The old way of selling by lining up client meetings and trekking to offices was incredibly inefficient and invasive. Having a virtual meeting that lasts 50 percent as long and is 90 percent faster to schedule has increased our ability to engage with clients by at least 75 percent. There's also the mental commitment of having a salesperson come into your office and take up your time. Virtual meetings in many ways are more personal than in-person meetings. In some cases, you enter someone's home. You often see their pets and even family. The overall tone is much more relaxed and disarming. I have found that it can lead to even deeper relationships. We still need in-person meetings to build relationships, but we don't need as many of them for routine discussions.[11]

- Consider how flexibility can impact your talent. Do you want to become more competitive in your recruiting efforts? Do you wish to retain younger employees who are very clear on enjoying a life outside of work, more women who leave their jobs after having a child, or more of your older workers who might feel their only options are to work full-time or retire?
- Consider how flexibility can benefit communication and collaboration among your team members. If you have a global or multi-site firm, flexibility can increase your ability to come together as one firm rather than just relying on the times you come together in person. For example, if you currently have an in-person company-wide retreat every other year, adding a flexible location option would allow you to get together online more often.
- Consider how flexibility can contribute to your business continuity plan. During the pandemic, those organizations that could shift their people to working from home immediately had better business outcomes than those that did not. In a post-pandemic world, flexibility should be part of an organization's business continuity plan. We now have the technology and skills available to continue doing business online, so it's become a business imperative for

everybody to be able to work online at a moment's notice. Can your organization continue operating if (or when) the next global challenge arises? Remember business continuity can save significant resources even during short-term office shutdowns due to weather conditions, building maintenance issues, and public transportation problems.

Your unique business case is the strong foundation for your flexibility strategy. The thread will also run through the entire Flex Success Framework. We'll return to it intentionally in step four, reintegrate, where you will create your implementation plan by aligning your purpose, principles, policy, practices, and people, and in step five, reinforce, where we measure the impact of your flex policy. Remember flexibility is not about what you're losing but what you have to gain.

Now that you understand how flexibility has benefitted your organization in the past, you've cataloged the needs and preferences of your current organization. You have constructed your organization's unique business case for flexibility; before creating the vision for the future, take a moment to assess where your organization is on the flexibility scale. This assessment will give you added information to take into the next step of defining who you want to be in the future—and how flexibility can make that vision possible.

ASSESS YOUR FLEXIBILITY CULTURE: THE FLEXIBILITY CULTURE METER

To create a strong foundation for what will ultimately be an organization-wide culture change, you'll want first to assess where your organizational culture is now related to flexibility so you know where you're starting.

Does your written policy match your unwritten rules? In other words, even if you have a robust flexibility policy, are people getting the hint that flexibility is *not* tolerated or embraced? I've heard countless managers say, "Yes, we have that policy, but you don't want to send *that* message about your commitment (or lack thereof) to the organization, do you?"

I've noticed that organizations tend to fall into one of several common flexibility profiles, as represented in the flexibility pyramid.

Before creating a flex strategy with an organization, I use the *flexibility culture meter* to help them identify their flexibility profile based on the flexibility pyramid and prepare them for the process ahead. Specifically, the flexibility culture meter assesses an organization's workplace flexibility culture by considering formal policies, usage, leadership support and communication, and policies, procedures, and infrastructure supporting flexibility. As a result, it reveals an organization's immediate and long-term priorities in its progress toward workplace flexibility.

There are six levels on the flexibility culture meter:

Level 1: Taboo

The lowest level on the flexibility culture meter is *taboo*, where the organization has no written flexible working policy, and leadership generally needs to support workplace flexibility. Leadership directives from Goldman Sachs CEO David Solomon in 2021 would fall into the taboo category: "[Working from home] is not ideal for us, and it's not a new normal. It's an aberration that we're going to correct as quickly as possible."[12]

Here's what a taboo work culture looks like:

- There are no written flexible work policies.
- Case-by-case workplace flexibility is generally not supported.
- Employees do not work on flexible schedules at any time.
- There is no leadership support for workplace flexibility.

Here are statements you might hear in a taboo culture:

- "We're not going to have a flexible work policy. It's not permitted or even discussed."
- "Eighty percent of infinity is still infinity, so we do not allow reduced hours."
- "We pay our people too much to allow them to work from home."
- "Our executive committee has given us a directive that we are not allowed to use the term *hybrid* to refer to the way we work."
- "Flexibility does not work in our organization. It is not our culture; it is not who we are."

Level 2: Scale the Walls

The next level is *scale the walls*, where the organization has no written flexible work policy but allows flexibility on an ad hoc basis. However, employees who use flexible work feel they have to hide when they are leaving early, coming in late, or joining virtually.

Here's what a scale-the-walls work culture looks like:

- There are no written flexible work policies.
- Some employees work on flexible schedules when a need arises.
- Employees who work on flexible schedules feel the need to be discreet.
- Some leaders support workplace flexibility, while others do not.
- Employees on flexible work schedules are rarely represented in leadership, or if they become leaders, they are asked to stop using flexibility.
- Some resources support flexible work schedules given on a case-by-case basis, and general resources may be applied for flexible work matters.

Here's what it sounds like:

- "I work from home sometimes, but I have to scale the walls to do it. No one can find out."
- "You can work from home this week, but make sure not to mention it to anyone."
- One associate told us, "I ask my assistant to turn on the lights in my office and put a hot cup of coffee on my desk so no one will know I'm working from home."
- "I don't want to indicate the days I am working from home for fear it will be held against me."
- "I would rather fly under the radar while working from home."
- "I work a reduced hours schedule, but none of my peers or clients know about it."
- "In my department, I allow people to work from home, but we do not have a formal policy set up."
- "I negotiated a deal with my supervisor that I would work a reduced hours schedule, but they asked that I keep it confidential."

Level 3: Paper Policy

The next level is *paper policy*. The organization has a written flexible work policy in place, but it is highly stigmatized, and only some people use it. As a result, there is a deep gap between policy and practice.

Here's what a paper policy work culture looks like:

- Written flexible work policies permit the use of workplace flexibility throughout the organization.
- Some employees work on flexible schedules when a need arises, and some work on flexible schedules consistently.
- Some employees who work on flexible schedules feel the need to be discreet.
- Some employees working on flexible schedules feel supported, while others do not.
- Some leaders support workplace flexibility, while others do not.
- Employees on flexible work schedules are rarely represented in leadership.

Here's what it sounds like:

- A talent leader says, "We have a reduced hours policy, but it is handed out with a wink and a nod that it would tank your career if you use it."
- When one associate asked about flexibility, he was told, "Those policies are only for mothers." Later, he found out that was not the case.
- When one individual said they were considering a reduced-hours schedule, their leader responded, "Are you really sure that you want to do that?"

Level 4: Leader-Specific

At the *leader-specific* level, the organization has a written flexible work policy in place. Still, the use of the policy depends on the acceptance or bias of the leaders in each group division. Leaders supporting flexibility implement structures to foster flexibility, whereas leaders opposed to flexibility do not make such structures available. As a result, when it comes to flexibility, there are pockets of excellence and pockets of resistance. Different applications of the flexible work policy lead to perceptions of inequality or disparate treatment among employees.

Here's what a leader-specific work culture looks like:

- There are written flexible work policies permitting the use of workplace flexibility throughout the organization.

- Some employees work on flexible schedules when needed, and others work on flexible schedules consistently. Still, these employees tend to be from specific departments or work under particular supervisors.
- Some employees working on flexible schedules feel supported, while others do not.
- Some leaders support workplace flexibility, while others do not.
- Employees on flexible work schedules are eligible to attain partnersip or senior-level positions, and partnership or senior leadership includes some employees on flexible schedules. However, these employees tend to be from certain departments or work under certain supervisors.
- Employees on flexible work schedules are inconsistently represented in leadership, with an over-representation from certain groups and an underrepresentation from other groups.
- Some resources and support structures (i.e., training, affinity groups, mentoring or sponsorship, work allocation, and evaluations or advancement procedures) might be in place around flexible work. Still, any such resources and support structures are applied inconsistently, with certain groups benefitting more from them than others.

Here's what it sounds like:

- "[In our practice group] it is more efficient to swap information back and forth in person," stated a practice group leader at an organization where several other leaders supported using flexible work.
- "In our office, I let my people work from home, but I know that people in the same practice group in another location all have to be in the office."
- "In our firm, we allow our individual practice group leaders to decide whether their people can work flexibly."
- "In our firm, we have partners who refuse to work with anyone on a reduced hours schedule. I feel bad for my colleagues, because I often work from home, but I know they work for partners who require them to be in the office every day."

Level 5: Flex Acceptance

The fifth level is *flex acceptance*. At this level, the organization has formal policies and leadership support for workplace flexibility, but it needs more infrastructure to support individual and organizational success.

Here's what a flex acceptance work culture looks like:

- There are written flexible work policies permitting the use of workplace flexibility throughout the organization.
- Many employees work on flexible schedules.
- Most employees who work on flexible schedules feel supported.
- Most leaders support workplace flexibility.
- Employees who work on flexible schedules feel supported by their supervisors but may not think that they have organizational resources to help them succeed.
- Employees on flexible work schedules are eligible to attain partnership or senior-level positions, and partnership or senior leadership includes many employees on flexible schedules. These employees represent a cross-section of departments across the organization.
- Employees on flexible work schedules are consistently represented in leadership, with a cross-section of departments across the organization.
- There is a lack of alignment of support structures fostering individual success (i.e., training, work experiences, mentoring or community, and evaluations or advancement) or organizational success (i.e., perceptions, usage, and experiences are not tracked and changes are not made to improve organizational outcomes) around flexible work. These support structures need to be created, expanded, and bolstered.

Here's what it sounds like:

- "I think a particular challenge is that the head of practices are responsible to create culture [in a hybrid work environment], and they don't [always] have people skills."
- "We allow flexibility, but we have not provided our people with the training they need to work successfully in a flexible environment."
- "We launched a new hybrid initiative, but we have not changed any of our practices to reflect the change."

- "We do not provide our people with the technology they need to work from home."
- "I wish I had some coaching on how to work effectively on a reduced hours schedule. My experience is very different from my peers."

Level 6: Flex Success

The final level, reserved for forerunners of workplace flexibility, is Flex Success. At this level, the organization has formal policies and leadership support of flexibility, and it has implemented infrastructure to support individual *and* organizational success. Individuals also have all the resources they need to embrace flexibility. In short, there is an alignment between policy and practice.

Here's what a Flex Success work culture looks like:

- There are written flexible work policies permitting the use of workplace flexibility throughout the organization.
- Many employees work on flexible schedules.
- Virtually all leaders support workplace flexibility.
- Leaders are held accountable for making flexibility work.
- Employees who work on flexible schedules feel supported by their supervisors and the organization as a whole.
- Employees on flexible work schedules are eligible to attain partnership or senior-level positions, and partnership or senior leadership includes many employees on flexible schedules. These employees represent a cross-section of departments across the organization.
- There is an alignment of support structures fostering individual success (i.e., training, work experiences, mentoring or community, and evaluations or advancement). For example

  - The organization offers a variety of training programs supporting its flexible work policy, including training programs on individual strategies for working flexibly successfully and training programs for supervisors on ways to best manage and lead teams that include employees on flexible work schedules.
  - The organization has a work allocation system, tracks work distribution to ensure it is equitable, and has managers and administrators in place whose role includes oversight such that employees on flexible work schedules receive proper work experiences.

- ◆ The organization has clear policies and practices related to resources for flexible work programs (i.e., technology resources, technology stipend, home office equipment, etc.).
  - ◆ The organization has affinity groups to support flexible workers, caregivers, and diverse employees.
  - ◆ The organization has management roles and responsibilities designated to support the flexible work program.
- Infrastructure is aligned to support organizational success (i.e., perceptions, usage, and experiences), data is tracked, and changes are made to improve organizational outcomes for flexible work. For example
  - ◆ The organization systematically and regularly monitors and measures the workplace flexibility program through pilot programs, flex program evaluations, employee opinion surveys, focus group interviews, stay interviews, check-in meetings, and productivity reports and reviews.
  - ◆ Workplace flexibility usage is tracked and tied to employee outcomes like turnover, performance, productivity, profitability, retention, recruitment, engagement, pay, promotions, or hours worked to inform decision-making.
- The organization regularly assesses market trends and implements novel strategies around flexible work.

Here's what a Flex Success work culture sounds like:

- According to Britta Lehn, a Systems, Applications & Products in Data Processing (SAP) employee, "I believe SAP's Pledge to Flex, our hybrid work model, and the hardware, solutions, and tools that SAP provides for flex work to be one of the great values of working at SAP."[13]
- "It is apparent our firm is supportive of flexibility because it touches everything that we do."
- "I feel fully supported in working a flex schedule."
- "We closely monitor everyone that is working on a flex schedule to make sure that they have all the resources that they need to be successful and that they are not disadvantaged in the way that they are working."

- "As a leader, I have all the resources that I need to support employees working flexibly."
- "We came together as a firm to reimagine the way that we collaborate, connect, and communicate in a hybrid environment."

Based on the six flexibility culture meter levels described previously, how would you rate your organization?

If your organization has room to grow, it's usually because of gaps in any of these five areas:

- You lack a clear purpose or business case for flexibility at your organization.
- You don't have a larger organizational vision for flexibility and lack leadership support.
- You don't have flexibility policies in place.
- You don't have the proper practices, tools, and resources to support flexibility across the entire organization (cultural support, technological infrastructure support, or both).
- You don't measure and monitor the use of flexible work options and make changes over time to improve them.

The good news is that each Flex Success Framework step aligns with the five gaps. In this step, reflect, you've deeply examined where you are today, built your business case, and defined your purpose. That leads us to the next step: reimagine.

REFLECTION QUESTIONS

This chapter asks you to reflect on several important questions that help uncover the *why* behind flexibility: how can flexibility drive benefits and positive outcomes for your organization and your people? Aside from looking at this through an organizational lens, examine it through the lens of the individual employee— what would flexibility do for *you* personally?

5

WHO DO YOU WANT TO BE?

I recently worked with a senior leader who told me from the beginning that he saw flexibility as a driver of talent. So when it was time to develop a flexibility initiative, it was easy to see how flexibility could help get them there. He wanted his organization to be the most competitive at recruiting and retaining talent, providing a workplace where employees could thrive and excel. He described the vision as being the "employer of choice" for the best talent. This clear vision made it easy for his organization to plan and implement their flexibility initiative.

In contrast, when another firm created its flexible work strategy, one senior leader commented, "We have to offer flexible work because other firms are doing it—otherwise we will lose talent. But I think it will cause a lot of issues in the long run." While this senior leader may have believed that flexibility was beneficial for talent recruitment and retention, he was looking at the process of creating a flexibility initiative as a problem to be solved rather than an opportunity to step back and create a vision of the future. This mindset set up roadblocks that had hindered progress from the start.

I've talked to many leaders creating and implementing their flexible work policies. *Reflecting* on the business case for flexibility combined with *reimagining* how flexibility can fuel their highest aspirations yields a much better outcome every time.

Now that you've reflected on where you are today and the purpose and unique business case of flexibility for your organization, you are ready for step two in the Flex Success Framework, *reimagine*. This is a time to look to the future and reimagine what work can look like and who you want to be as an organization in this new environment from a place of strength.

Next you will consider alignment between what your organization says about its culture and how your employees see it. You will uncover whether you need to bridge any gaps.

You will also look at your flexibility non-negotiables to know what you want to honor and preserve. This step is about giving your team clear guidelines for equity and accountability.

Typically, vision and planning work is limited to the leadership team. But as discussed in chapter 3, an effective flexibility strategy must be inclusive, which means bringing as many voices as practical into each step of the process as you did in step one. To ensure you include all voices in this step, you will gather input from other employees and stakeholders on these questions: What do they believe the organization's vision, values, and culture should be? And what are their biggest flexibility non-negotiables?

Finally, as a working group, you will extend your flexibility vision into a set of clear, powerful flexibility principles to ensure you align your flexibility strategy with what matters most to your organization.

With your purpose and business case from step one, your vision and flexibility principles will provide a strong foundation for designing your flexibility policies in step three: redesign.

REIMAGINING WHO YOU CAN BE

In his classic book *The Fifth Discipline*, Peter Senge notes that the organizations with the highest competitive advantage are the organizations that learn the fastest. One of the five disciplines needed for these "learning organizations" is *building a shared vision*.

> *If any one idea about leadership has inspired organizations for thousands of years, it's the capacity to hold a shared picture of the future we seek to create. One is hard-pressed to think of any organization that has sustained some measure of greatness in the absence of goals, values, and missions that become deeply shared throughout the organization. . . . When there is a genuine vision (as opposed to the all-too-familiar vision statement), people excel and learn, not because they are told to, but because they want to.*[1]

As Senge says, "People need visions to make the purpose more concrete and tangible."[2] There are several ways to go about visioning for the future. In this stage, I want companies to ask themselves critical questions that help to make that vision clear.

Articulate Your Positioning: What Do You Want Your Employees to Say About Your Organization?

As you consider creating your shared vision, think about how you want your employees to talk about your organization.

- What do you want employees to tell friends, family, and industry colleagues about your organization? What do you want to see posted on websites like Glassdoor?
- How do you want your employees to describe their workplace when talking to clients?
- What would best capture the best of who you want to be? What will set you apart?

Clarify Your Positioning: What Do You Want Others to Say about You?

Consider your positioning or industry reputation as you think about your shared vision for flexibility.

Consider the following questions:

- What do you want the market to say about you?
- What do you want your clients to say about you?
- What awards do you want to win?

As with articulating your position, you can answer these questions as a leadership team and then ask others in your organization the same questions.

How might you sum up the responses?

Now draft your vision in a way that paints a clear and compelling picture.

MAKE SURE YOU ARE WHO YOU SAY YOU ARE: ENSURING ALIGNMENT

The biggest mistake organizations make is to quickly draft a policy that is not based on their own vision, values, and culture. But in a culture of Flex Success, the unwritten rules match the spoken rules. Who you say you want to be and who you are must align.

The step of reimagine allows you to create alignment between who you say you want to be and what you do regarding your flexibility strategy. For example, you might say you value innovation as a company but do not implement the latest technology to support your employees working effectively online. This lack of alignment can damage your reputation and trust with employees, colleagues, vendors, clients, potential clients, and even your industry.

Many organizations fall into this trap. Organizations may tell me that their culture is human-centered. Yet there is no evidence of it. Recently a senior leader at a firm told me he was mandating that all their employees be in the office five days a week. Yet one of the values they express to employees and potential employees is that they have a culture of autonomy. Those two things are not in alignment. In a case like that, employees will lose trust in the company because the words and actions don't sync up.

In the previous stage, you compared how leaders' descriptions of culture sync with employees' views and experiences of the culture. Were company descriptions of culture aligned with employee descriptions? This information will reveal any gaps that your written policy should bridge.

Are your people connected to your culture? According to Gallup, when people are connected to their organization's culture, they are 3.7 times as likely to be engaged at work, 5.2 times as likely to recommend their organization, and 55 percent less likely to be looking for a job.[3] Both connection and alignment matter.

If you want to change your organizational culture in any other way, you'll want to make sure that your flexibility principles, policies, and practices are all reflective of your aspirational culture. We'll discuss this kind of intentional alignment in steps three and four.

OUTLINE YOUR NON-NEGOTIABLES: WHAT DO YOU WANT TO PRESERVE?

Regardless of how the future of work changes, it's essential to define what needs to stay the same. Identifying these non-negotiables is critical to protect them as your organization changes in other ways.

Ask yourselves, what do you want to honor and preserve? What cultural attributes, working methods, or strengths do you want to protect? The answers to these questions ultimately help you to ensure that your flexibility initiative will strengthen your organization without compromising what's important to you.

For Jenn Flynn at Capital One, preserving corporate culture and in-person collaboration was most important.

As a leader, I believe it is important to preserve what is special about our corporate culture in this hybrid environment. We've found hybrid work can be both effective and empowering. Work-at-home days provide flexibility, heads-down time, and efficient daily schedules without time spent commuting. In-office days provide unique opportunities for planned collaboration, innovation, personal connection, and mentorship. We continue to be compelled by both ways of working and the powerful benefits that hybrid enables.[4]

Another way to identify your non-negotiables is to consider your concerns about flexibility. This step is revealing because it uncovers fears leaders may have about how flexibility might change things that are working well now. When leaders tell me about their fears, I don't try to convince them not to have them. I encourage them. Why?

First, because they're right to be concerned, because by default, some of these scenarios are likely to happen. But by design, they don't have to. You can intentionally design a policy to preserve everything you're most concerned about losing. That's what you'll learn in the remainder of this book.

Second, I encourage leaders to express their concerns because this also gives important insight into what matters most so that we can design for that.

In one recent example, an executive committee member expressed that he worried about his team not being as responsive to clients if they work outside the office. Responsiveness is critical, so this was at the top of his list of non-negotiables.

In another example, before COVID-19, I spent over an hour talking to a senior leader who was very opposed to telecommuting. After hearing him out and then working to show him how those fears can be translated into non-negotiables and effective policy, he told me that he saw the light! He is now one of the biggest proponents of flexibility in his firm.

You're not alone if you have concerns or fears about flexibility as a leader. I've talked to hundreds of leaders about their flexibility fears and noticed several common fears emerge (as mentioned earlier in the book). They are so common I've started calling them the five Cs: loss of control, loss of contribution, loss of connection, loss of collaboration, and loss of culture, which are part of a framework I described in an article in the *Harvard Business Review*.[5]

Let's see if any sound familiar.

Loss of Control

Executives often worry that if they allow some employees to work flexibly, they will open a flood gate of issues that they won't be able to control. They fear that if they allow people to work on reduced hours schedules, everyone will want reduced hours, and they will not be able to support it. With hybrid policies, they worry they will never know where people are on any given day or that people will never come into the office.

When loss of control is at play, people start discussing attendance policies and monitoring where people are. They fear losing control of knowing where their people are.

Yet, before COVID-19, leaders expected people to abide by policies but were not constantly patrolling who was in the office and who wasn't—or verifying they were really at the conference or client meeting they said they were.

The answer to this fear is *structure* and *clarity*. Any organization that correctly designs and implements its flexibility initiative will not lose anything. To maintain control and smooth operation of your organization, you must set standards and communicate them clearly. We'll talk more about how to do this in chapter 7.

Loss of Contribution

Leaders often fear that if their employees are not physically at their desks in the office, they won't know if they are actually working.

With endless distractions on computers (from online shopping to social media), even if your people are sitting at their desks working on their computers, you really don't know if they're working for your company. They could be searching for a new job (that offers flexibility!) right before your eyes.

At the same time, Vernā Myers has found that a highly flexible environment can result in more significant contributions from employees. Giving people a choice of where or when to get work done instills trust and empowers them.

"That choice is such a powerful feeling," Myers states. "It makes me want to work harder. I have the freedom to [set personal appointments] and then come back to work. The more you use that freedom, the more you trust yourself and appreciate your company and your leader.

"The question is, do you see the people you work with as professionals? Do you believe they are going to do their best for the company and for the team?"[6]

Loss of Connection

Many individuals feel the greatest sense of connection when in person, so it's unsurprising that many leaders fear losing connection when considering flexibility. However, the loss of connection is also a myth. With technology from laptops to conferencing apps, individuals today can connect at any time of the day in almost any location.

Loss of Collaboration

Loss of collaboration is a frequent fear that emerges when leaders consider a hybrid work environment. They're concerned that people will be siloed and team collaboration will suffer. But as long as teams working a flexible schedule commit to regular meetings and consistent communication, collaboration does not have to be compromised.

Loss of Culture

This fear may be the most prevalent, especially when discussing a hybrid work environment. Yet many leaders who have told me they are most concerned about losing their culture are also unable to articulate exactly how to describe their culture.

The first thing to remember is that culture is not a place. Culture is about your set of values, relationships, behaviors, and habits. It is evidenced in the way that you treat people and the way that people feel. Certainly offices can enhance it, but they alone do not form your culture. This is why it's so important to define your culture and values, as you have been invited to do in chapter 4, so you can design flexibility to honor and enhance your culture.

Identifying your non-negotiables is so essential that I urge everyone to take their time on this step. The following exercise is one way to discover what your flexibility fears have to teach you. This exercise can be done by leaders individually or as a working group.

1. Write out your biggest concerns about what might happen if you allow flexibility in your organization.
2. Next to each fear, write down why you're afraid this will happen.
3. Reflect on whether this reason is true for everyone or just true for you. For example, let's say you wrote down you were afraid you would lose connection with flexibility because we can only build relationships in person. Think about whether that reason is true for just you or everyone. Does everyone build relationships in person? Do some people connect online first? Digital-first generations can be very comfortable building relationships digitally. Consider your own experience. Did you have to build new client relationships virtually

during COVID-19 when you could not meet in person? Have you built strong relationships with colleagues in different offices with whom you have had to work closely but never met in person?

4. Once you determine whether the reason is true for everyone or just true for you, identify what each fear reveals about what you value most:

   ◆ In light of this fear, what do you want to preserve, no matter what?

   ◆ Regardless of what changes, what needs to stay the same?

Here are examples of flexibility fears shared by leaders in their own words:

- We won't be able to connect as a team.
- We won't be able to maintain our productivity.
- We won't be able to be as responsive to clients and team members.
- We won't be able to maintain our apprenticeship model.
- How will we be able to provide mentoring?
- How will we retain boundaries on vacation?
- We'll lose our edge with client service.
- Our unique culture will fade away.
- We'll lose our ability to collaborate.
- We'll miss out on developing our professional relationships.

Hidden in all these fears are the things these leaders value most: connection, productivity, responsiveness, the apprenticeship model, mentoring, boundaries, client service, unique culture, collaboration, and professional relationships. These are all important qualities, and they're right to value them.

The good news is that now that these fears are clear, they can intentionally design an initiative that preserves what they value most.

So after leaders write down all their fears, I facilitate the process of reframing their fears as opportunities. Here's one example:

Wherever we go from here, we must maintain:

- Commitment to our mission. Continue to be accountable to yourself, to the team, and to the organization;
- Commitment to our members. Exhibit flexibility, nimbleness, and agility in our work for our members;

- Our culture; and
- Employee expectations and the need to remain competitive. We're expected to do exceptional things and to deliver and perform at very high standards.

For this organization, performance and high standards cannot be compromised. And I agree 100 percent: flexibility is not a trade-off for performance, as we'll see in the following section.

Here is another example:

We struggle with maintaining connection: How do you, with newer, younger talent, replicate the culture of when people are all together? Personalities and humor come together when you're all in the same room. We want to make sure we still have those forward-thinking in-person sessions.

Connectivity is also essential. And especially as new people have been onboarded in the past year, we value being a collegial and supportive workplace with coworkers and the individuals we work with. All the members are professional, courteous, friendly, and helpful. We also need to make sure this stays the same.

This is how you can make the shift to intentionality. Instead of fears, you now have a list of what matters most to you and a list of opportunity areas for your initiative.

CREATE YOUR FLEXIBILITY PRINCIPLES

Now that you've clarified who you want to be and what you want to preserve in the context of flexibility, you'll create a set of flexibility principles that will become your guiding lights that govern how you behave as an organization. These are meant to be shared with your entire organization when you roll out your flexibility initiative to ensure everyone is on the same page with what you expect and allow.

The following are flexibility principles that are important in almost every organization. You might adopt some or all of these along with any you develop that are specific to your organization. You may notice that some of these were discussed earlier in chapter 3 in the section on essential reframes leaders need to make to embrace flexibility. Many are crucial to entire organizations, which is why they might also appear here in the form of a principle, as is the case with this first principle.

Flexibility Is Not a Trade-off for Performance

One leader told me that an employee told them they couldn't take notes on a client call because they were working from home.

"And what did you say to them?" I asked.

"I didn't say anything," they admitted, "because I didn't want to seem anti-flexible."

I reminded this leader that they are allowed to have expectations with flexibility. That's part of what it means to be a business. The business can have needs, just like employees can have needs.

Many leaders are fearful about pushing back when employees don't meet expectations. Some of that pushback is legitimate. People committed to the same mission and vision should be committed to finding a way to achieve critical outcomes together. Just because you want to be flexible doesn't mean you can't create clear guidelines about expectations. If you discover someone isn't producing or reaching their goals, you need to ask them what's going on. Don't assume it's just because they're working flexibly. If you've set expectations, created support, and ensured they have what they need, and they still aren't producing, then it's more likely that they're not the right person for the job. Ultimately this is an employee performance issue, not a flexibility issue.

Flexibility doesn't mean everyone does whatever they want, whenever they want. You can design your flexibility strategy for productivity, which may include requiring people to attend specific meetings or be at their desks at certain times.

Flexibility should not impact productivity or performance. That's where intentionality comes in: you can design a policy to protect what matters most to you, as you'll do in chapter 6.

And if you notice an employee's responsiveness, availability, or quality of work has decreased after implementing a flexibility strategy, those aren't failures of flexibility. They are failures of performance. Bringing them back into the office won't necessarily solve those problems, as we'll see in the following principle.

Facetime Is Not an Indicator of Commitment

"I just don't want people sitting around the pool in flip flops doing their work." Yes, this is an exact quote! A quote from a leader of a multinational organization on why he just didn't think flexibility was right for his organization.

First of all, I thanked him for his honesty. I was glad that he felt comfortable saying what he thought (and what I'm sure a lot of people believe but are not comfortable expressing.) I explained that with a flexible working strategy, the emphasis must shift to the *end product* rather than where and when that product was produced.

The real question is, are your employees producing high-quality work and contributing to the organization's vision, regardless of where, when, or how they work? With the technology available today, there is no reason someone working from home cannot be as engaged, productive, and available as someone working in person. And as we saw in chapter 2, the option to work from home can make us more productive, not less.

A recent study from Gartner has indicated that *not* requiring facetime for every collaboration increases quality results.[7]

Plus *facetime* and *time in the office* are not necessarily the same. Someone may work full-time in the office but walk straight to their office, shut the door, work all day, and then leave without engaging with anyone. In essence, they are telecommuting from the office.

Is that employee more committed than the one who works from home twice a week, produces the same quality work, and regularly mentors others through video calls? Does it matter if your employees are sitting by the pool in their flip-flops if they are completely immersed in their work and producing top-quality results?

As long as employees can be *trusted* to deliver top-quality work by the deadline and actively contribute to the organization's goals, time and location are less important.

One Size Does Not Fit All

Individuals will need flexibility for different reasons and at different times. To map out the components of your flexibility initiative, it's helpful to look at the needs of your employees while keeping in mind the organization's needs as a whole.

While Jenn Flynn notes that, in her opinion, certain types of work are best handled in person, other leaders may collaborate best virtually for other types of work.[8] One size of flexibility does not fit all. Sometimes it may be better for some people to do their deep-focused work in the office, while at other times, it may be better for a team to work together at a certain time to meet a specific objective. It's best to provide the type of flexibility where individuals have the autonomy to get their work done as efficiently and effectively as possible and for teams also to set norms for completing work together as efficiently and effectively as possible.

Remember that work preferences do not necessarily correlate with demographics or identity. Not all parents prefer working at home, and not all men want to work in the office full-time. Some Baby Boomers may prefer working online from home, while some Gen Zs prefer the office. And all want the autonomy to choose within a framework.

Remember our definition of holistic flexibility is a full and complete approach to working that meets both organizational and employee needs in a way that produces a healthy culture, employee loyalty and productivity, and a profitable bottom line.

Holistic flexibility includes a wide range of work options like virtual work, reduced hours, job sharing, flexible start and end times, full-time flex, annualized hours, and all kinds of long- and short-term leave. We'll cover all these options in detail in chapter 6.

Flexibility Is "Yes and"

We often hear debates about whether it's better or worse to work at home. It is better to find the higher ground by asking, "How can we make it work?" Yes, some people are more productive at home, and others are more productive at the office. Yes, some have their best ideas during meetings, while others have their best ones in solitude. Yes, we can intentionally create meaningful connections online and in person. If we can bring together the best of who we are while working online, in person, at different times, and beyond, we can have the best of all worlds.

Work Is Not a Place, and Culture Is Not a Location

We all remember the phrase *return to work*. What did you think when you heard that phrase? I know what I thought: "Was I not working at home?" Most people would say they worked harder and longer at home during the pandemic than they ever had. We can work effectively in a variety of places, and not just at the office.

If work can be done at any time and everywhere, that also means culture is not dependent upon your location. As discussed in chapter 4, culture is what we do when nobody's looking—wherever we are. Culture is shaped by your values, how people experience a sense of belonging, how you treat one another, your relationships, and what you stand for. Yes, being together in person can enhance culture, but you can also create and build culture effectively online. We'll talk more about this in step four: reintegrate.

Flexibility is Continually Improving

Some leaders say, "Well if our flexibility strategy doesn't work, we'll just go back to requiring everyone to work in the office." The truth is a flexibility strategy is by nature iterative. No one gets everything right from the beginning. Acknowledge that you're almost certainly *not* going to get it right on your first attempt, but that you can commit to continuously improving. Then when things go wrong, as they certainly will, your first response will be, "How can we make it better?" Thus your organization will continue to get better and better at this new reality of holistic flexibility.

Flexibility Is a Shared Responsibility

This principle—also covered in chapter 3—applies to every organization and everyone in the organization. To make flexibility work, everyone—organizations, leaders, and individuals—must take responsibility for the initiative's success.

Organizations are responsible for putting structures, systems, guidelines, and training in place to foster the success of workplace flexibility. Leaders are accountable for their teams' success. Employees' loyalty and perceptions about their organization are often rooted in the opinions of their leaders and supervisors and the tone they set. Leaders must take responsibility for embracing the new work environment and shifting their behaviors to lead differently.

Finally, individuals are responsible for success in this new environment and prioritizing their career goals and team or organizational needs. We'll discuss leaders' and individuals' responsibilities in chapter 7.

Flexibility Is Flexible

Finally, flexibility is flexible. That's because flexibility is a two-way street. On one hand, nobody should be using flexibility as a reason why they cannot do something within their job description (see "Flexibility Is Not a Trade-off for Performance"). On the other hand, the best policies allow for autonomy and are not overly rigid (see "People Want Autonomy Within a Framework"). To be effective, flexible work programs should provide what the employees want while meeting the organization's needs.

To meet the needs of individuals and the organization, Susan Neely at the American Council of Life Insurers (ACLI) notes that she has had to learn when to be flexible and when to hold the line. "I've always been committed to making [flexibility] work, while at the same time maintaining high productivity and related to that, accountability," said Neely. "We as the organization set the weather, but people also have to own it, make it work, and be committed to our high level of performance."[9]

To meet the dynamic needs of clients, employees, and the organization, flexibility has to be flexible. No one can use it as an excuse not to get the job done or not to meet with someone. "I can't make that meeting because I'm working from home" should never come out of the mouth of anybody. Communicate clear principles to guide your policy and practices to avoid this behavior.

But even as you map out specific flexibility objectives like usage rates and advancement of employees working flex, remember that the program should be adaptable and evolve with the organization as the needs of its employees change. We'll talk more about this throughout the book.

When I share these principles with leaders, many breathe a sigh of relief. You can have expectations of your employees in your flexibility strategy, and some pushback to employees' requests is legitimate. Flexibility doesn't mean anarchy!

Keep in mind these principles are not just recommendations; they are expectations. They determine who you are and who you will be as an organization. To that end, feel free to include any existing principles from your values or vision statement you've already created. For example, a leader who is worried about their team's level of responsiveness might develop a principle like "flexibility and responsiveness must go hand in hand," or for those who fear a loss of collaboration, "We will use the best of who we are in the office and online to collaborate optimally as an organization."

Because these principles will determine who you are and who you will be as an organization, you can see why it's so essential for top leadership to be part of your flexibility working group. If top leadership is not involved for some reason, make extra sure your leadership team is also going through this visioning exercise.

With your flexibility purpose statement and flexibility principles in hand, flexibility is now not just a business imperative but a strategic one.

Remember you're designing more than a policy—you're designing a system change and a culture change. Now that you have established a strong foundation of the purpose of your flex policy and who you want to be as an organization, you can begin to redesign not just your flex policy but also the infrastructure, office space, and other resources you need to make it successful.

REFLECTION QUESTIONS

This chapter asks you to create a vision for the future and includes many reflection questions to help you and your team do this. Before you get started with your team, consider this from your perspective. What do you envision for the future, and what are parts of the culture that you personally want to preserve? What aspects of the culture would you like to change? What new aspects of culture would you like to create?

6

WHAT FLEXIBILITY INITIATIVES WILL SUPPORT YOUR PURPOSE AND PRINCIPLES?

In step three of the Flex Success Framework, *redesign*, you will design your flexibility initiative based on the flexibility purpose statement you established in step one and the flexibility principles you established in step two.

In this stage you'll tap all the data and inputs, as well as the purpose, values, and principles you've established or articulated in earlier steps, and from those you will craft the initiative that will support your goals and vision. Importantly this step also includes developing plans for the infrastructure—the policies, people, systems, and structures needed to make flexibility work.

A word of caution before we dive in: if you're like some clients I've worked with, at this point, you may start thinking that this process is more involved than you thought, or you might think that it isn't necessary to be as thorough as I recommend. I've seen this go both ways: companies that shortcut the process run into plenty of implementation issues down the road they could have prevented, or alternately, clients who do the essential foundation-building work upfront come back to me after implementation and say, "We had an exact roadmap to follow that made implementation successful."

Consider the countless headlines and quotes we've read or heard in recent years about chief executive officers (CEOs) or leaders demanding their employees get back into the office because they felt they lost productivity, or their employees felt disconnected or less engaged. As I've mentioned, so many of these issues are not failures of flexibility. They are failures of implementation. For example, some organizations offered their employees virtual work options but didn't support them by training their managers on how to stay connected in a virtual world. The result: lack of connection. Or companies offered hybrid schedules but then micromanaged employees by making them swipe in and out of the office. The result: employees felt disconnected from their leaders because the leaders' actions expressed a lack of trust. This is why it's so important to be thorough and intentional when you design and implement your flexibility initiative. The time and effort invested is well worth it. Now let's dive in.

REDESIGNING YOUR FLEXIBILITY INITIATIVE BASED ON PURPOSE AND PRINCIPLES

To ensure that your flexibility initiative is successful, it's essential that the organization considers all aspects of the initiative and then articulates the details clearly. This provides a full opportunity to optimize everything that flexibility offers to the organization and each employee.

An initiative that is well thought out and detailed, with a formal, written policy that can be shared by all, has clear benefits for everyone:

- It signals the importance of flexible work as a business initiative to the organization.
- It lets all employees know what options are available and how to use the program.
- It encourages consistency by preventing flexibility from being a series of one-offs or secret side deals.
- It gives the employer control over the policy's specific terms and provides concrete guidelines for managing it.
- It allows the employer to encourage all employees to use the policy to reduce the stigma associated with a flexible schedule.
- It gives the employees clear guidelines on what is expected of them.
- It allows the organization to create a detailed roadmap that sets them up for a smooth and successful implementation.

This chapter will summarize the elements necessary to support the initiative's success.

GETTING STARTED: WRITING YOUR FLEXIBILITY POLICY

Writing your flexibility policy is when you take your raw materials—your goals, principles, strengths, vision, and ideas—and craft them into a clear, detailed model that everyone can understand, embrace, and utilize. A flexibility policy must be tailored to the needs of each unique organization and its employees, led by the flexibility working group. While the substance of the policy should be uniquely yours, I can provide the framework.

I recommend every flexibility policy include the following provisions:

- Purpose;
- Structure;
- Eligibility;
- Approval process;
- Compensation and advancement;
- Review schedule; and
- Legal considerations.

Developing thorough policies that consider all essential details upfront sets your organization up for success. Next I'll cover considerations of each of the provisions.

State the Purpose of the Policy

Begin drafting your policy by stating your flexibility purpose statement from the reflect stage: your organization's unique business case for flexibility. This business case should specify why flexibility is vital to *your* organization. Are you creating this policy to invest in talent recruiting and retention? Support the diversity of your workforce? Foster wellness and work-life autonomy? Enhance productivity and profitability? By connecting flexibility with business benefits, you help reduce stigma and increase acceptance of the policy.

Choose the Types of Flexibility You Will Offer

When leaders thought about flexibility options after the COVID-19 pandemic, most were thinking about a hybrid or virtual policy or flexibility in *where* you work. But it's important to remember that there have been successful flexible work arrangements for decades that cover many forms of flexibility. In many law firms, for example, reduced hours options were more commonly utilized before COVID-19. It's important here to think about *holistic flexibility*—including all the models and structures that flexible work offers.

As discussed in chapter 1, holistic flexibility includes flexible work options for *where* you work, *when* you work (synchronous vs. asynchronous hours), and *how long* you work (part-time options, job sharing, etc.). As you begin crafting your policy, you'll want to consider all possibilities.

Many organizations include many or all of the above, like Microsoft, which describes their approach as "At Microsoft, we value and support flexibility as part of our hybrid workplace where every employee can do their best work by working the way they work best. A hybrid workplace is a mix of workstyles across work site, work location and work hours."[1]

Here are specific models to consider that represent flexibility in where, when, and how long you work:

Flexible Location: In-Office, Hybrid, and Virtual Policies

Firms can create flexible arrangements that include in-office, hybrid, and virtual work all in the same policy. For example, some organizations ask all employees to be in the office a few days per week. So the company is 100 percent in the office during those days. The rest of the week, perhaps everyone is working from outside the office, so they are 100 percent online or virtual on those days. Overall, the employees work on a hybrid schedule in any given week. Organizations can further modify or customize among these categories to include percentage of time, percentage of days, anchor days, and any combination of these—options I will explain next. The goal is to create a policy structure that allows your organization to reach the objectives aligned with its purpose and principles.

For example, Capital One's flexible hybrid model helps maintain its corporate culture and offers the benefits of in-person collaboration in an office environment.

"The hybrid model gives us a chance to match the work we're doing with the environment that best supports that work," said Jenn Flynn, Capital One's head of Small Business Bank. "Needs change on a daily basis—the needs of your team, the needs of your work, the needs of your family—and we have two environments that allow us to accommodate those needs—creating the best of both worlds. Our hybrid approach concentrates the time when we are in the office in order to maximize the collaboration and human connections that we know are an important part of Capital One's culture."[2]

For different individuals at different organizations doing different types of work, it might be the opposite—perhaps collaboration is best done virtually if teams are dispersed geographically, and focused work is best done in the office if the home is chaotic during the day. One size does not fit all.

To design the flexible location policy that fits your organization best, consider the following options that have worked well for different organizations with different needs.

Percentage of Time. There are a few ways to structure the percentage of time model. One approach is for the organization to require a certain percentage of time in the office, but the individual has free choice about when to work there. Many who use this model will spend 50 percent of their time in the office and 50 percent working virtually.

Another approach is to use a number-of-days option. In this setup, sometimes the days are designated, and in other cases, they are not.

- *Benefits*: The percentage of time model considers that every week may have different personal and professional needs. In the case of client services industries, like law firms, consulting firms, and financial services, client needs can change from week to week, making a percentage of time model easier to manage. This model may be especially attractive to organizations with many offices, where hybrid and virtual meetings are already commonplace.
- *Drawbacks*: Employees working in this model may come into the office when others are away, reducing the benefits of being in the office. Also, the percentage of time model is more abstract and harder to track for employees.

One example of a percentage of time policy is law firm Arnold & Porter's Remote Work Options Policy, which allows attorneys and professional staff to work 50 percent of their time in the office, leaving 50 percent each month for virtual work.

From the beginning Arnold & Porter's flexibility initiative was strongly supported by leadership. "Our leadership very strongly believes there are benefits from working from home, and there are benefits from working in the office," said Ellen Kaye Fleishhacker, co-managing partner at Arnold & Porter. "We learned during the pandemic that we can provide excellent client service even with everybody working remotely. We feel very strongly about finding a balance between people having control over their schedules and continuing to do excellent client work."

Arnold & Porter also developed their policy in collaboration with their people from the beginning. "There are so many constituencies within any organization, and we really wanted to put together a policy that worked for those constituencies," said Fleishhacker.

> *So we started with focus groups: we had focus groups for our partners and counsel, we had focus groups for our associates, we had focus groups for our professional staff. We really tried to get the input of virtually every single person in the firm, as we were thinking about the policy we were putting together. People met in small groups, talked about a set of questions, and then reported back. Then as we were developing the policy, which was an iterative process, we would reach back out to representatives of each constituency and get their input.*[3]

Arnold & Porter received the Diversity & Flexibility Alliance's 2021 Flex Impact Award for their inclusive hybrid initiative.

Anchor Days. In chapter 2, we noted a potential downside for diversity when it comes to flexible work locations: without intentional design, siloes and ingroup versus outgroup divisions can form. We've also noted leaders' general concerns about connection and collaboration when implementing a flexible work initiative. One way organizations can intentionally design for connection is to include anchor days when offering percentage of time options.

In the anchor days model, organizations allow people to work away from the office, but the organization decides when people will work at the office and when they will not. For example, an organization might require everyone not to work in the office on Monday and Friday and everyone to work in the office on the Anchor Days of Tuesday, Wednesday, and Thursday. I note here that though some companies allow individual teams to set their anchor days in addition to the organization-wide anchor days, be careful about how it works in practice. Ensure there is still equity in policy utilization, plenty of opportunities for cross-pollination of ideas, expertise, and opportunities among teams, and greater overall connection across organizations.

Another note about anchor days: I've noticed some organizations call the days when everyone is in the office *connection days* or *collaboration days*. I wouldn't recommend that terminology because it implies that we are only connecting or collaborating when we're in person. Flexibility is yes, and yes, we can connect in person, and yes, we can connect online. And if we feel disconnected online, we can learn skills to increase connection wherever we work. We'll talk more about this topic in chapter 7.

- *Benefits*: The anchor day model levels the playing field and reduces the chance of creating an ingroup and outgroup. It also reduces organizational costs, as you can turn down the thermostats and use less power at the office when everyone is working elsewhere. It also means you don't have to navigate hybrid meetings, where some people are online, and others are in person. This type of model is especially beneficial for organizations with one office.
- *Drawbacks*: By deciding which days people must work at the office, the organization has taken away people's autonomy in choosing where they work at least some time, a key motivator for success. For example, if someone prefers to work in the office full time, they no longer have that option.

The American Council of Life Insurers (ACLI) uses an anchor day model, with Wednesdays and Thursdays each week required in the office. But even this arrangement is flexible. "Our language says we have two anchor days in the office to maximize collaboration and working together," said Susan Neely, ACLI's president and CEO. "But we have flexibility with that. If you need to be at a doctor's appointment or your kids' soccer game at three o'clock on a Wednesday, you can use your judgment on whether you need to come in at all, as long as you get the work done. Likewise, if a customer or stakeholder needs to meet on a non-anchor day, we do it.

In addition to their two anchor days, ACLI allows the organization to work 100 percent virtually during July, a characteristically slow month in their business year, plus every major holiday.

"I think it's working really well," said Neely. "Most importantly, everybody in the organization is owning how they're going to work and how to make the most of it."[4]

Perkins Coie modifies the anchor day model further. To avoid the siloes that can unintentionally form between those working in the office and those working away from the office, especially for underrepresented individuals, Perkins Coie encourages teams to set their own anchor days without requiring the same anchor days for everyone.

"[For our team], we ask people to try to coordinate and have everyone come in at least one or two of the same days," said Genhi Givings Bailey, Perkins Coie's chief diversity and inclusion officer. "We also ask other leaders to do the same thing and support them with resources to help them do that."[5]

Combination: Percentage of Time plus Anchor Days. As a combination of those two models, another option is to set a specific anchor day each week where everyone is in the office but allow free choice with a percentage of time in the office beyond that anchor day.

- *Benefits*: This model allows for both some autonomy and in-person connection. It offers both benefits by enabling employees to make some choices of when to come in and having specific anchor days when they will have the time for in-person connection.
- *Drawbacks*: Anchor days take some autonomy away from employees. Plus employees may feel more dissatisfied coming in on non-anchor days as they can compare attendance and engagement with others.

Saul Ewing developed such a model, called the 4+4 flexible location policy, where people work in the office every Wednesday and can choose four other days to work in the office each month, equaling approximately four plus four days in the office per month. "The idea was that for those Wednesdays, you would know people were going to be in the office, so you could plan meetings," explained Jason St. John, managing partner at Saul Ewing and recipient of the Alliance's 2022 Flex Leader Award. "Then you pick four other days where you could work with your teams, go to lunch with folks you might not have seen on Wednesdays, collaborate with larger groups, or just be in the office to work in a different environment. It's four plus four, and nothing more than that."

It was intended to apply to everyone as a policy and a new way of working. "What was really important to our leadership team was that the rules applied to everybody the same," said St. John. "For those very few people with jobs that require being in the office, such as those in the mailroom, we talked with them about how we tried to be as flexible as we could, but four plus four wasn't going to apply to them. But for everybody else, it applied exactly the same."

Saul Ewing has also made Wednesdays Zoom-free days "unless, of course, client demands dictate otherwise, because clients do feed our families," St. John added. "But we really looked at them as community days, days to collaborate with each other and break bread with one another. It's really been a terrific success."[6]

In chapter 9, you'll learn the full story behind how Saul Ewing developed their organization-wide flexibility shift, detailing how one organization implemented the Flex Success Framework from beginning to end.

Work-from-Anywhere Weeks. Regardless of the hybrid or virtual model they choose, some organizations add work-from-anywhere weeks, where people can choose two, three, or four weeks where they can choose where to work. Some organizations decide when these weeks will be, such as the week before Labor Day, the week of Thanksgiving, or the week between Christmas and New Year's Day, while others allow their people to choose.

In my work with organizations and leaders, I've heard many employees mention the attractiveness of work-from-anywhere weeks. During the pandemic, some employees traveled to different places and worked in different locations.

Before moving on to flexible time models, note the language you use in your location policy. Many terms describe when employees work outside a company's physical offices—online, virtual, remote, work from home, work from anywhere, off-site, telecommuting, digital nomad, and more. Some of these have specific connotations that can be either positive or negative. For example, calling an employee's work situation *remote* can raise feelings of disconnection or isolation, as mentioned earlier in the book. Or an employee might say they are working *virtually*, with many others assuming they are working at home, but they could be at a client site in a different time zone. Whatever words you use, they should be precise. I often suggest people use *insert location*—meaning, be specific about where you're working so that others know how to reach you, what time zone you're in, and if you're in proximity to the physical office in case you're needed on site. The more specific the communication is, the more seamless the collaboration.

Flexible Time: Shifting Hours and Compressed Workweek

Flexibility in *when* you work is desired by many because it offers autonomy. This type of flexibility is especially useful for caregivers, employees with outside interests (i.e., writing, marathon running, community service), and those with strenuous commutes. It also allows workers to work when they are naturally most productive.

However, productivity and engagement could be negatively affected if proper communication and guidelines are not associated with this form of flexibility. I hear from leaders that they had a difficult time when employees worked virtually because they would not work regular hours. I recommended that working virtually should not change employees' hours (unless that is part of the agreement), and this behavior should be addressed with the employee. For this reason, flexibility in when you work must be separate from flexibility in where you work.

Flexibility in when you work comes in two forms. The first is shifting hours, where employees work different schedules, such as coming in earlier, leaving later, or taking a break in the day. The other is a compressed workweek, where employees work a full-time schedule (what is traditionally done in five days) on a shorter workweek (three or four days) by completing more hours per day.

When offering this type of flexibility, I suggest that team workload and considerations are involved in the approval process. Additionally, a clear work schedule must be communicated to all. For example, if an employee is not working on Fridays but will complete all work Monday through Thursday, the whole team needs to be in the loop so that their schedule is honored.

Flexible Number of Hours: Reduced Hours and Job Sharing

Flexibility in *how often* you work offers employees the work-life autonomy they might need to attend to other personal obligations, needs, or desires. Caregivers often use this type of flexibility to manage domestic, family, and work obligations. Employees with special outside interests can also greatly benefit from this. This form of flexibility comes in two forms. The first and most common is reduced hours, where employees work less than a full-time schedule or take on a lower billable-hours requirement in a client services organization. The other, which is much less prevalent, is job sharing, where two employees work together to complete one job.

Reduced hours flexibility is an important way to retain valuable employees, as was the case with Lisa Madden, vice chair of risk management at KPMG. When she began her career at KPMG over thirty years ago, she assumed working and parenting couldn't mix—until extraordinary support from her husband and boss proved otherwise.

> *After I got married, my intention was to stop working when I had children. My mother was a stay-at-home mom, and I thought I would be a stay-at-home mom. I loved the idea of being a mom, and I had no qualms about that notion. It was my husband who kept saying to me, "I don't think you'll be happy being a stay-at-home mom. You know I'll support you whenever you want." So I*

thought, all right, with my first child I'll try a three day a week schedule. I was so fortunate that my boss and mentor cared so deeply about my continuing to work that he recommended his nanny when he learned I was looking for childcare for my family. He knew I cared so intensely about being a mom and was so inter-ested in supporting my continuing professional success after his sponsoring me for promotion to the partnership, that not only did he want me to continue working, but he also had a wonderful nanny to recommend to me![7]

As important as flexible options have been for women leaders like Madden, too often they are still *only* positioned for women with young children—which virtually guarantees that they will fail. In these cases, men who ask for flexibility face biases: "Oh, that's not for men; that's just for moms."

Whether it's to care for a child or an ailing parent, to avoid wasting time in traffic, to pursue a new interest, or to get more work done, all of us need work-place flexibility at some point in our lives. For that reason it should be *degendered* and *deparented*.

Flexibility should also be destigmatized, as it still has the potential to result in stigma. Leaders and supervisors (even coworkers) might question the commit-ment of reduced-hours employees. Do they really care about their careers? Will they soon quit altogether? How can they work an intense career part-time when client needs are full-time? These are just a few of the criticisms I hear.

In practice, employees working reduced hours often face being passed up for top projects, are less likely to develop meaningful mentoring and sponsorship relationships, and are not advanced on time or even on a pro rata basis. Therefore organizations offering this form of flexibility must combat the associated stigma to ensure employees working reduced hours develop and advance like their peers.

I've referenced several examples of successful reduced-hours policies, such as those at KPMG (Lisa Madden), Akin (Kim Koopersmith), and Hogan Lovells (Eve Howard).

Hogan Lovells implemented a flexible work initiative that incorporated many of these flexible work options. Its Global Agile Working Initiative allows every attorney and business services member in all offices worldwide to develop their flexible working plan. These plans can include any aspect of flexible working, such as virtual work, reduced hours, staggered arrival and departure times, and job sharing. In the development of the initiative, Hogan Lovells created a toolkit to help explain and implement the policy. They initiated a pilot program with a large group of corporate transactional attorneys, each adopting their unique agile work plan.[8]

"Agile working at Hogan Lovells is about embracing ways of working that are more innovative and efficient and are designed to give each member of our firm more control over how to balance personal and professional lives while continuing to deliver outstanding service to our clients," said Eve Howard, who accepted the Alliance's inaugural Flex Impact Award on behalf of Hogan Lovells in 2017, the year after this initiative was implemented. "We are committed to supporting our employees in their professional development—whatever direction that might take—and we have found that agile working has allowed us to foster a range of needs and interests, improving our talent retention and promoting stronger engagement while maintaining our sense of community."[9]

In 2011 PwC launched Flexibility™, another comprehensive flexible work program "that allows employees to control when and where they work while ensuring excellent client service and maintaining the quality of their lives."[10] The *everyday flexibility* portion of the program included a variety of options such as year round flex days, teaming culture (which advocates shared responsibilities), and unprescribed paid leave for self and family care. The *formal flexibility* portion included options such as reduced hours, flexible start and end times, a formal virtual work option three or more days a week, working from home one or two days a week, job sharing, compressed workweek, and sabbaticals. The recipient of the Alliance's 2019 Flex Impact Award, the program led to better morale, increased productivity, improved overall satisfaction, and higher retention rates.[11]

"Having flexibility at work is a centerpiece of our culture at PwC and is available to everyone starting on their first day at the firm. Flexibility at PwC is not about working less, but it is about encouraging people to work differently, in a way that fits their personal lives," said Anne Donovan, the former US people experience leader at PwC. "A culture of flexibility creates a happier and more productive workforce and is essential to recruiting and retaining the best talent."[12]

Understanding the business case for flexibility, PwC made a multi-year $2.4 billion investment to expand its flexibility program in 2022 with the My+ program, which received the Alliance's 2022 Flex Impact Award.[13] My+ allows PwC employees to create their own personalized careers by choosing their assignments, where and when they work, as well as customized rewards and benefits.[14] Key elements include enhanced leadership development programs, personalized and customized benefits to support well-being, two week-long firm-wide shutdowns per year, robust flexibility programs, and more.[15]

"We've worked hard to instill a culture of everyday flexibility across our firm and will continue to offer customized work options and a variety of benefits and resources that support all 65,000 of our people," said PwC Chief People Officer Yolanda Seals-Coffield.[16]

Once you've decided which flexibility model(s) you will offer, consider the implications and expectations for each one. For example, regardless of which form of flexibility you institute, it must be considered from a team perspective. Is there enough backup on days certain employees will not be working, or can your organization work to help create such backups (i.e., team arrangements for assistants and secretaries, contract workers, or offering different days off for different employees based on team schedules)? Consider a shared work plan for your teams like the one PwC instituted. What other expectations or support are required for this model to be successful both for the organization and the individual?

Remember the importance of alignment: be sure the flexible work models you include align with who you say you want to be as a company.

Determine Who Is Eligible

Next articulate who is eligible for each type of flexibility you will offer. Ideally organizations should have one strategy that covers the organization. However, offering a flexibility policy to all positions does not mean all positions have the same options. Remember one size does not fit all. For example, if a receptionist's job is to greet people entering the office, they may not be able to work from home, but if you had more than one receptionist, they could have flexible start times or shifting hours, or two people might job share. The flexibility options you offer for each position should be based on the needs of the job and the people doing the job.

So based on your flexibility purpose statement and flexibility principles, audit each position to decide what forms of flexibility you can offer.

Here's what that process can look like, step by step:

1. Articulate the job function.
2. Determine any limitations regarding where, when, and how often with this job function.
3. Determine whether any limitations could be offset by partial flexibility in location, schedules, and hours.
4. Determine if other team configurations could offset any limitation noted.

The topic of eligibility deserves special attention because in some companies, even some industries, some groups of people are given more benefits or more flexibility than others. If you offer this kind of disparity in your flexibility policy, if you haven't seen evidence of resentment yet, I can virtually guarantee that you will—whether they express it in the form of telling you directly, through quiet quitting, or through quitting and then posting about it on Glassdoor.

I can't say this strongly enough: if your organization believes flexibility is a business and strategic imperative, you must offer flexibility to all your people.

All your employees play a role in the success of your organization. The good news is that if you adopt the holistic flexibility approach outlined in this book, you will not only create an intentional and inclusive flexibility strategy, but you will also improve the health and success of your entire organization.

Another requirement that can be hard to implement successfully is a tenure requirement, requiring employees to work full-time in the office for at least one or two years before accessing flexible options to ensure they could get to know others.

Based on my experience, you should not have a tenure requirement. First, a vital part of the business case for flexibility is recruitment, and most new employees will not want to wait a year or two to access flexible options. Second, the argument for requiring employees to work in the office to get to know their colleagues made sense when most employees worked full-time in the office. But if tenured employees have access to flexibility, that means they're less likely to be working in the office at the same time, which means new employees will be less likely to get to know them.

Articulate the Approval Process

Next clarify how a request for flexibility is made and who must approve it. Specific reasons for denying a request should be clearly outlined in the policy, and they should be clearly related to your flexibility purpose and flexibility principles.

I recommend submitting requests first to talent or human resources professionals who can serve as the gatekeeper to ensure the approval process is consistent. Even if supervisors or department heads are ultimately approving requests, submission to talent or human resources first can help monitor that particular supervisors do not regularly deny requests. These professionals can also provide input on how to craft the requests.

The request process should also be reason-neutral (i.e., the request does not require a reason for the proposed flexible work schedule). If employees are required to include a reason, flexible work will become more stigmatized, as there is a higher likelihood that the process will be subjective. For example, caregivers might get access to flexible work more often than other employees.

Finally, the approval process should be simple and clear. Requests should be approved unless there is a conflicting business need, team need, or issue due to the employee's function based on an audit. When a flexible work request is not approved, the organization should offer another flexible work option.

Clarify the Relationship to Compensation and Advancement

For each flexibility model you offer, clarify its relationship to compensation and advancement. Overall, we recommend making compensation and advancement proportional to the work done. Flexibility should not derail someone's career path.

That means for all full-time, flexible work options, we recommend no impact on compensation and advancement because those flexibility models should result in an equal or greater amount of work done. If those working these flexibility models are less productive than those working full time in the office, that is more appropriately addressed as a performance issue.

The two forms of flexible work that need special clarification are the reduced hours model and job sharing. Here, too, compensation and advancement should be proportional to work done. For example, for a 75 percent reduced-hour policy, proportional compensation would be 75 percent of that position's full-time pay, and proportional advancement might mean spending roughly 25 percent longer at your position level to be considered for advancement.

However, "proportional to work done" doesn't have to be measured strictly by time. If you're working at a law firm where it typically takes eight years to become a partner, your policy might proportionally increase time spent at the same level for employees in the same position doing the same kind of work. But the impact of work could also be considered. For example, if one attorney working at 75 percent reduced hours was primarily doing document review, while another attorney working 75 percent reduced hours had significant first-chair trial experience, the attorney with litigation experience may advance more quickly than the one doing document review.

In organizations with a billable-hour model, proportional can sometimes get complicated. Sometimes reduced hours employees are under-compensated when they bill for more hours than their target. For most client-facing professional services organizations, the culture tends to be client-first, which means schedule creep is common. If the full-time billable-hour target is 2,400 hours, employees often exceed that number, and when they do, they are often compensated with a bonus. However, organizations typically do not track when reduced-hour employees exceed their target, so if their target is 80 percent and they end up working 90 or even 95 percent, they are still often paid at 80 percent.

For that reason we recommend having a *true-up policy*, where, at the end of the year, organizations review the actual number of billable hours and compensate reduced-hour employees accordingly. Employees who billed 90 percent should be compensated for 90 percent. And if their vacation or other benefits are proportional to billable hours, those benefits should be increased proportionally as well.

Document Legal Considerations

Once you've clarified all aspects of what types of flexibility you'd like to offer and what they will look like in practice, consider the legal implications. In consultation with legal counsel, include issues such as tax implications or confidentiality concerns based on flexible working locations, impact on employment status due to flexible hours, and any other relevant legal considerations based on the types of flexibility you will offer.

Establish a Review Schedule

No matter how detailed your policy is, unexpected issues will arise. For that reason we recommend that managers set up reviews with employees on a set schedule to keep their problems small.

When beginning a flexible work arrangement, I typically recommend that supervisors meet with individuals at three-month, six-month, and twelve-month intervals to address any issues and make adjustments. Once the employee has worked in their flexible arrangement for a year, we recommend doing yearly reviews.

IMPLEMENT STRUCTURES AND SYSTEMS TO ENSURE FLEX SUCCESS

Next in light of the preceding ideas, you'll assess and design the infrastructure to support this initiative. What systems and structures do you have in place? What do you need to add? Consider the following starting roles and functions that will support your initiative.

Roles, Functions, and Human Resources

Once you have your policies in place, you will need to identify who will manage them. In all successful flex initiatives, everyone in the organization is responsible for its success. Beyond that, some specific responsibilities should be owned by existing leaders and managers as part of their current jobs. Consider adding roles as well, depending on the size of your organization and its resources.

Dedicated Flex Resources

It's helpful to invest in an individual dedicated solely to overseeing the program on a day-to-day basis. Large organizations may, in fact, hire a flexibility program manager. Smaller organizations may task someone in human resources to oversee the program as part of their job. Either way, this person must be able to coach, educate, and monitor those working a flexible schedule and report on and troubleshoot any issues.

In addition I recommend that you identify flex program advisors who are members of senior leadership who can provide operational and organizational support. Some organizations also identify flex ambassadors who are executives in each office who can serve as the eyes and ears for the program and lead efforts to identify and avoid flex stigma. They can be seen as the troubleshooters or ombudspersons for flex. The flex ambassadors can also help identify individuals who are serving as roadblocks to the success of the flex initiative, reinforce the message, and support the initiative.

State of Flexibility Committee

At this stage, consider creating a state of flexibility committee that will be charged with rolling out and implementing workplace flexibility policies. I recommend organizations create this committee to operate for the long term, at least five years, instead of dissolving it after rolling out a new flexibility policy.

This committee will continuously develop and revamp workplace flexibility by developing new policies, systematically gathering and implementing feedback, and changing necessary infrastructure to make workplace flexibility succeed. To ensure flexibility remains intentional, inclusive, and iterative, I recommend that this committee be diverse, consisting of professionals of different functions, levels, and demographics, and include powerful leadership who can (and will) champion change. This committee might be the same as your flexibility working group or might evolve from it.

Additional Roles and Responsibilities

In addition to the dedicated roles and state of the flexibility committee, consider the following responsibilities that can be owned by dedicated flex resources or existing employees to integrate your flexibility initiative into your culture further and reinforce it over time. These functions include

- *Onboarding and integration*: This role ensures new employees receive orientation and onboarding involving firm policies and work environment, receive necessary technology, and connect with peer advisors and mentors. The talent and recruiting teams likely assume this function.
- *Culture and connection*: This role organizes and hosts in-person and virtual events to foster connection.
- *Ombudsperson*: This role serves as a point of contact for employees regarding issues and challenges.
- *Flexibility champions*: These partners and leaders support hybrid and flexible work (and might serve on the state of flexibility committee) to advise employees, communicate the business case for flexibility, and report matters to the executive committee.

LEVERAGE TECHNOLOGY

Technology infrastructure is critical in setting up your organization for Flex Success. You'll want to consider what kind of technology you'll need in place to enable and ensure seamless communication, collaboration, and connection. You will also need to ensure your people are trained in all the necessary skills to leverage the technology effectively. Also, consider any equipment you will need to provide employees: hardware, laptops, monitors, apps, or any technology for virtual offices.

Leveraging technology is a necessary skill for everyone, no matter what role they play in your organization or what type of flexibility strategy you have. Even if you're in a single-location organization and your organization requires all people to work in the office at the same time, employees will still need to leverage technology to work effectively with distributed teams or clients. Any leader who says that people have to be in person to work together effectively is essentially saying that if they are not in person with those they are working with, they cannot work effectively. But what does this say about their ability to work effectively with clients or other partners or stakeholders who may not be available to meet in person due to schedules or geography? At this point it's fair to say that this would not be a viable way to work. The ability to use technology to collaborate and communicate is an essential skill.

The same is true for functions like sales and business development. When pitching and selling, many potential clients may not want you in their offices for every meeting, because they feel like having you on Zoom or Teams is just as, or even more, effective, both time- and cost-wise. Leveraging technology is no longer about creating a competitive advantage; it's about staying in business.

Organizations may provide budgets and training for technology and infrastructure, but it's up to leaders to identify exactly which tools will support their team's specific work and make sure your people have the access and training they need. This is how you can make hybrid the best of both worlds. You won't always be working online, but when you do, you can leverage technology to make your work as effective as possible.

If you're working in a hybrid environment, many technology tools exist that can enable connection, collaboration, communication, and contribution, as well as or even better than working in person. Here are a few that I recommend (and I suggest you get employee feedback here, too):

- *Scheduling communications*: Many platforms, including Google, allow e-mails and communications to be scheduled. This is incredibly helpful for employees working flexible time and a flexible number of hours, as they can work off hours but still have communications sent out during typical office hours.
- *Alerts*: You can schedule alerts when emails are received from specific people. This step reduces the worry regarding being offline during your flexible schedule.
- *Work location notifications*: There are technology tools that indicate everyone's work location, allowing people to meet in person with those in the office, connect virtually with those working virtually, and save time from trying to track down someone who is off due to a flexible schedule or vacation. Some teams, such as Jenn Flynn's at Capital One, have a standard practice of adding their location to all meeting invites. That way, an individual can see whether people will attend the meeting virtually or in person. "We've learned that people want to come in the office to see other people," explained Flynn. "So if you're sending a meeting invite to fifteen people and ten accept in-person, the other five on

the fence are likely to accept in-person to be with the group. That transparency is important. Alternatively, nobody wants to be the only one who came in for a meeting when everybody else is on screen."[17]

- *Switcher, document camera, and split screens*: When presenting online, it is helpful to utilize a switcher and document camera so you can zoom in on a document while still being present and zooming yourself in and out so your presentation is more interactive.

By providing technology infrastructure, training, and access, while ensuring individuals know what is available to them, both the organization and the leader are ensuring their flexibility strategy is inclusive. The intention is that all people have the tools that allow them to be seen, heard, and aware of crucial information.

Another question you'll need to ask: will you provide people with the same technology setup at home as they have in the office? I believe that you should. If you're telling your people they can work from home, you must ensure you give them the technology to support that option.

Organizations should provide technology stipends for any other tools needed to ensure a fair and inclusive workplace. If you don't, you may create an ingroup and outgroup of those who can invest in extra monitors or those who can pay for high-speed internet, for example, and those who can't.

On the other hand, some organizations that provide technology stipends tell me many employees don't take advantage of them and are literally leaving dollars on the table. Others tell me they haven't been trained in using their online meeting equipment or software so that although they have a seat at the table, they can neither be seen nor be heard.

So encourage and re-encourage your people to use any available technology stipends, get trained, and make sure they've set up their systems so they can be most effective.

ESTABLISH LEADERSHIP ACCOUNTABILITY STRUCTURES

An increasing number of organizations are holding leaders accountable for supporting flexible employees. Leadership controls assignments, opportunities, access to information, evaluations, compensation, and promotion—which means they can undo even the best flexible work program through bias, inattention, or worse, in how they treat professionals who work flexible schedules. Senior leaders, partners, and other executives must be invested in making flexibility work.

Accountability requires setting goals or creating other methods to determine whether top executives have supported the flexible work program. Some firms and corporations provide their leadership with suggestions for showing their support—leaving room, of course, for leaders to create their own ways to advance their organization's flexibility objectives.

Compensation Structures

Best practices from Corporate America align compensation and promotion with achieving organizational goals. Some industries are catching up, like professional services industries. Some professional services firms are increasingly using various methods to ensure that their partners are responsible for retaining and developing flexible professionals and supporting the firms' flexible work programs. These methods include

- Requiring leaders to include in their annual compensation-setting narrative a statement of how they supported flexible work at the firm during the year;
- Providing bonuses or additional compensation to leaders in recognition of their efforts to support flexible work; and
- Deducting compensation from leaders whose departments experience significant attrition among flexible professionals.

Define Work Allocation, Performance Reviews, and Advancement Structures

One of the promises of flexibility is an increased level and quality of individual contribution. Organizations must set themselves up with the systems required to ensure optimal success to reach that promise. Organizations can set up universally implemented structures in several key areas, including work allocation, feedback, performance reviews, advancement structures, and reviews to identify unconscious bias:

- Establish equitable work allocation practices. Organizations are responsible for addressing biases in workload allocation so that employees utilizing flexibility have the same opportunities. At a minimum, organizations should review workloads regularly to

ensure assignments are evenly distributed and have a system to
remediate inequitable work distribution.

- Ensure regular feedback. In a flexible environment, people may
notice that they are not getting the same frequency of feedback that
would happen in person. To ensure people are getting quality
feedback and continue improving, organizations need to support
leaders by investing in mechanisms that make feedback accessible.

  For example, consider investing in real-time feedback applications that can make it easy for people to submit feedback after
every assignment that they can immediately incorporate into future
performance. These systems and applications can also alert the
organization of any challenges with flexibility and allow continuous improvement and iteration. Alternatively, organizations can
make sure providing employee feedback is part of their job goals
and responsibilities.

- Establish fairness and equity in performance reviews and advancement structures. Are your employee performance evaluations and
advancement systems based upon objective benchmarks or competencies, and do you have measures in place to reduce unconscious
bias? Develop organization-wide reviews to ensure equity.

- Review your organization-wide performance evaluations for
stigma. Nearly invisible and yet very powerful, flexibility stigma
can infiltrate employee evaluations and undermine even the best
flexible work program. Organizations must provide training to
managers at every level and implement organization-wide reviews
of individual employee performance reviews to ensure equity
across the board.

Consider Additional Implications

Finally, you'll want to examine whether your flexibility initiative raises additional
considerations or implications, the most common of which is real estate implications. Perhaps your flexibility models will allow you to lessen your real estate
footprint. Or you may need to redesign your office space to include larger conference rooms or collaboration spaces, where people working at home can be
included online during in-person meetings rather than assuming everyone will
always do their work in their own individual office.

  Now that you have a clear flex policy, it's time to integrate that policy into
the fabric of the organization with step four: reintegrate.

REFLECTION QUESTIONS

Like each step of the framework, this chapter challenges you with many questions to consider as you articulate a flexibility initiative and policy. For further reflection and to make sure you are always challenging your own unconscious biases, list what you think would be an ideal policy or outcome, then step back and consider what objections you might hear from others. Consider if there are additional nuances or implications that you haven't yet included in your thinking.

7

HOW WILL YOU INTEGRATE FLEXIBILITY INTO YOUR CULTURE?

At this stage, you, your leadership team, and your flexibility working group have taken the time to create a strong foundation with your flexibility purpose, vision, and principles and you have established a detailed policy with infrastructure and systems to support it. Now it's time to develop specific *practices* to implement your policy effectively and to train your *people* in these practices as an integrated part of your overall flexibility strategy.

In step four of the Flex Success Framework, *reintegrate*, you'll be rolling out your organization-wide culture change (also known as your flexibility initiative) by intentionally aligning the five Ps:

- Purpose (step one: reflect);
- Principles (step two: reimagine);
- Policies (step three: redesign);
- Practices (step four: reintegrate); and
- People (step four: reintegrate).

Remember the Flex Success Framework is not only about creating a flexibility initiative; it's about creating a future of work that drives your business objectives and enhances the experience for your people.

In this chapter, you will learn how to enroll your people in each aspect of your flexibility policy, allowing them to connect to and own its purpose. This starts with organization-wide *strategies* and practices that your flexibility working group, human resources (HR) and talent team, and senior leadership instill universally throughout the organization. Then you'll extend and enroll your people through training, particularly by providing your managers and leaders with individual strategies that will help them make your flexibility initiative successful.

This enrollment and empowerment creates industry-leading organizations, no matter what external changes are on the horizon.

PLAN YOUR ROLLOUT: ALIGNING PURPOSE, PRINCIPLES, AND POLICY

I have seen it countless times: Organizations invest a great deal of time to build their business case for flexibility, develop leadership buy-in, research the components, conceive of an initiative perfectly tailored to their unique needs and objectives, and carefully draft the language of their policy. But when it's time to implement, they give in to time pressures and rush the launch. Often they announce their policy in one mass email, and that's it. Not surprisingly, they don't get the response they hoped for or the success they envisioned.

Your time investment in developing your unique business case and communicating your flexibility initiative deserves to be commensurate with the time invested in the development of the initiative and with the results you hope to obtain.

So as you prepare to implement your flexibility initiative, begin with a well-planned and clearly communicated rollout. Develop a multi-pronged communication strategy to make your workforce aware of your flexibility initiative, including the flexibility purpose, principles, and policy you developed in steps two and three.

I recommend you focus on connecting flexibility to purpose and macro business benefits. Gather a variety of data points to show those benefits. Most importantly, emphasize your goal to utilize flexibility to create or deepen your organization's commitment to human-centered values and to help improve employee engagement, job satisfaction, personal and professional growth, and overall well-being. This may be a time to work with your communications team to help clearly and powerfully articulate the why behind the initiative, what it includes, how it works, and what's in it for the organization and the individual employees.

Anything that's a business imperative should come directly from senior leadership. Flexibility is no exception! I strongly recommend the first line of communication come from your chief executive officer (CEO), managing partner, or other top leader to gain traction and buy-in. However, a one-and-done email is not enough! I will talk later in this chapter about various communication strategies. You need to choose the communication methods that work best for your organization. At the very least, be sure all your leaders know your flexible work policies and can speak to them, and enlist various leaders to communicate these flexible work policies throughout your organization.

Finally, intentionally include your people during the rollout. The goal is to inform them and *enroll* them in the flexibility purpose, principles, and policy your flexibility working group has designed (with their input at every step) and continue to solicit their input and buy-in.

When your people are fully enrolled and included in your organization's flexibility purpose and vision, they will begin to take personal ownership and responsibility for it. In this way, flexibility will not be an initiative that is launched and quickly forgotten but will become part of your organization's culture that's invested in and improved over time (we'll talk more about how to do this in step five: reinforce).

The following are guidelines that have been helpful for leaders I've worked with over the years as they rolled out their organization-wide flexibility initiatives.

Design Shared Experiences

During your rollout, avoid sending out an edict or any one-way communication; instead, focus on connecting with your people and allowing them to connect with each other.

The way to do that is to *design shared experiences* that allow people to reflect on what they're hearing and then allow them to interact with and learn from each other. Create space for pairs or small groups to have conversations and allow them to share what they've learned with the larger group.

In rollout experiences like these, leadership is not the expert, commander, or sage on the stage, but a *guide on the side*, as they say in educational circles.[1] Leaders serve as facilitators, crowdsourcing wisdom from all participants, who are the experts on their own experience. This approach allows employees to directly engage with the organization's flexibility purpose, principles, and policy, make it their own, and invest in it over time.

Here's a sample outline of a town hall-type rollout event that illustrates how you can create space for your participants' experience while still achieving maximum buy-in.

Exercise: Town Hall Rollout Event

One way to share your flexibility initiative with your entire organization (or, if you have a multisite organization, one entire location) is a town hall-type meeting led by top leaders but with active participation from your people.

Leaders can ask participants to read through the policy before the meeting, as there will be opportunities for discussion during the meeting. At the meeting, explain the purpose of the policy, your principles, and the business case for it. Share how the policy works and clearly communicate that it is not just a policy but a culture shift, a new way of working, and the future of work at your organization.

Also, emphasize the organization's long-term commitment to flexibility's success. Describe how you will continue to monitor its implementation and follow up with individuals about how it's working for them.

Then leaders can give participants opportunities for small group discussions. Consider splitting participants into groups of two to five, ideally. Consider asking the groups the following questions:

- What do you hope to gain from this flexibility policy? How would you use it?
- What would help you succeed when working flexibly (i.e., technology, supervisor support, training, mentoring, workload support, etc.)?
- What are some ways that flexibility can help your teams, clients, and organization?
- Which principle do you resonate with the most? Are there any you would like to add?
- What excites you or concerns you about this new policy?

Then ask groups to designate a group leader and report back to the larger group. Participants often find it interesting to hear everyone's feedback. By doing so you help gain buy-in and support and get feedback on types of support structures that would be helpful. Consider the suggestions and inform your organization about the support you added based on their feedback.

Finally, in addition to creating interactive time for sharing, leave plenty of time for questions at the end.

I want to add a quick note for companies that already have many virtual employees, perhaps because of pandemic-era policies. I generally advise against a digital-only rollout or leaving the rollout to an email for those who work virtually while the remainder of the organization is attending an in-person rollout event. Whenever possible, if your resources and geographic footprint allow it, invite those employees to an in-person event. If that's not possible, find other ways to communicate interactively with those employees, perhaps with virtual small-group discussions led by executive leadership, ensuring every employee feels the same level of engagement with the process.

Continue Clear and Consistent Communication

Don't rely on just one event or launch announcement to adequately communicate your flexibility initiative. *Continued* clear and consistent communication is crucial for your initiative's success, especially in the early stages when you're trying to get people on board. I recommend launching via multiple channels at multiple times, including at small and large group meetings, quarterly meetings, in internal newsletters, on internal web pages, and via personal emails or videos.

For example, after a rollout event, leadership can continue to support the initiative through ongoing strategies like the following:

- Continuously educate your leaders at trainings, orientations, and meetings so they know the details of your flexibility policies.
- Enlist champions among your leaders who will host office or department meetings that specifically communicate flexibility policies to employees so they understand that there's support for these policies and are more likely to use them.
- Discuss flexibility policies at new hire orientations to familiarize new employees with flexible work options.
- Include updates and success stories in organizational newsletters.
- Maintain a website on flexible work so that policies, guidelines, and resources are readily available.

ALIGN YOUR PRACTICES WITH YOUR PURPOSE, PRINCIPLES, AND POLICIES

If you have been using the Flex Success Framework to build your initiative one step at a time, your purpose, principles, and policies are aligned by design because you have built each step upon the foundation of the other.

In this section, we get to the heart of implementing your flexibility initiative: the *practices* that align with your purpose, principles, and policies and connect with your *people*. For organizations that embrace flexibility and understand its potential, it's an exciting time when you bring your initiative to life.

Although what works in practice is different for every organization, I can give you some common guidelines to help you determine your organizational best practices for yourself.

When looking at developing practices, your flexibility working group can look at what might be implemented on an organization-wide basis to help provide guidelines and guardrails for individual leaders and employees to follow. These would follow the policy, systems, and structures discussed in the previous step. You can consider these using the four Cs—connection, collaboration, communication, and contribution. These correlate with four of the five Cs mentioned in chapters 3 and 5. This is because the five Cs represent some of the most critical aspects of culture that organizations most want to preserve.

Connection

When instituting organization-wide practices, remember that one of leaders' and employees' biggest concerns about flexible work is losing connection. Considering opportunities for connection at every level in your organization should be a priority. Here are components to consider building into executive leadership responsibility and HR or flexibility management roles and responsibilities:

- *Training*: The skills of key connection goals like online mentoring and relationship building are not always innate, and organizations that provide such training will help foster these necessary relationships. Design and offer training that can be offered organization-wide and specific training for different roles when needed, like for managers and supervisors.
- *Spotlights*: Focus on the positives and gather success stories along the way. Share stories of employee resource groups or mentor/mentee relationships that thrived in flexible work arrangements. Make sure to publicize these successes so others can replicate them. Create an internal HR or workplace hub highlighting Flex Success stories, or include these in employee newsletters or company meetings.
- *Programs*: Create or leverage existing programs, such as employee resource groups, mentoring programs, onboarding and integration programs, and sponsorship initiatives. Consider how you can add virtual activities and events through existing programs. Also consider how you can charge senior leadership with responsibility for implementing and supporting these important avenues for connection.

- *In-person events or retreats*: Organizations need to host in-person events or retreats in a flexible work environment, and employees should be required to attend. Consider hosting monthly or quarterly in-person department events, periodic social mixers, and team and organization-wide retreats to foster in-person connections.

Collaboration

In a flexible work environment, organizations must be very intentional about collaboration. In the previous stage of redesign, you will have considered technology solutions that can facilitate collaboration. Organizations can also train leaders to vary how people can collaborate during meetings so that those with different styles can participate optimally.

I often recommend *Smart Collaboration*, a system and book by the same name developed and underpinned by years of research by a distinguished fellow at Harvard University School of Law, Dr. Heidi Gardner. Her research shows that when organizations invest in this type of collaboration, they deliver higher profits, develop greater innovations, and do a better job of retaining and engaging their employees who see the opportunity to collaborate across groups and functions as valuable for professional growth.[2]

This approach emphasizes hyper-intentional collaboration that brings together diverse groups of people (different backgrounds, life experiences, job roles, and areas of expertise) to solve problems or pursue specific goals. One of the things that I find most important about this approach is the awareness that the key to better collaboration is not as much about whether your group is communicating via an in-person meeting, online meeting, or asynchronous phone calls or emails. Instead it's about intentionally putting together diverse groups and setting them up to succeed. Thinking about collaboration in a flexible workplace will certainly need an infrastructure and will include meetings, but it's a myth that collaboration is *about* in-person meetings.

This is underscored by a recent research project that looked at successful teams and included survey data from 2,000 executives and thought leaders. The study, led by global consulting firm and applied research institute on the future of work Ferrazzi Greenlight and its founder, Keith E. Ferrazzi, showed that virtual and hybrid working teams can be as successful at connecting as those working together in person based on factors having nothing to do with location.[3] In fact, according to an article by Ferrazzi published by the World Economic Forum describing the research, world-class teams see collaboration as a stack, "each level of which needs to be purposefully engineered for what that type of collaboration is best used for. At the top of the stack is asynchronous. Asynchronous collaboration is working as a team on a project but not in real time."[4] In this format, everything other than what requires an active discussion happens before any meeting.

According to Ferrazzi, another key is how an online meeting occurs. Too many online meetings don't take advantage of the powerful feature of breakout rooms. In the same article, Gary Sorrentino, the global chief information officer (CIO) of Zoom, is quoted as saying that the most utilized feature of Zoom is turning meetings on or off. He says, "There's a genuine superpower for higher psychological safety in the shape of break-out rooms. You can ask a bold question in a twelve-strong group and get no reply. But if you send two or three people into a break-out room, open a Google Doc, now we find the courage to speak is 85 percent higher. Return to the main room and it's game-changing."[5] So I recommend focusing on what you can do as an organization to support highly successful teams and effective collaboration overall.

Dr. Gardner emphasizes many keys to effective collaboration. I'll mention two of those here. One is trust—both competence trust, which refers to one's belief in the expertise and professional capability of others in the group, and interpersonal trust, which is more about one's trust in another to follow through, show up, or have integrity. Organizations can help build a culture of trust in part by allowing employees plenty of intentional opportunities to interact and get to know each other so that trust can develop.

Another key is incentivizing people to help each other. In her work, Dr. Gardner sees that one barrier to collaboration in law firms specifically is a lack of incentive for a person in one business unit or practice to help a person in another unit or practice. This lack of incentive stymies important collaboration or cross-selling opportunities. Organizations can get around this by intentionally creating incentives to support collaboration.[6]

For example, Morgan Lewis designed their compensation system to reward people for collaborating. "Collaboration is emphasized here," according to Grace Speights, partner at Morgan Lewis, "In our compensation system, people are rewarded for collaborating. We train our associates that way." This incentive encourages partners and associates alike to reach out to each other, to refer clients, and to do pro bono work and outside activities to expand their connections. Having more meetings online has increased the opportunity for collaboration.

"The fact that people don't have to travel as much, that we can just pull them into meetings," Speights noted, "[collaboration] has only gotten better."[7]

Communication

Clear communication is crucial in a flexible work environment. Organizations must intentionally set communication norms that apply universally. This might include setting expectations for management's communication of cultural values, employee expectations about response times or how frequently to communicate with their managers, and where managers and employees can go for help or support.

Consider what would fall under the category of universal communications expectations, and then consider strategies for individual managers separately. Communications is covered later in this chapter.

Contribution

Every leader's job is to enable their people to succeed and contribute at their highest possible level. When discussing this with clients, I often ask, "Are you FOR your people?" FOR is an acronym that represents *feedback*, *opportunities*, and *relationships*, essential things a leader is responsible for.

Much of this responsibility falls into individual strategies for managers later in this chapter. However, organizations should support their leaders by setting universal best practices and systems and by reviewing implementation across the whole organization in these key areas: feedback, opportunity for equitable work and advancement (by looking at work allocation, performance reviews, and advancement), and relationship building such as networking and mentoring.

When it comes to feedback, the key from an organizational level is to ensure that every employee gets feedback in a clear and timely manner. Organizations can set up systems to review each manager's communications about expectations and to deliver feedback about how an employee is doing in the context of those expectations. I often hear managers complain that their employee hasn't been performing after they've started working virtually. When I ask about how often or how specifically they've communicated the issues to the employee, they sometimes say they haven't communicated it at all. Managers must create this expectation feedback loop, and organizations must ensure it is happening.

When it comes to opportunity, it is an important organizational responsibility to review work allocation. Some managers unknowingly favor on-site employees over those who work elsewhere when assigning work. This is a bias that should be prevented or stopped. Help employees and managers by setting up a review process with managers, asking

- Do employees working a flexible schedule have the same access to key assignments?
- Do leaders hold check-in meetings with these employees to address satisfaction with projects received?
- Do leaders allow workers to regularly indicate availability and areas of interest, such as weekly or biweekly?

Pay attention to schedule creep—the tendency of reduced hours or part-time roles to creep back up to full-time levels while pay remains decreased. It starts for several reasons: unavoidable demands and deadlines, accepting too much work, senior executives who are unaware of junior professionals' schedules, and possibly supervisors who are passive-aggressively expressing their distaste for reduced hours. When it happens over a sustained period, it undermines an individual's reduced hours agreement and can lead to negative consequences for the whole organization, such as decreased engagement, frustration, or burnout, and can damage the effectiveness of the flexible work program itself.

Fortunately, there are solutions:

- Assess the reason for the schedule creep. Find out why the increase in hours has occurred and whether this is happening across the whole organization or in specific groups.
- Schedule creep often happens due to forgetfulness. Flexible work managers may need to remind senior executives of the reduced hours professional's schedule.
- If excessive work seems to result from the senior executive's resistance to the reduced hours program, the flexible work manager can remind them why the reduced hours program exists and the business benefits of it. If necessary, the manager can offer coaching or involve senior management.
- Develop alternative ways of accomplishing work. If schedule creep results from multiple senior executives assigning work at once, the flexible work manager can ask to modify or coordinate assignments. If schedule creep is the product of too much work, the flexible work manager can help senior executives think through alternative ways of accomplishing the work: shift some of the work

to a more junior employee, outsource rote aspects of the assignment, use other staff, cross train underutilized employees, or job share.

- Assist with scheduling compensatory time off. It can be difficult for reduced-hours professionals to arrange compensatory time off. The idea of time off often seems illusory and can leave the individual feeling discouraged. A flexibility manager can have the senior executive commit that the reduced hours professional can take compensatory time off once the assignment is complete. This will make the option more viable and will also communicate to reduced-hours employees that the organization values them.

ALIGN YOUR PEOPLE WITH YOUR PURPOSE, PRINCIPLES, POLICY, AND PRACTICES

Now that you've aligned your purpose, principles, policies, and organizational practices, it's time to align your *people* with all of the above.

According to Gallup, when it comes to flexibility success, "managerial support is the most critical element. One big finding of Gallup is that 70 percent of variance in workplace performance can be traced back to the person you call manager."[8] It's critical that you *train your leaders, especially middle management and supervisors*, to ensure that they can effectively support the initiative.

When Arnold & Porter rolled out their flexibility initiative, they understood the importance of training in making their flex initiative a success. "We had a lot of internal communications with everybody," said Ellen Kaye Fleishhacker, co-managing partner at Arnold & Porter. "We also started a series of trainings with Manar and the Diversity & Flexibility Alliance, with a set of trainings for our leaders, a different set of trainings for our lawyers, and a different set of trainings for our professional staff."

The purpose of the training was to ensure everyone was enrolled in making the flexibility initiative a success. "We really wanted to make sure that our leaders were sensitive to all the different factors that go into this hybrid experience," explained Fleishhacker. "For example, we wanted to make sure that if our leaders have a meeting in the office that some people may not be able to attend, they know how to make that meeting inclusive, so that whether or not someone's literally in the office that day, they can still participate. We were trying to sensitize our leaders to their role in making sure that *flexible flexibility*, as we keep calling it, is reinforced, that it's a cultural value, and that it's a priority."

In their transition to flexible work, Fleishhacker saw the primary role of leadership as creating a positive return on experience (ROE) for their people and enrolling them in the positive benefits flexible work can provide.

> *How many times in your career do you have an opportunity to build what your work experience looks like from scratch? This is probably the only opportunity we're ever going to have. So we've been working very closely with our leaders to make sure that we all share the same common values of making sure people are included, making sure people feel comfortable, making sure client service excellence is paramount, and trying to combine all of that into a set of best practices in our hybrid work model.*[9]

Following are strategies for managers and supervisors to optimize their flexibility initiative no matter what flexible arrangements they have adopted.

Connection

It's a manager's responsibility to establish best practices for connecting as a team and ensure they are implemented. To provide additional guidance, next are strategies around key connection points: meetings, networking, employee resource groups, mentoring, and choreographed connections.

Create Connection in Meetings

To build connection in meetings, I recommend that leaders focus on *experience*, *expectations*, and *engagement*, whether the meeting is in person, online, or hybrid.

Experience. First is the *experience* of our people in meetings. How many meetings have you sat through, thinking, "This could have been an email"? And how many email strands have you waded through, thinking, "This multi-day email chain could have been dealt with in a quick meeting!" So as you contemplate a meeting, ask yourself

- Is a meeting even necessary? According to research from Microsoft, when we lost in-person interaction during the pandemic, meetings increased by over 150 percent.[10] Not surprisingly, many employees experienced Zoom fatigue. Develop your own protocol to decide when meetings are necessary. For example, Dropbox suggests the following: if you have to decide it, debate it, or discuss

it, it should be a meeting.[11] Anything else can be done through
asynchronous communication, whether phone, email, or chat.

- Should the meeting be in person, online, or hybrid? Determining what
type of meeting you should have should be guided by the purpose of
the meeting. Do you just need to give some updates that might not
require many follow up questions? Perhaps that suggests you can do
this meeting online rather than having people commute into an office.

To decide the form of the meeting, you can also think back to meetings you
have led in the past and when you were at your best, both in person and virtually.
Where did you see the most participation? What situations generated the best
results, and why?

In addition to noting when you were at your best, here are some other guidelines leaders have found effective:

- If you believe the meeting will be highly contentious, in-person may
be best to allow participants to read body language more easily and
perhaps meet afterward for a cup of coffee to defuse any tension.
- If you're considering a hybrid meeting, where some participants are in
the room, and some are not, the key is ensuring all participants can
have the same experience. If your meeting will include participants at
multiple offices, I recommend meeting 100 percent online to equalize
how everyone shows up. When everyone has their own device and can
show up full screen, participants can see individual reactions clearly
instead of having a camera in a conference room with multiple
participants, where individual reactions are hard to see. You also don't
want some people to feel comfortable participating (those who are in
person) and others to feel like a fly on the wall watching the meeting
(those linking in virtually). Another way to think about this is that
everyone in your meeting should be participants, not spectators.
- Importantly consider your team's schedules. In addition to hybrid
and virtual schedules, what other types of flexibility do your team
members use? If you have people on reduced hours, compressed
work weeks, job sharing, or shifting hours, when would be the best
time and day to schedule a meeting? Also, schedule important
meetings ahead of time so those working flexibly can change their
schedules or join virtually. Consider providing everyone with
materials and ways to provide input.

Expectations. Be sure to communicate meeting *expectations* to the participants ahead of time. For example, communicate the goal of the meeting, whether it's in person, online, or hybrid, what type of preparation is necessary ahead of time, and how participants should present themselves (i.e., cameras on for online participants or attire necessary for client meetings).

This last point deserves some attention. During the pandemic, all norms went out the window regarding online presence as we collectively figured out how to survive working from home while social distancing. If your organization hasn't set online meeting expectations about how employees present themselves online, set them yourself as a team. A rule of thumb we recommend is to treat your online virtual space as an extension of your office.

Remind your people how they show up both in the office and online matters. If you have specific expectations regarding online presence, share them with your team. Sylvia Ann Hewlett, the researcher and thought leader who wrote a book on *executive presence*, asserts that how you show up impacts your effectiveness and success. How you communicate, the way you interact, and how you look together influence how people perceive you. Appearance also includes things like attention—are you leaning forward and engaged or is your head down?[12] Help your employees put their best foot forward by setting clear expectations.

In addition to virtual meetings, consider your expectations for meetings involving those with flexible time and flexible number of hours. Consider holding such meetings on days and times when most team members are available. Think about ways those unavailable can provide input and still participate before or after.

Engagement. Finally, intentionally *engage* meeting participants not just during the meeting but before and after as well:

- *Before the meeting*: For an in-person meeting, we naturally chitchat and say hello before the meeting begins. So why, for an online meeting, do we so often enter a moment of silence? If you're leading the meeting, build engagement before the meeting by humanizing it. As each individual enters the virtual room, say hello. Ask them about their day. Chitchat.

   If you're running a hybrid meeting, be sure you're engaging online participants as much as in-person participants. Welcome the person entering the virtual room just as you would the person walking in the door. As the leader of the meeting, you're bridging the two worlds.

Another important way you can engage with participants before the meeting is to send meeting expectations ahead of time, as mentioned in the previous section. If you're sharing the meeting goal and recommend preparation ahead of time (i.e., submitting thoughts, coming to meetings with questions, and even asking members of the team to be prepared to share information during the meeting), you're empowering them to be active participants. This step is especially important for introverts, those new to the team, and others who may feel less comfortable voicing their opinions in a public forum, as it will help level the playing field.

- *During the meeting*: Prioritize making sure all voices are heard. Whether in person, online, or hybrid, direct questions to all participants. For online and hybrid meetings, encourage and monitor the chat discussion (those leading the discussion may find it helpful to tap another meeting participant to monitor the chat and ensure all insights are shared). Additionally, for hybrid meetings, level the playing field for online and in-person participants by intentionally bringing online participants into the conversation and ensuring technology allows online participants to actively engage.

- *After the meeting*: When I ask people, "What's the most important part of a meeting?" they often say, "It's the meeting after the meeting." It's who you walk out with. It's who you keep talking to. It's how that meeting continues in conversation. Many are also quick to say, "With virtual meetings, we lost that." You can still engage people in the meeting after the meeting if you're intentional. One way is to invite people to stay on for an extra ten minutes or set up a separate Zoom link to debrief the meeting after the meeting (if debriefs are necessary).

Provide Connection Through Networking and Employee Resource Groups

Employee resource and networking groups can be valuable sources of connection. Roles of employee resource groups include several important functions: building community by creating a safe space for discussion during meetings; fostering professional development by spearheading surveys and interviews to understand experiences and holding trainings or discussions to fill in any gaps; and advocating for its members by raising any concerns or challenges to the state of flexibility committee and leadership team.

Eve Howard, partner at Hogan Lovells, leveraged technology to launch the virtual community Women in Capital Markets Alliance (WICMA), which offers networking and mentoring opportunities and skills training.

"One of the silver linings of the pandemic is our ability to make connections across the globe," said Howard. "I'm a firm believer that to foster retention, development, and diversity of talent, we have to be able to form communities and make connections. My practice group happens to have a lot of women coming up the pipeline, so we launched the Women in Capital Markets Alliance. It has really taken off."[13]

In addition to its networking, mentoring, and skill training opportunities for its approximately one hundred members, WICMA also includes virtual peer circles of eight women each, facilitated by a more senior member, that create a deeper sense of community.

Grace Speights, a partner at Morgan Lewis, notes that virtual communication tools have allowed her to experience even greater connection in her networking relationships. "Our Black lawyer network gets together once a month on Zoom from around the world. We didn't do that before. All of our network groups get together virtually to see each other and talk, and it's allowed us to do programming we have never done before and bring in speakers we never would have gotten before."[14]

To focus on the intersection of diversity and flexibility, create caregivers; reduced hours; women; lesbian, gay, bisexual, transgender, queer, or other (LGBTQ+); flexible working groups; and racial and ethnic diversity employee resource groups.

Be Intentional About Mentoring

In addition to meetings, make sure you're intentionally creating connections through *mentoring*. I was talking to one partner who told me that he'd always had an open-door policy. During the pandemic, he was the one who continued to come into the office, even when he was the only one there. "I really miss having an open-door policy," he said. "I still have an open-door policy, but nobody shows up."

"Have you thought about how to recreate that open-door policy online?" I asked. He admitted he hadn't. "You could schedule open-door hours online, where people can Zoom in. You could reach a whole new group of people that way," I suggested.

Because many professional services organizations, especially law firms, are based on an apprenticeship model, the loss of mentoring opportunities is of particular concern when not everyone is in the office at the same time.

Though online mentoring doesn't feel the same as sitting next to someone, it offers a huge hidden upside. For example, Grace Speights increased mentoring opportunities for associates since many of her client meetings moved online. "To the extent our clients are willing to do virtual meetings, I normally invite my associates, which I wouldn't always have had the opportunity to do at in-person meetings. The technology has allowed us to bring associates into more things. Instead of just getting me ready for the meeting, they're participating in the meeting. And they're learning."[15]

With online mentoring as a team, you can mentor at scale. You could establish one-to-many mentoring relationships, create peer circles, or hold informal office hours available to individuals outside your local area.

For example, Nancy Laben at Booz Allen has an online calendar for office hours and freely shares that link with team members, which increases her accessibility for mentoring. "People can click on that link that goes to a calendar that says where I'll be and when I'm available to talk. If you're in person, great. If you want to talk virtually, that's fine too."

However, Laben notes that just because the link is available doesn't mean junior associates feel comfortable using it. "The more senior I am, the more people say, 'You're really busy. I don't want to disturb you.' We have quarterly in-person team meetings. I try to attend those and then the next time I send out an office hours link, I'll get more uptick, because they see I'm a real person and they feel more connected."[16]

Kim Koopersmith, chair of Akin, notes the connection between investing in mentoring and retaining talent.

> *Whether you call it mentorship, sponsorship, or investing in people, we do a ton of that, because to me, that is what makes you feel most connected. For the women who really loved what they were doing and left, I've found the reason they leave is less about spending more time with their kids, and more about not finding the job as fulfilling and not feeling as engaged as they once did. Intuitively, I've always felt that sense of connection and engagement is the guiding principle of success for people's careers because it fuels their desire to stay. And that's a battle in this [hybrid] environment.*[17]

Online mentoring opportunities have led to more mentoring across offices, increased mentoring efforts of senior executives and partners, and allowed for more seamless group mentoring moments that deepen and extend connection.

At the same time, mentoring in person has its advantages. As Nancy Laben shared with me, it allows you to observe real-time reactions to situations.

> *One of my team members said, "The best thing about you, Nancy, is you take bad news really calmly." He's seen me do that any number of times, but it's been when we've sat down to talk through an issue. I was modeling the behavior you really need to have if you want to be a general counsel.*
>
> *With technology, I find I have to be more intentional about teachable moments—to the point of saying, "Hmm, that's interesting. Let's talk about that for one second." I literally sometimes have to call it out: "Let's have a teachable moment." 80 percent of our communication is nonverbal, so I have to make more effort to translate, because they can't see my whole body.*[18]

Consider where you and your team have experienced your best mentoring relationships both virtually and in person, take advantage of organizational mentoring resources, and create the best of both worlds.

From Serendipitous to Choreographed Connections

One of the things people tell me they miss the most is serendipitous interactions: "I miss seeing people at the elevator" or "I used to love running into people at the coffee machine."

In a flexible work environment, there will still be serendipitous connections when people are all in the office at the same time—you will still run into people at the elevator and coffee machines. However, there will indeed be fewer impromptu run-ins in a flexible work environment since people aren't together all the time. Although, this new environment allows us to recreate such interactions with intentionally choreographed connections. An added benefit is reducing ingroup and outgroup dynamics that sometimes occur in in-person serendipitous connections.

Here are some ways to create choreographed connections:

- Leverage online meetings. See the earlier suggestions in this chapter for connecting during meetings. Use breakout rooms for small group discussions and ice breakers. With planned virtual connections, you can create interactions between people who might never have sat next to each other in an in-person meeting.

- Intentionally network during in-person meetings and retreats.
  When organizations schedule in-person meetings or retreats, make
  sure to leave time for networking and plan connections as well.
  - Consider seating assignments at in-person meetings to facili-
    tate introductions between people who have not met.
  - Plan small group breakouts, choreograph group discussions,
    and allow some to meet organically.
  - Create post-meeting groups to meet virtually or in person.
- Host virtual meetings and events. Make sure to leverage virtual
  platforms to allow people to regularly meet. Facilitated meetings
  work best where there is an agenda or meeting plan. Some successful virtual events have included cooking classes and tastings, where
  participants could do an activity together and have time for talking.
  But remember, don't overschedule!
- Train your people. Offer training on how to carve out time to
  socialize and connect—it does not come naturally for many.
- Provide budgets to connect. If you're able, give your people budgets
  to connect in person or virtually. Think creatively. Perhaps people
  can use these budgets to have coffee or lunch with other employees
  who live close by during virtual days.

Facilitate Collaboration

When it comes to effective collaboration in a flexible work environment, be
intentional and generative. So many organizations are focusing on what they're
losing. For managers, consider that you can create much better results if you focus
on what you're gaining. How might this new environment enhance collaboration
on your teams? Here are a few considerations:

- Be careful not to overschedule meetings for the general sake of
  collaborating. Make sure if you're having a meeting, it is intentional,
  organized, and the facilitator engages as many voices as possible.
- As stated earlier in the chapter, utilize the power of breakout rooms
  in your online platforms. Even if you have a larger group session,
  when it's time to develop or debate ideas, shift to smaller groups,
  then come back together again to share ideas or conclusions that the
  group arrived at in breakouts. This allows more input and greater
  interaction and trust-building among those who are in the breakout
  rooms together. It also generates more input and ideas.

- Just as you are intentional about collaborating online, do the same with in-person collaboration. Make sure the agenda is designed around a goal and find ways to get as many people to give input as possible.

Ensure Inclusivity

In collaboration, we want to be inclusive. Online collaboration practices can offer a huge advantage in terms of diversity and inclusion. They can offer opportunity to interrupt or alleviate forms of bias. For example, if an employee always feels they are constantly being interrupted, which studies show happens more to women and underrepresented groups, they can use the chat function to make sure their input and ideas are included.

This can be effective for those who may feel a lack of confidence in meetings or those who are introverts and don't feel comfortable interjecting during an in-person work session. Their input often goes unspoken. But online meetings have been a huge benefit for them because they've been able to engage through chat. They've been able to take the time to compose what they want to say in writing and share it publicly with the group when they're ready, and they know it's exactly what they want to say.

Optimize Team Interaction

As a leader, consider how you might leverage all the different personalities you have on your team to get the best out of everybody. Perhaps you can assign roles on projects or ask for specific feedback or input at meetings from those who are less likely to participate. If you go that route, giving assignments or asking for feedback ahead of time will make this much more successful.

Managers can utilize these concepts and those discussed earlier in the chapter with their own teams.

Set Team Communication Norms

Next how do you plan to communicate as a team across location and time, whether you're a permanent team or an ad hoc group working on a time-limited project?

As we discussed in step three: redesign, flexibility isn't just about where we work; it's about when we work as well. People are not only working in different locations; they're working asynchronously. Some leaders have told me they have shifted to 100 percent asynchronous work, while others have told me they expect their people to work within defined working hours.

Either way, you'll need to clarify what type of flexibility you'll be using as a team and then set up expectations about how to communicate team members' work hours and locations.

Communicate Where and When

I typically recommend people overcommunicate about where they're working and when. In the past, people didn't want to be too forthcoming. But to function well in a flexible environment, we need to know where people are. It's not about watching. It's about planning.

Before flexibility, when we all worked in the same place at the same time, we didn't have to communicate at this level. In a flexible environment, the rules of engagement have changed. Now we do need to know where people are. Why? Because for us to work well together, I need to know if I can leave something on your desk and expect you to see it before the end of the day. Or if not, I know I need to send it by email or other electronic method. Similarly, if I know I need an in-person interaction for maximum effectiveness, I need to know if that person will be in the office the day I go in.

So if your people are resisting your requirements to consistently communicate when and where they're working, give them specific reasons why it's important to know when and where they're working. It's not to invade their privacy. It's to allow them as much autonomy and flexibility as possible and still work effectively as a team.

Be Explicit About How the Team Should Communicate

Once you clarify when and where your team is working and how you will know, establish some common norms for specific communication methods, including messaging, phone, email, and meetings.

During the pandemic, it seemed like everything that used to be a phone call became a Zoom meeting, and everything that used to be an email became a Zoom meeting. We now have the opportunity to intentionally decide what type of communication fits our needs best.

In the earlier section "Create Opportunities to Connect," we discussed how you might decide whether something is best communicated in a meeting. I recommend that individual managers go several steps beyond that and set norms for whether a communication should be a text, phone call, video meeting, or instant message as well. With so many communication options, people are getting inundated with "urgent" communication to the point that they are becoming meaningless.

Reclaim the true meaning of urgency and set specific norms for each type of communication.

For example, one leader created a communication framework with a clear response time: they would respond to an email within one day, to a text within a couple of hours, or if an immediate response was needed, they would respond by phone as soon as they were able.

Another team got more specific. They would schedule a meeting if their communication required more than three total emails; they would schedule a phone call if it involved only two people, it was a quick check-in, and it would take prohibitively long to type out what they wanted to say; and they would schedule a video call for longer conversations between two people or where a quiet environment was needed.

Finally, be sure to communicate clear expectations and take full responsibility for your communication. Make the implicit explicit. Overcommunicate. Be exceptionally clear when sharing expectations.

Taking full responsibility for your communication means you're responsible not just for what you say but for how it's received. If you're delivering content through slides, you're not just responsible for what your slides are saying; you're responsible for how they are being received. Are people getting the message? Are they resonating with it? It all comes back to giving people clear expectations for what they should expect when engaging with you as a leader.

Ensure Contribution by Providing Opportunity and Accountability

As mentioned earlier, many managers with hybrid or virtual employees ask, "How am I going to know people are working?" Remember rather than measuring face time, measure output or impact.

However, you and your team can achieve even better results if you shift your question from "How do we avoid the worst-case scenario?" to "How can we become the best we can be?" To do that, ask yourself, "How might I provide opportunities for people to contribute at their highest level?" Remembering the acronym I mentioned earlier in the chapter, ask yourself, "Are you FOR your people?" Make sure you are providing them with feedback, opportunities, and relationship-building. The following sections include some considerations.

Individual Productivity

When it comes to contribution, remember that different individuals are productive in different environments. As mentioned earlier in the section on collaboration, introverts may be most productive in a quiet space alone, while extroverts may need a lot of in-person interaction to do their best work. The question is, does your team experience the psychological safety they need to ask for the work conditions that make them most productive? That responsibility rests with the leader.

Work Allocation

We've mentioned the organizational responsibilities of setting equitable work allocation guidelines. As a leader, you'll want to measure and review the data on work allocation with your own team. To avoid confirmation bias, don't rely on your impressions or memory. Look at real data on who's getting work and who's not, who's getting opportunities and who's not, and who's being promoted and who's not.

Also measure and review the data from the perspective of inclusion. Are your work allocation and contribution practices hindering your opportunities for diversity and inclusion on your team or enhancing them? When allocating work, are you defaulting to the people who are right next to you, or are you giving everybody a chance to contribute in some way? Are you providing people on reduced hours schedules the opportunities they need to develop?

Grace Speights admits she is concerned about virtual work's impact on diversity. "I will be frank about that: that's what worries me," said Speights. "I worry that our diverse associates, especially those who are first generation coming into a law firm, can get lost in the virtual and flexible world. Many of them don't take charge of their current career and their development. [During the pandemic], it was very rare for diverse associates in my group to proactively reach out to me. I had to proactively reach out to them. But the nondiverse associates were reaching out."[19]

To address this concern, Morgan Lewis chair Jami McKeon emphasizes the impact of having leaders like Speights visible to people of color and underrepresented groups, in addition to having an intentional plan for inclusion and advancement.

"We're really lucky because one of the leaders of our firm is Grace Speights, one of the best lawyers in the country," said McKeon. "And so to have a leader of Grace's stature, a Black woman, on our advisory board and our compensation committee, that is a blessing. She's a fantastic leader. If you believe you can't be it unless you can see it, you can see it with Grace.

"But it's never enough to have a limited number of people in those roles," McKeon continued. "So every one of our practice groups has a plan both to attract and then advance top talent, including lawyers of color and other underrepresented groups. We must make sure that all of our top talent is getting the same exposure and the same opportunities to move forward in their careers, rather than hoping it happens by happenstance."[20]

Ensure Equity in Performance Reviews

As mentioned earlier in the section on organization-wide practices, organizations should set up systems to monitor for equity in performance reviews, but it's the individual leader or manager who must monitor this day-to-day.

Here are five mistakes supervisors can make when evaluating individuals who work flexibly—and how to fix them.

- *Attributing missed deadlines to reduced-hour schedules*: Research has shown that when individuals who work standard schedules miss deadlines, their supervisors are likely to attribute the lateness to the individuals' busyness, poor time management, or uncontrollable events such as sickness. On the other hand, when individuals who work reduced-hour schedules miss deadlines, their supervisors are likely to assume that the lateness is due to the fact that the individual worked fewer hours. This assumption can cause supervisors to attach their frustration over late work to the individuals' schedules and undermine the supervisors' support for flexible work. It can also prevent the supervisors from uncovering the real reason for the lateness.

  The fix: Talk to the individuals about why their work was late. If they have too much work on their plates or are trying to juggle too many high-priority projects, the cause can be corrected. If they need some coaching in managing their time or becoming more effective in the way they work, discovering the deficit is the first step toward getting the individuals the help they need.
- *Not giving honest feedback*: Supervisors often shy away from providing negative feedback, and even more so when giving feedback to individuals who are in traditionally underrepresented groups. It may be because of a fear of being labeled biased, a desire to appear understanding and supportive, or an unwillingness to spend effort on an employee who is perceived as likely to leave the firm. Whatever the reason, the lack of feedback can make it much more difficult for individuals to learn and develop.

The fix: Ideally, feedback should be given frequently and close to the event so that there are no surprises at annual evaluation time. Plan feedback ahead of time, focusing on providing specific information that is focused on behaviors and not on personality or character. For example, rather than saying, "You have no regard for deadlines," say, "You were two days late with the Smith brief." State that change is needed and what the outcome has to be for satisfactory performance. For example, "When we give you assignments, we give you deadlines that you need to meet so we are able to meet court deadlines." Ask the employee to tell you how they will fix the situation going forward, set a timeframe, and follow up.

- *Not suggesting next steps*: It is common to include at the end of performance reviews the next steps the associate should take to gain the necessary experience or skills. A side-by-side comparison of performance reviews given to lawyers who work standard schedules and lawyers who work flexibly frequently shows that the flexible schedule lawyers are not given this next-step information. This may be because their supervisors assume they do not have time to take on additional tasks, or it may be because they do not believe the lawyers want to advance in their legal careers.

  The fix: Supervisors can check their reviews of individuals to make sure that all are given the same type and quality of suggestions for improvement, as appropriate. Firms can help by creating evaluation forms or checklists that include suggestions for improvement and by reviewing all performance reviews for consistency before they are given to the individuals.

- *Torpedoing evaluations with schedule-related comments*: I have seen more than a few well-done evaluations of flexible-schedule individuals undermined with comments about the individuals' schedules. For example, a generally positive evaluation that focused on the skills the associate had demonstrated and their positive relationships with colleagues and clients was undone by a gratuitous observation that they had been able to complete all their work on time and professionally despite working from home one day a week. Such comments, while usually intended as compliments, shift the focus from performance to schedule and telegraph an opinion that nonstandard schedules are unprofessional hindrances.

The fix: Stay away from comments about schedule. After all, supervisors do not ordinarily comment on a standard-schedule associate's arrival or departure times, lunch hours, gym schedule, or vacation time. Schedule-related issues should be addressed separately from performance evaluations, particularly when the schedules are newly instituted, and frequent and timely feedback is important.

- *Providing an evaluation that appears adequate until compared with others*: Often the deficiencies in an evaluation of a flexible schedule employee do not become apparent until the evaluation is compared to those of a standard schedule employee. Differences can include lower numerical ratings given to flexible employees for the same level of performance, a willingness to overlook the mistakes of employees who work standard schedules, and less specific feedback given to flexible schedule employees. A comparison may also reveal that flexible schedule employees are not getting the same types of assignments, opportunities, or mentoring as standard schedule employees.

  The fix: Compare the evaluations before they are given to the individuals and reflect deeply on differences. Are the differences the result of different expectations, stricter standards, or more leniencies being given to one group? Do they reflect a willingness to put forth more effort to help the development of some individuals over others, and if so, are there legitimate, defensible reasons for the difference? Use the answers as signs showing where more effort is needed to eliminate flexibility stigma.

Interrupt Bias

Leaders are responsible for interrupting bias. As covered in earlier chapters, managers should watch out especially for proximity bias and confirmation bias in flexible workplaces.

As a leader, look first at your own practices and tendencies. Challenge any proximity bias by regularly asking yourself the following questions: Am I mostly giving work to those in closest proximity to me, or am I distributing work intentionally? Am I just mentoring the people right down the hall from me? Am I working with individuals on a reduced hours or flex schedules? Do I mentor individuals with different schedules than my own? What opportunities do I have to mentor more broadly?

Challenge your own confirmation bias by asking these questions: When am I assuming someone working at home isn't actually working? Do I assume those on reduced hours are only partially committed? Do I believe that only those who come into the office are going to be successful? If that's what you believe, that's likely what you will perceive.

Be sure to challenge these biases when you see or hear them from others. How will you monitor and measure evidence of biases in others? How will you interrupt them while being a resource for your people? How will you train your people in bias awareness and encourage them to point it out where they see it as well?

Kim Koopersmith had an opportunity to interrupt bias the moment she became chair at Akin. Her new position had just been announced, and she left a discussion on new partners to sign off on the press release. By the time she walked back into the partner meeting, the committee had decided to turn down the two potential partners who were working flex schedules. Kim decided that the meeting should begin again. She told the committee, "We will discuss their performance and not their schedule."[21]

Respect Boundaries

Leaders are responsible for respecting boundaries—both others' and their own. One of our key flexibility principles is that flexibility is not a work-life balance tool; that's where boundaries come in.

The truth is, as a society, we've lost all sense of boundaries when it comes to work. People are calling at all hours, working at all hours, and setting up meetings at all hours. In this new flexible work environment, we must reclaim them. And it starts with leaders leading by example. Set your own clear boundaries and be respectful of others' boundaries.

For example, if you want to respect someone's boundaries around work time, it takes more than just an email subject heading that says, "Don't look at this until Monday." By sending that email over the weekend, you've already intruded on that person's time. What I hear from people receiving those kinds of emails is, "I can't unsee that. I get that they've told me I shouldn't look at it, but of course I'm going to look at it anyway."

Instead use the simple strategy of *schedule send*. Write the email at midnight, or when it's convenient for you, and instead of hitting send, use schedule send so it automatically goes out at 8:00 a.m., or the beginning of their scheduled workday. It amazes me that one of leaders' biggest takeaways from these strategies is schedule send, because they had never heard of it before! It's another reason leveraging technology is so important for leaders. If schedule send sounds like a helpful boundary tool, use yourself to lead by example but also offer a quick training on schedule send for your people.

In our communication, as well as all our practices, we as leaders must be very intentional about the example we're modeling and the influence we have on people's ability to continue working productively and sustainably. When virtual work became a regular practice, many of us saw high levels of productivity. And many of us said, "Wow, this really works." And it does really work—to a point. Those high levels of productivity often result from people working all hours of the day. That level of productivity is not sustainable, as we're seeing in the impact on mental health and burnout rates. If we don't begin reclaiming healthy work boundaries and deeply rethinking how we define and measure productivity, flexibility will not be sustainable for our people.

Just as the leader is responsible for respecting boundaries, the individual is responsible for articulating them. I've heard from so many people who are overwhelmed or burned out to the point of helplessness that they feel they can't say anything. At the same time, I hear leaders say, "If only I had known how much was on their plate, I wouldn't have pushed them."

Leaders, encourage your employees to communicate with you about boundaries and give them a safe space to do so. Also provide guidance on how they can successfully communicate boundaries with others. Remind your people that nobody can enforce boundaries for them. Someone may knowingly or unknowingly ask them to cross a boundary, but they are the ones who decide to do what someone is asking or not (I'll discuss more about boundaries in the context of well-being in chapter 10).

Set Clear Expectations

In our work, one of the most common complaints we hear from individuals after a new flexibility initiative is implemented is that they don't know when they're supposed to come into the office—an observation supported by research.[22] If they don't even know where they're supposed to work each day, it's probably safe to say they don't know about many other expectations their leaders have.

Managers should help professionals working a flexible schedule learn about the specific strategies that are key to their Flex Success. These include paying particular attention to communicating proactively with your supervisor and team, maintaining visibility even when you're physically outside of the office, being adaptable and flexible when there's a need for a schedule adjustment, and leveraging technology whenever possible. This training should also focus on ways they should carve out time for business development, professional development, and mentoring.

Even so, individuals are ultimately responsible for their own executive presence. Here are some general recommendations:

- *Attire in virtual meetings*: Norms for attire are continually evolving, but when meeting online, remember that virtual meetings should be treated like any other meeting. Present yourself in accordance with the purpose of the meeting.

- *Cameras on during virtual meetings*: To increase connection, I recommend all individuals keep their cameras on during meetings. By doing so, you show you are fully present, committed to enhancing connection, and engaged face-to-face, just as you would be for an in-person meeting.

- *Background in virtual meetings*: Make sure your surroundings are suitable for a professional environment. If you cannot create a separate virtual office in your home, consider blurred filters or background images to help with the background.

- *Attention during virtual meetings*: Another reason many feel disconnected during online meetings is that some attendees are clearly doing other things. We don't expect people to be driving while attending an online meeting. I've had a number of people who will do that and say, "Well, isn't this what flexibility is about?" My response: "No, this is what gives flexibility a bad name." Make sure that you're giving 100 percent of your attention to your colleagues. Avoid phone calls, texts, emails, and other distractions during virtual meetings, as you would during meetings in your conference room.

- *Participation during virtual meetings*: Be intentional about your participation, and make sure that you come to all meetings prepared to contribute. When attending virtually, share your thoughts either by speaking up or using the chat function. Show that you care about your own professional development as you network and build relationships by starting or joining in on the serendipitous discussions before and after the meeting.

- *Maintain visibility when coming into the office*: In a hybrid environment, employees must prioritize intentional connections when coming into the office. Who else will be coming into the office that day? When are colleagues you should connect with coming into the office, and can you schedule the same in-office days? Have you planned lunches and coffee breaks with colleagues? Are there any work events you can attend?

Provide and Solicit Feedback

The organization is responsible for soliciting feedback on the flexibility initiative as a whole, but how do we as leaders make sure flexibility is an iterative process for our people? In addition to regularly offering feedback, create a process for soliciting feedback, whether it's an ombudsperson appointed to receive and share feedback with you or a more informal process. Even more importantly, talk to your people regularly. Ask them about their work experiences—what's working, what's not working, and how can we improve the experience?

Now that we've focused on how managers and supervisors can best manage teams and set up practices for their employees, the last essential step for leaders is to look at how they work to ensure they are embodying and exemplifying flexibility themselves.

HOW LEADERS EMBODY FLEXIBILITY

Many leaders I talk with agree that flexibility is the path forward for their organization and fully support their company's flexibility strategy. What they struggle with is developing new habits to shift the way *they* work daily, the choices they make in how they show up every day, and how they communicate with team members.

Though changing how we work and lead can feel hard sometimes, our society's ever-increasing rate of change requires *adaptive leadership*, something important for leaders and individuals alike.

If you are leading long-term change at your organization, your personal work habits and expectations of your people must also be aligned with your organization's flexibility purpose, principles, policies, practices, and people. If not, you risk losing all the business and visionary benefits of the flexibility initiative you've worked hard to create and roll out.

Are You a Demand or a Resource?

Your most important responsibility as a leader: Be a resource to your people, your clients, and your organization rather than always a demand. Focusing on how leaders can be a resource to their people is an essential part of humanizing the workplace.

Daniel Friedland, MD, author of *Leading Well from Within*, often asks leaders, "Are you being a demand or a resource?" because how they interact with their employees creates conditions that impact that employee's satisfaction, engagement, well-being, and productivity. Friedland defines stress as a state where demands exceed resources, so it's particularly important for managers and leaders to work in ways that provide resources to their teams instead of stressing their teams with too many demands.[23]

Of course, ideally, the organization has created a flexibility strategy that serves as a resource for leaders and individuals alike. But remember the data from Gallup: 70 percent of the variance in workplace engagement can be attributed to the manager.[24] You as the leader play a huge role in your team's and organization's experience.

The following leadership strategies will support you in balancing these needs and more consistently being a resource for your team, your clients, your organization—and yourself.

Lead by Example

Even if your organization has a new flexibility strategy, flexibility itself may not be new to you. You may have already realized that your team has been using technology to work effectively across office locations or asynchronously. In other words, you may know a lot more about leading in a flexible work environment than you realize.

The difference is that now it's intentional, and it is organization-wide. All eyes will be on leaders, asking, "Do our leaders really believe this? Is this something they're actually going to support? Am I really allowed to use this flexibility policy, or will there still be the silent stigma?" Your people will be looking to you for these answers, not just through your words but through your actions.

Recently a colleague shared a story with me about her new boss and how thankful she was that he understood flexibility. How did she know? He spoke regularly about his family and didn't hide when he was leaving early to attend a child's event.

One day, when she was packing up her belongings at 4:00 p.m. to leave for a meeting at her child's school, she realized that for the first time ever, she no longer had heart palpitations at the prospect of walking past her boss at an early hour. She so appreciated that her new boss got it when it came to flexibility and the need to be at her child's school. "What a gift!" she told me.

When it comes to leading a flexibility shift, let your actions show your embrace of flexibility. Model behaviors that interrupt flex stigma and unconscious bias and set the tone for the rest of the organization. This shows individuals that they can feel comfortable using the policy.

What might this look like? You can be unapologetic and transparent about your schedule. You can be proud you have a family, special interest, or hobby and that you value your life outside the office.

Most importantly, lead with empathy. We live in an era where the personal and professional are blending. Take the time to understand what your people are experiencing both in and out of the office and show them flexibility is here to stay with your words *and* actions.

Be Strategic about When, Where, and How You Work

When we begin to wrap our minds around the new possibilities offered by flexibility, as leaders, it's very natural to focus on personal preferences. Where do I prefer to work? At what times am I most productive? Do I want to give up my commute? What's easiest for me?

While taking full advantage of the autonomy flexibility offers is an important consideration (even for leaders!), it's not the only consideration. You might prefer to be home for that meeting, but what would be most beneficial for your team, your clients, and your organization? If you showed up in person, would you have a bigger impact? Or would working virtually produce better results?

As we create our new work habits, it's important for leaders and individuals to balance their personal needs, team needs, client needs, and organizational needs. Here are some things to consider when deciding where, when, and how to work each day:

- *Personal needs*: Leaders and individuals need to get their work done—and they also need regular breaks and healthy boundaries. When assessing personal needs, consider the following questions: Where will I work best? Where will I have the greatest impact?

  For example, if you need to concentrate and work on a brief, perhaps working from home is the best place to focus with the least distractions. On the other hand, if you're presenting a training where the majority of attendees will be working from the office, maybe coming into the office will be most beneficial.
- *Client needs*: When serving clients directly, consider how you can create the best possible impact from the client's perspective. Ask yourself what will be most effective in meeting your client's needs.

  For example, if you meet with your client virtually, you might be able to include team members from other locations that bring value to the meeting. Or if you are focusing on developing a deeper individual relationship with your client, perhaps you suggest an in-person meeting.

- *Team needs*: Also, consider what will best meet the needs of the team. Are there in-person meetings or collaborative discussions that would benefit from being face-to-face? Are most team members working in the same office, or are they across locations?

  For example, if you are holding a meeting with team members across offices, perhaps it is best to host the meeting virtually so all members can equally participate. Also, consider where you can collaborate best: Does your home office have the same technology tools? Are there any benefits to taking a virtual meeting from the office (i.e., to chitchat with those in the office)?

- *Organizational needs*: Finally, consider the needs of the organization. Are there organizational attendance requirements that need to be considered?

  For example, during recruiting season, individuals may need to be available for interviews, be present for questions from new recruits, and help integrate new team members by meeting for coffee or lunch.

"It's incumbent on every single person to figure out where the best place is for them," agrees Nancy Laben, general counsel at Booz Allen. "If you joined a year ago and haven't been with anyone live, come to the offsite. Have a cup of coffee with your colleagues to build that rapport. But if you're writing a protest, feel free to go home, turn your phone off, and don't take calls." It's up to the individual to find the right balance and get the most value out of each location.[25]

Now that you've aligned your flexibility purpose, principles, policy, practices, and people, you're well on your way to integrating flexibility into your organizational culture. But you want to make sure you maintain your flexibility shift—which brings us to the final step in our framework, step five: reinforce.

REFLECTION QUESTIONS

The reintegrate step of the framework is where the rubber meets the road at implementation. I share many ideas and best practices to help make sure you're setting your organization up for success in areas like connection and collaboration in a flexible workplace. There are many more ideas that are in practice today at other organizations. What additional ideas do you have to improve communication, connection, and collaboration among your teams?

8

HOW WILL YOU MEASURE, MONITOR, AND ITERATE OVER TIME?

After developing and rolling out their flexibility initiative, one executive committee member confided in me, "I'm concerned the firm will shoehorn old practices into our new environment and assume everything is working." Her concern was that people would not change their behaviors and, because of that, flexibility would not succeed at the firm in the long run.

How can we know flexibility is working and having the intended business impact? And how can we ensure people are not disadvantaged by how they choose to work?

A flexibility shift is an iterative process, which means it must be measured over time to learn what is working, what isn't, and how to keep improving.

One recent study indicates that although 54 percent of organizations report increased productivity due to hybrid work, only 22 percent had established quantitative metrics to measure that improvement.[1]

If you are committed to ensuring that your flex initiative is successful, it's essential to continue to follow up and reinforce the Flex Success after the launch. Reinforcement is a step that many organizations let slide. To ensure that your flex policy is successful, effective, and meeting your organization's and your employees' needs, you must develop a system for measuring and tracking metrics that demonstrate quantitative and qualitative success. This tracking system must be embedded in your flexibility initiative to ensure systematic and effective monitoring.

The good news is that if you have followed the process outlined in this book and built your initiative on a solid foundation, you know why you created your initiative in the first place, which means you know exactly what outcomes to measure.

In this chapter, you will develop an intentional, inclusive, and iterative process to reinforce your flexibility initiative so it will become more and more successful over time.

Here are the steps we'll cover:

- What to measure;
- How to measure and monitor; and
- What steps to implement so you can iterate over time.

This final step in the Flex Success Framework, *reinforce*, ensures your entire flexibility initiative is iterative so your process *and* results continue to improve.

WHAT TO MEASURE

I once worked with a corporation that had rolled out a flexibility initiative. One of the department leaders was concerned that not all employees were taking advantage of it.

The leader called all their direct reports into their office and posted each department's flex policy usage rates on a large screen. They used the data to point out opportunities some departments were missing and even called out each department head to own their percentage rates. The leader then issued a directive: for people whose usage rates were low, they needed to come back with a plan for how they would address it. The data provided a very clear message.

You may not choose to be this direct with your team, but this kind of data is valuable for any team. Data tracking and sharing are all part of reinforcing and iterating your flex initiative.

Gather Data from Your Own Organization

In step four, we emphasized the importance of knowing general data and trends to bust myths about flexibility. But to make the best decisions for your organization, you must go beyond broad studies or statistics and gather data from your people.

According to a Future Forum study, "workforce policy planning is largely happening at the executive level, with 60 percent of executives saying they are designing their company's policy with little to no direct input from employees."[2]

The reinforce stage offers an opportunity to be curious about what is *actually* happening in our organization rather than settling for what we *think* is happening based on our own limited experience or assumptions. Then it offers us clear direction on how to iterate as a result. For example, if you want to know how your flexibility initiative impacts engagement, use surveys, check-in interviews, and focus groups to get input directly from your people.

Ask them directly:

- Where do you feel most engaged?
- What aspects of your work environment cause you to feel engaged?
- What do you enjoy most about being in the office?
- What do you enjoy most about working virtually?
- What other forms of flexibility would help you bring your best self to work?

Gathering data directly from your people will remind you that different individuals have different experiences at the office. Some will say they enjoy going to the office to build connections and build their network, while others say it's an opportunity to put their heads down and get their work done. It all depends on how the office's resources compare to those available at home, and that value equation is different for everyone.

Similarly, some may bring up that reduced hours, compressed work weeks, or job sharing helps with work-life control. If these employees can better manage work and personal obligations, they can be more present and committed when working. You might learn that there are barriers to using flexible options under certain managers or technology issues lowering productivity. These are all valuable inputs that can shape how well your organization adapts and fine tunes your programs.

So to get the organizational data we need to make good decisions about reinforcing this new way of working, you'll start by defining what outcomes to measure. Defining your outcomes will help you see how all the steps of the Flex Success Framework pay off.

Measure the Key Business Outcomes from Your Flexibility Purpose

In step one, you outlined your flexibility purpose and your organization's unique business case for flexibility. Because your flexibility purpose defines why you created your flex initiative in the first place, you'll first want to measure your initiative's impact on these key outcomes.

To measure the impact of your initiative through the lens of your flexibility purpose, you can ask the following questions:

- What business outcomes did we initially believe flexibility would make possible for us?
- What business outcomes has this new way of working made possible for us based on organizational data?
- Are there any gaps between the two?

Also, when measuring these business outcomes, remember that both leadership and employees contribute to those outcomes. For example, instead of measuring engagement based on whether people are in the office, as some organizations do, Morgan Lewis measures whether leaders are reaching out to develop mentoring relationships.

"It's got to come from the top," said Grace Speights, partner at Morgan Lewis.

> There isn't a partner meeting or a week that goes by that doesn't have a reminder for partners to engage with associates as opposed to putting it on the associates to engage with the partners. We have a talent office, and part of that office's job is to reach out to associates to see if partners are connecting with them. The talent office reports up to leadership, and then they reach out to partners to encourage them to be more engaged.

Speights also notes that this data can impact compensation and bonuses for leaders.[3]

Morgan Lewis has been a pioneer in virtual work well before the pandemic, and firm chair Jami McKeon credits the feedback they received from their employees.

"I especially want to echo the iterative process," said McKeon.

> A driving force for us was our junior associates. One of the lessons we learned from the pandemic was that junior associates were not getting as much guidance as they needed. It doesn't do our juniors any good to be in [the office] on their own. Everybody else has to be with them too.

Initially, we tried the concept of "all in" days once a week—figuring that people could select their other in-office days. What we quickly learned, however, is that everyone wanted to be in the office at the same time, and that the process of people trying to meet up when they didn't know the schedules of others was cumbersome. So ultimately, we decided that as a general rule all the lawyers would be in the office on Tuesday, Wednesday, and Thursday, and were free to work in the office or at home on Monday and Friday, subject to client and firm needs. That's working well for now.[4]

This example truly shows the value of measurement and feedback.

Measure the Impact on Your Flexibility Principles

Next you'll want to measure the impact on your flexibility principles from step two.

Your flexibility principles were based on your values, culture, strengths, market positioning, and non-negotiables. They answered the questions, "As an organization, who do you want to be? Regardless of how flexibility evolves in the future, what do you want to preserve, honor, and maintain no matter what?"

To measure the impact of your initiative through the lens of your flexibility principles, you can gather data on the following questions:

- Have our values changed or evolved since implementing our flexibility initiative? If so, how?
- Has our culture changed since implementing our flexibility initiative? If so, how?
- Have our strengths changed since implementing our flexibility initiative? If so, how?
- What is the market and our industry saying about us? Has that changed since implementing our flexibility initiative? If so, how?
- Review the original flexibility principles. Are we showing up as who we want to be? Are we preserving what's most important to us in terms of flexibility? If not, what principles are at risk?
- As the rate of change continues to increase, are there any principles we can appreciate that got us to where we are today but are now working against us? Are there any new principles emerging that we want to adopt to be who we want to be moving forward?

Measure the Usage of Your Flexibility Policies

In step three, you created your flexibility policies. To assess their effectiveness, you'll want to measure how many people use them, who uses them, and how often.

- How many individuals are using your flexibility policies?
- Who is using them? Look closely for differences in gender, positions, demographics, departments, and office locations. In addition to measuring the number of women and underrepresented groups working flexibly, be sure to measure the number of men working flexibly. If no men work reduced hours or work from home, then chances are that working flexibly is too stigmatized for your program to be a retention tool.
- How often are your flexibility programs used?
- What gaps do you see between actual usage and intended usage?

Measure the Effectiveness of Your Flexibility Practices

To assess the effectiveness of your flexibility policies beyond usage, you'll want to review for other critical metrics such as productivity, allocation, and unconscious bias.

- Assess evaluations for evidence of any unconscious bias related to flexible work.
- Regularly review productivity reports to address any ingroup and outgroup issues.
- Drill into workload allocation to ensure everyone has access to high-quality work—determine your top clients and projects for skill development and see who is staffed on them.
- Look closely at your pipeline—ensure employees with flexible work arrangements are on track for promotion by providing them with leadership and work experiences typically necessary for advancement.
- Understand trends in attrition reports and exit interviews to see if flexible workers are impacted at a greater rate.

Measure the Impact on Your People

Finally, it's important to monitor and review how your flexibility strategies are affecting your people.

- Understand the experiences of flexible workers by regularly soliciting input (we'll talk more about how to do this in the next section).
- Conduct a deeper dive on flex employees with positive experiences to understand what supports have helped.
- Drill into flex employees with negative experiences to better understand what factors were at play.

HOW TO MEASURE AND MONITOR YOUR FLEXIBILITY METRICS

Now that you know what metrics to measure, how exactly do you measure and monitor them over time?

I recommend using the same intentional and inclusive approach you used for the first four steps: include all voices in the data you gather and meet as a leadership team to review the data and address any gap areas.

Include All Voices

First you'll want to regularly receive input from all your people on your key metrics and their general work experiences. This doesn't happen enough. According to a 2022 Microsoft Work Trend Index special report, 43 percent of employees say their company solicits feedback at least once a year, and 57 percent say they rarely do.[5]

Closing the feedback loop is critical in retaining talented employees. According to the same Microsoft Work Trend Index special report, "Employees who feel their companies use employee feedback to drive change are more satisfied (90 percent vs. 69 percent) and engaged (89 percent vs. 73 percent)."[6] To close the feedback loop and create a feedback cycle, you need to ask for feedback regularly and share what you're seeing and how you're responding with your people.

Following are some ways to regularly measure and monitor all voices when it comes to your flexibility initiative.

Surveys

You can use surveys to efficiently collect information and metrics from a large workforce. Gather data on the importance employees place on flexibility, whether employees have the flexibility they need, the types of flexible work arrangements most appreciated, how often formal and informal flexible work options are utilized, additional types of flexible work arrangements needed, what types of infrastructure has been most helpful, and what other types of infrastructure are needed. These responses help build a business case to offer and expand flexible work arrangements. If you conduct a general employee opinion survey, see if flex-related questions can be added and compared with responses from other questions related to employee satisfaction and commitment to demonstrate how flexibility impacts these areas.[7]

If you use surveys to monitor your flexibility initiative, conduct them at least annually. These can include any of the following surveys:

- *Workplace flexibility surveys*: Include your key metrics for impact on purpose, principles, policies, practices, and people.
- *Employee engagement surveys*: Include a section on workplace flexibility.
- *Program surveys*: Include questions about participants' flexible work experiences.

Interviews

Interviews and focus groups with employees are a great way to gain more detailed information about what's working and what's not. You can include questions about your flexibility initiative in the following types of interviews:

- *New employee interviews*: To understand the impact of flexibility on recruiting, ask new employees during check-in meetings why they chose to join your organization and how important flexibility is to them.[8]
- *Exit interviews*: To understand the impact of flexibility on turnover, ask employees during exit interviews if they felt like they had the flexibility they needed if they would have stayed, and what types of flexible work options they would have wanted.[9]
- *Stay interviews*: In addition to new employee interviews, 360 evaluations, and exit interviews, more organizations are conducting *stay interviews*, which are one-on-one conversations with all levels of employees intended to understand what factors are leading them to stay at the organization, show appreciation, and invest in their future.
- *Check-in interviews*: Use these to assess specific challenges or successes as they arise with individuals (i.e., women, employees from all demographics, specific departments, new employees, certain positions and levels).

- *Focus group interviews*: These interviews will assess specific challenges or successes with specific groups (i.e., women, employees from various demographics, specific departments, new employees, certain positions and levels) or the whole organization.

Some leaders wonder how to be sure you're getting truthful input from employees, especially during exit interviews. Jami McKeon shares a few ways Morgan Lewis creates an environment that encourages honest feedback.

> *First, we ask pretty close to the exit. And second, we don't circulate it. Nobody gets confronted in their office. Also, our HR [human resources] people do most of the interviews. I think people feel comfortable talking to them, because they're not talking to their practice group leader.*
>
> *But when somebody's leaving and I'm worried that there's more there than meets the eye, I'll ask our chief engagement officer, or somebody who knows the person well, to talk to them. Then I write to them and say, "I really appreciated your candor; we only get better if you tell us what we should be doing." We also do an upward review, where our associates do upward feedback of our partners. We've tried to create an atmosphere where we're encouraging people to be honest. I'm sure there are people who aren't 100 percent honest, but I get some pretty candid answers.*[10]

Pilot Programs

Pilot programs can be helpful when specific departments or offices are more eager to adopt flexibility than others. They're also beneficial if you want to test the program with a small sample to gather sufficient information about what works and what needs to be adjusted or to build momentum before rolling it out across the organization.

When creating a pilot program, it's essential to assess experiences, usage, and perceptions regularly; this allows for adjustments and data collection to build momentum for the program. This data also provides helpful input for monitoring and reinforcing flexibility in your organization.

For a pilot program, consider the following process:

- Implement a pilot program for workplace flexibility with a group(s) most amenable to this arrangement, with leadership support.

- Regularly monitor and report results.
- Assess productivity and performance by looking at collective time or billing as well as evaluations before and after the program's implementation.
- Understand experiences regarding work-life control, satisfaction, and engagement by conducting check-in meetings.
- Roll out programs more broadly, based on iteration and results.

Meet Regularly as a Leadership Team to Measure, Monitor, and Iterate

At least annually, you'll want to meet as a leadership team to review your key flexibility metrics based on data and employee input. Consider what's working well and what's not, and iterate accordingly.

For those annual meetings, I encourage leadership teams to follow the following process.

Prepare participants before the meeting for best results. Before you meet, the leader or facilitator of the meeting should be sure everyone has access to all data (reports, statistics, surveys, interviews, etc.) that will give them a complete, inclusive understanding of the key flexibility metrics you want to measure. Be sure to provide them with enough time to review the data. Also, to make the most of your time, consider sharing in advance the questions you intend to discuss at the meeting.

Begin with a question of purpose. Where you start determines where you end up. When you "start with why," as Simon Sinek puts it,[11] you can create meaningful change that matters to your leaders, people, and organization. Begin by inviting participants to reflect on why this meeting is essential in the first place and to share with the group.

- Why is it essential for us to meet as a leadership team to have this conversation about our flexibility initiative?
- What does *getting it right* mean to you individually, our organization, our people, our stakeholders, and our industry in terms of our strategic priorities?

Review business outcomes related to your flexibility purpose. Once your team is connected with purpose, review your first set of metrics related to your flexibility purpose or business case. As most of us know from experience, when people are asked for feedback, they tend to forget the positive and focus on the negative. You will have plenty of time to discuss what hasn't gone well, but to give yourselves the best chance of seeing the *whole* truth of what your flexibility initiative has made possible; I recommend intentionally focusing on the positive impact first.

Remind your team of your flexibility purpose. Next share business outcome highlights from the data and the voice of the organization. Then ask the team the following questions:

- Based on your experience, what positive business outcomes did you see as a result of our flexibility initiative? (Encourage them to share an example or a story.)
- What specifically about flexibility do you think led to this positive business outcome?
- What else would you like to see?

Review the impact on your flexibility principles. Then review the next set of metrics related to your flexibility principles with your team. Even though I encouraged you to think of your flexibility principles as non-negotiables, the truth is that in our society of ongoing rapid change, even tried and true principles need to be revisited from time to time.

To practice adaptive leadership and to allow participants to consider their principles from a curious, iterative perspective, you can ask questions like the following:

- Which core principles continue to be an important part of our culture?
- Are there any principles we can appreciate that got us to where we are today but are now working against us?
- Are there any new principles emerging that we want to adopt to be who we want to be moving forward?

Review usage outcomes related to your flexibility policies. To review the metrics related to your flexibility policy, first share key usage highlights from data and organizational input. Then ask the team the following questions:

- What did you like about the policy or the way in which work has evolved?
- What would you like to see?

- What types of workplace flexibility were most utilized?
- Were these forms of workplace flexibility used equally across the organization? Or is there evidence of more robust pockets of usage by specific departments, positions, offices, or demographics?
- What flexibility policies were not as well utilized? Why do you think that was the case?
- What can we as an organization do to foster greater usage?

Theme opportunity areas into the five Ps. Along the way, you and your team have shared what you liked and what you would like to see. Now is the time to clarify any gaps between what you intended for your purpose, principles, policies, practices, and people, and what is actually happening so you can iterate and continue to improve your initiative.

Remind your team that you will get better outcomes when you ask questions that lead you in the direction you want to go. If you see challenges and want to go in a positive direction, you can ask questions, framing gaps or challenges as opportunities.

In light of the conversation so far, ask the team to share the opportunity areas they saw based on the data and the voice of the organization. Then theme their responses based on the five Ps:

- *Purpose*: A purpose gap can result from forgetting why the organization decided to launch this flexibility initiative in the first place. For example, some may still believe flexibility is a perk or an accommodation instead of a business imperative.
- *Principles*: A principles gap might result when a shift has occurred away from an organization's original principles, or when policies are not being implemented in alignment with their articulated principles.
- *Policy*: A policy gap can result when someone doesn't understand the specifics of the policy and more clarity or education is needed.
- *Practices*: A practices gap can result when implementation practices aren't clear, there's a lack of training, or there's a lack of infrastructure. Note: Gaps in practices are often perceived as people problems, such as when an employee has not attended meetings consistently but may not have received invites. This is, in fact, a practices issue, not a people issue.

- *People*: A people gap involves keeping individuals accountable for following the policies and practices and providing them with the right tools to succeed. Because many gaps first appear in people's performance, before assuming you have a people problem, ensure the individual has access to the same information, training, technology, and infrastructure as all other individuals do.

While facilitating this conversation, someone may say, "The problem isn't one of the five Ps; the problem is that flexibility isn't working." Spoiler alert: The problem is never a flexibility problem. You can remind them of the data we reviewed in chapter 2 and from your own organization: We know flexibility works. But it will take some time to implement it properly, which is why we need to measure, monitor, and iterate continually.

Ensure you have easy access to industry and organizational data to challenge opinions and bust myths when needed. For example, a common unconscious bias is *rosy retrospection*, or viewing the past with rose-colored glasses. At a leadership team meeting, one leader stated that their flexibility policy had hurt their mentoring ability. Another leader responded, "We were never good at mentoring!" It can be easy to blame flexibility for problems that were already there, but that doesn't make it true. So if the group starts reminiscing about "how great it was when we all worked together in the office," have organizational data and surveys ready to show why working at home is actually much better for many people, for logical and measurable reasons.

Groupthink, another form of unconscious bias, may occur if your leadership team is relatively uniform regarding age, position, gender, ethnicity, generation, or another differentiator. If you notice the team engaging in unconscious groupthink, keep bringing in the voice of the organization, especially voices that are not otherwise represented by the leadership team.

Most importantly, lead with empathy. Give everyone an opportunity to share their perspective and stay curious to understand other people's viewpoints.

The Importance of Employee Resource Groups

Many organizations find that employee resource groups (ERGs) are critical to supporting a flexibility initiative. I mentioned ERGs earlier as one way to build connections in an organization, whether employees are in the office, working virtually, in distributed offices, or some combination thereof. ERGs provide support, relationship building, and tips for their members, and they can also be used as built-in focus groups for getting feedback and tracking the success of the flex-ibility initiative.

ERGs are also safe spaces for those working a flexible schedule to address challenges within a particular context and unite around opportunities that advance their careers. It's best if members of the ERG can meet face-to-face, either in-person or through video, on a regular basis for fellowship as well as professional develop-ment and education. The ERG members should decide what educational programs are needed, and it's helpful if the organization helps fund the events.

I recently heard a great example of the value of an ERG. An attorney, pro-moted to partner while working a reduced hours schedule, gave a presentation during an ERG meeting to highlight the initiative's success. Another woman present had always believed the firm would not promote those on reduced hours schedules. If it hadn't been for the ERG, these two women may never have spoken and shared their experiences, which in turn helped retain a valuable employee.

I recommend that organizations create flex ERGs so employees working in flexible arrangements can share tips and build community. In that latest bench-marking report from the Alliance, we saw that only 16.2 percent of law firms had flex ERGs, but our members who have these groups find them invaluable.[12]

Law firm Crowell & Moring has offered an employee resource group for those who have flexible work arrangements for many years and has a significant number of employees who utilize it, according to Don Smith, talent and inclusion officer at the firm. He has found many benefits to this: not only can participants share best practices, but the organization has a built-in focus group that allows them to understand how people are experiencing flex and to quickly refine or respond to any issues or opportunities. Smith says, "In the affinity group, people come and share best practices. We openly discuss promotion paths for people in non-traditional work arrangements and highlight people who have made reduced hours work successfully. These are really important things."[13]

Further Integrating Flexibility throughout the Organization

As you integrate flexibility throughout your organization's culture and structure, you'll want to regularly monitor whether it is being implemented equitably and iterate accordingly. Here are some areas to pay close attention to and ideas for effective monitoring.

Recruiting

When monitoring flexibility and recruitment initiatives

- Include leaders on flexible work schedules on the hiring committee and interview panel.
- Systematize interviews such that all interviewers receive training to understand how to conduct interviews and be aware of biases, and standardize interview questions so that they are focused on skills, past performances, and behaviors to reduce biases against flexible workers.
- Assess the number of candidates interviewed, offers extended, and offers accepted, broken down by workplace flexibility, especially with lateral candidates.
- Conduct check-in meetings with candidates who rejected offers and new hires to understand how workplace flexibility played a role.

Equitable Workload Allocation

In a flexible work environment, we strongly recommend work allocation support. The level and type of support needed depends on your organizational culture, but at a minimum, include the following work allocation measures:

- During performance reviews, establish clear goals related to projects, experiences, and competencies needed to advance during the upcoming year so both employees and managers understand what types of experiences are necessary.
- Review projects and time worked weekly.
- Review flexibility utilization reports monthly to see who is getting too much work and who is getting too little, as well as who is getting the right experience and who isn't.
- Review and discuss over- and under-utilized employees.
- Monitor schedule creep regularly for employees on a reduced-hours schedule or in a job-sharing position.
- Check in regularly with employees who are under- and over-utilized, and regarding any ingroup or outgroup concerns.

Fairness in Evaluations

Flexible employees often face bias in the evaluation process. Thus, it is helpful to implement the following measures:

- Link evaluations to clearly delineated benchmarks and competencies to reduce bias and make evaluations more consistent.
- Provide training on writing and delivering feedback so leaders understand the importance of providing specific, measurable, and timely reviews.
- Review evaluations for bias prior to evaluation meetings.
- Address any bias directly.
- An HR or talent professional should sit in on evaluation meetings to ensure there is no bias.

Parity with Promotions

Tracking, measuring, and monitoring usage, retention, and compensation rates will help you identify problems early and allow you to fix any issues before they truly impact your organization. This type of regular self-evaluation can be valuable in correcting issues at minimal expense. Consider the following operations:

- Clarify in flexible work policies that full-time flexible work options (i.e., hybrid work, virtual work, compressed work week, or shifting hours) do not lead to delay in advancement timing, and part-time flexible work options (i.e., reduced hours or job sharing) may lead to delay in advancement timing only if it impacts critical experiences received.
- Include a leader currently or previously on a flexible work schedule on the promotion committee to help reduce any bias.
- Define clear metrics for promotion, to reduce any bias.
- Communicate these metrics.
- Assess with each promotion cycle the number of employees promoted, up for promotion in this past cycle, and in the pipeline for the next three to five years, broken down by workplace flexibility, to ensure fair representation.

CELEBRATE SUCCESSES

Sharing your success stories is an excellent way to reinforce Flex Success. Shine a light on the individuals who are successfully navigating their careers while also working a flexible schedule to prove to others that flexibility does not have to be a hindrance to careers. These role models can also help to spread the word that the organization completely supports working a flexible schedule. By sharing the success stories with others in the organization, you are helping to build momentum, trust, and support for the initiative. In addition to celebrating individual successes, be sure to celebrate successes of the initiative itself—the *bright spots* or areas of flex impact.

When it comes to flexibility initiatives, it's critical to identify, celebrate, replicate, and share your organization's successes. Whether they are small improvements or large achievements, any action or flexibility initiative that impacts your organization in a positive way is a bright spot worth acknowledgment.

Bright spots can be minor adjustments that ultimately have a major impact on your organization's bottom line, recruitment and retention capabilities, and employee satisfaction. Perhaps it's an individual who has maintained a successful career path while working a reduced-hours schedule. Or perhaps you've developed a new family leave policy that has had a serious impact.

It's so important to share information about your policy or initiative and the impact it's had on both internal and external audiences through newsletters, press releases, social media posts, and presentations. When you share your bright spots, you're building support and momentum for future initiatives.

REFLECTION QUESTIONS

One important step that can make or break your flexibility initiative is gathering employee feedback. This chapter highlights common methods like employee surveys and other examples beyond the survey like Morgan Lewis's exit interviews and upward reviews, or Crowell's affinity groups. Can you identify additional opportunities for employee feedback in your organization beyond the survey, perhaps with approaches that also make employees feel valued and engaged? How might you measure the usage of your flexibility policies? How might you measure the effectiveness of your flexibility policies?

9
PUTTING THE FLEX SUCCESS FRAMEWORK INTO PRACTICE

Even when following a framework like the Flex Success Framework, one size doesn't fit all. Flexibility is flexible and customizable and should be implemented in a way that best reflects your organization's goals, values, purpose, business case, and workforce. The framework's fundamentals should be in place, but how it comes to life will be unique to each organization and will evolve over time.

To illustrate how the process looks in practice, I'll share the journeys of two different organizations, one a professional services organization and one a financial institution. These companies, like hundreds of others I've seen go through this process, have approached the journey a little differently and learned different lessons along the way—many of which are universal and can apply to any organization.

SAUL EWING EMBRACES A NEW WAY TO WORK

Like many organizations, Saul Ewing began developing a larger vision for flexibility as a result of the pandemic, and they successfully used the Flex Success Framework to develop the initiative and to roll it out. Jason St. John, chair of Saul Ewing, generously agreed to share how his firm implemented the framework step by step.

"When I started my career twenty-three years ago, there was no concept of flexibility," said St. John. "People came in and worked in the office five, six, even seven days a week. All work at every level was done in the office.

"In the last ten years or so, things started to change. You started to see partners not coming into the office every day, working from home or some other location. If we had measured it, I think we would have found that offices weren't just empty on Fridays, but any day throughout the week that partners found they could work from home."

Then came the pandemic. "That was the pivotal moment that showed us the technology and resources were there to allow us to serve our clients from home or anywhere," said St. John. "That is when the idea of flexibility was born for me within a professional services model.

"As the pandemic evolved, we started to talk about what it might look like to come back into the workplace. Health and safety were our first priorities. We wanted to ensure that people were safe and that we had protocols in place to safeguard health. That is easier said than done in a firm like ours that practices in so many different geographies with divergent attitudes about pandemic safety protocols, proximity, and regulation."

In 2021, Saul Ewing began to look at how they might get people back into the office. "That's how we had done it forever before the pandemic," St. John said. "The world was getting back to normal. Kids were back in school. It seemed like it was time for us to get back to business as usual.

"But as we tried to do that, it became really clear just how much good came from working from home. We weren't ready to give up the autonomy and flexible productivity that the pandemic gave us. As long as the work was getting done, the clients didn't seem to care. So why should we go back to business as usual?"

The idea of preserving the benefits they received from the pandemic was one thing, but creating a policy to preserve them was quite another. Fortunately they didn't jump straight to a policy, but first laid a foundation of purpose and principles.

Step One: Reflect

"Even before we came up with a policy, it was important for us to engage with our colleagues about this idea of how we work and what it would look like in a hybrid environment," said St. John. So they invited the Alliance to do a series of five training sessions, one for each employee group, on how to lead and thrive in a hybrid world. St. John says,

> *By doing this, I wanted to signal two things. One, the pandemic had moved us away from the old way of working, and we were never going back to the old way. Two, we were moving towards another way of working, a new normal of hybrid work.*
>
> *It was helpful to have Manar come in and talk about how we would actually work together in this new hybrid world. For*

*example, if we had a meeting in an office but some of the attend-
ees were remote, how do we make sure everyone is included in the
meeting? It was a whole new concept and a whole new way to
work, and it was important to engage with everyone about these
issues.*

Each of those five sessions were designed for a different group in the firm,
such as the executive committee or the staff, so everybody could attend a session
and address questions or concerns specific to that group. But the ideas and goals
for each session were the same.

"It was an important message to our staff that before we created a policy, we
were going to listen to everybody's concerns and ideas," said St. John.

At the end of each session, each group was asked to send written feedback
to Saul Ewing's chief talent officer about what they planned to do with the information they learned, and especially what they intended to do differently. By
asking everyone to reflect on how they could contribute to the success of the work
environment, Saul Ewing was intentionally emphasizing from the beginning that
the most important thing wasn't the policy, but what individuals would do to
make it work.

These firm-wide trainings and discussions began to shift the conversation
from "How can we get people back in the office?" to a higher purpose conversation of "How do we move forward with flexibility as a business imperative now
that we see what flexibility makes possible for us?"

"Once again, we realized we had picked up so many positives through working in the virtual world," said St. John. "We began to ask ourselves, 'What do we
want to keep from the virtual world? And what do we really miss from being in
person?' From there, we thought, let's build this hybrid model based on maintaining what worked really well for our clients and colleagues in the virtual world,
and bring in the things we missed from being in person. And that's how we started
to think about flexibility as creating the best of both worlds."

That discussion led to recognizing some real business benefits of flexibility,
including talent retention and productivity.

"Some say clients don't care about whether we work in a hybrid environment,
but I believe they do. Clients do care about whether their law firms retain people
who are happy, because that leads to continuity of service, which leads to more
productive, efficient work for clients."

Reinforcing what they were already noticing, a few of Saul Ewing's clients
told St. John that a common measure for law firms was the happiness of their

people, particularly their associates. "We've been proud to see our ranking increase based on that measure, and I do think it's because of this greater desire to maintain a flexible workplace," St. John said.

Step Two: Reimagine

As a result of defining the business benefits flexibility provided, Saul Ewing began to think bigger about what flexibility could do for their firm in terms of their position in the marketplace and their larger vision.

"We started to ask, 'What do we want our people to be saying and feeling about this experience?'" said St. John.

> *That was the purpose of flexibility for us—we wanted it to be a differentiator. We wanted to say to the market that we were putting our people first, and that by putting our people first, we were really putting clients first, because clients want happy, engaged people working for them on their matters. We wanted our staff and our practice assistants to be saying, "I talked to my colleagues, and they don't have that kind of flexibility." We thought it would be a competitive advantage for us to provide greater autonomy to everyone.*

Step Three: Redesign

According to St. John, this reimagining resulted in the following flexibility principles: "We wanted to create a workplace that strikes a balance between autonomy and the benefits of being in person without compromising our high standard of excellence and performance for our clients."

Now that the firm was clear about the purpose and principles of flexibility, the executive committee turned their attention toward drafting a policy. As a first step, they researched what policies were emerging among similar firms and what they could learn from them. Many policies seemed to be mandates requiring people to return to the office two, three, or four days a week, and in some cases, staff who had been working effectively at home were required to come back five days a week.

"While this policy by proclamation was easy enough to make, the firms never seemed to address why they were rolling these requirements out, and the approach didn't seem to fit what we wanted to accomplish," explained St. John.

> *So we started with this question: why do we want people back in the office, and what do we hope to gain? This question turned out*

to be a good foundation for a policy that was purposeful and intentional, and that the entire company could plan around.

That is how we came up with the new idea of anchor days. When we did this, we didn't know that word. But we picked Wednesday to be our in-person day as a company each week. It was simply a day to get out of the house and come to your local office to meet with clients, work, and dedicate some time to experiencing community. And community could be the office as a whole, a group of coworkers, or one-on-one with a mentor.

They called their policy 4+4, based on the fact there were approximately four Wednesdays in a month, and then four other days in each week. They chose one consistent day each week so colleagues could plan around it. Because it was always the same day each week, they encouraged people not to schedule personal appointments on Wednesdays, and later, as everyone became more aware of Zoom fatigue, they encouraged people not to schedule video calls that day, unless client needs required it.

"It allowed a level of predictability, which we thought was helpful. It also allowed people who had been working from home for two plus years every day to ease into the idea of coming back to the office, as opposed to saying, 'Okay, your life is going to completely shift again,' without having a reason for it." However, although 4+4 was a strong recommendation, it was not a mandate.

Another intentional aspect of their policy was that the 4+4 policy applied to everyone, including leadership, attorneys, and staff.

"We really wanted to live equity," said St. John.

So while we didn't promote our policy as part of our DEI [diversity, equity, and inclusion] strategy, an important component for us was having everyone play by the same rules.

As a quick footnote, some positions, such as receptionists and those in the mailroom, require being in person. And we were going to include them, but the rules were going to be a little bit different for them because their job required it. Putting that group aside for a second, who are critically important to what we do, saying to our staff that they were going to have the same rules as the lawyers and the partners spoke volumes about how we view our people. Rather than just saying to the market that we believe in equity, we thought it was important to show the market by creating a policy that was inclusive for all.

As a result, Saul Ewing created a policy that was both a mirror and a window into their culture and their vision of who they wanted to be as a firm. Even though each member of the executive committee sat as one person around the table as they drafted their policy, they represented hundreds, thanks to the input they had been gathering all along from their people.

Step Four: Reintegrate

Once the policy was created, the firm made an announcement, and St. John went on a road tour to visit each office to explain why they created the policy and why everyone's involvement was key to its success.

"Sometimes people will look at a policy and say, 'Okay, this is on leadership to make it successful,'" St. John said. "But this was one policy we felt our colleagues needed to be invested in. As we rolled 4+4 out, we formed a task force that included people with all different titles across our footprint to listen to our colleagues and help us think about how we could help people work 4+4, which I think was particularly helpful."

Also, to reinforce their intention to make this policy a market differentiator, they refrained from responding to the many calls from journalists asking them about their hybrid approach, and instead announced their policy during rollout.

"I wanted to instill a sense of pride in our colleagues," said St. John. "I wanted everyone to know that we were listening to our people, that our policy was intentional, purposeful, and flexible, and that our colleagues should be proud they created this policy, because they really did create this policy. [The executive committee] came up with the name and picked the day, but it was all based on colleague input, like 'Don't just tell me to come in because we're checking a box. Let's make it valuable and purposeful.'"

After the rollout, Saul Ewing worked with directors, managers, and at the office level to integrate the policy into their culture and intentionally create a return on experience (ROE) for their people.

"We did some easy things, like feed them," said St. John.

> *That was particularly nice during a time when some folks were still concerned about being outside or in a restaurant. We would provide Starbucks gift cards for folks at all levels to use, so they could go out with a colleague for a walk and grab a cup of coffee or an iced tea. The idea was to get out of our office environment and spend some time together one on one, which facilitated mentoring relationships.*

We got a lot of really good feedback around that—not just because we paid for people to get coffee, but because we were giving people autonomy and flexibility around how and when they would engage with each other, rather than saying, "It's 11:00 a.m.; everybody take your break and mentor." We had folks who would go for a walk at 7:00 a.m. to exercise together, which had never happened before, folks saying it was a really nice way to end the day, and everything in between.

By giving their people the resources to connect and the autonomy to choose how and when to connect, Saul Ewing allowed them to design their own ROE.

Another practice was to encourage everyone to pick three people they hadn't talked to in a long time and go to lunch together to get acquainted. Even though they had no requirements to report back about the experience, St. John found that in addition to getting caught up on each other's lives, people also naturally began talking about clients, matters, and opportunities.

"Those conversations we didn't script or tell people to have happened naturally," St. John said. "And that was what we wanted: we wanted people to feel like they came in for a reason."

In this way, Saul Ewing was creating a work environment that wasn't just about getting the job done, but about building relationships and therefore building a career—and elevating the work of the firm as a whole.

They also kept the task force active to continue making suggestions about how to make 4+4 more meaningful for people, as well as scheduling regular trainings to help people run hybrid meetings and generally understand how to work effectively in the hybrid world. "We didn't just say 4+4—go," said St. John. "We tried to provide tools along the way to make it more effective."

One of those tools was a custom app that allowed people to update their weekly schedule to let others know when they would be in the office. It also allowed them to check into the office each day, so that if anybody was in the office or planning to be in the office, they could easily see who else was there.

"We did that for a lot of reasons," said St. John.

One was transparency. Knowing who was in allowed people to be more purposeful and intentional about the days they also chose to be in. Also, the check in feature in the early days was related to health and safety. Because let's not forget when this all started— lots of folks were masked in our offices. So people knew when it

was worth it to walk down three flights of stairs to go visit with
someone, because they knew someone would be there.

Step Five: Reinforce

Saul Ewing began measuring and monitoring their initiative from the first weeks. "We told people from the beginning that this was going to be iterative," said St. John. "We needed to see how the way we worked evolved and how that would impact our ability to deliver excellent client service as well as our lives."

Initially, St. John's only concern was that productivity would decrease on Wednesdays, so they monitored productivity very closely.

"In the first few weeks, productivity did not dip at all," said St. John. "Wednesdays looked like Tuesdays and Thursdays. Some folks were thrilled, but I actually started to get concerned, because I had now been to enough offices and I had seen the engagement on that anchor day. I just couldn't understand why productivity was looking the same."

As St. John dug deeper, he discovered that people were maintaining their productivity levels because they were going home on Wednesdays and working later. Now that the firm had motivated their people to come in on Wednesdays, he realized that they needed to be more intentional about expanding community efforts to the other four days, so Wednesday didn't simply extend the workday.

"I feared people would start to dread Wednesday," said St. John. "Fortunately, we haven't had that. People are still loving Wednesdays, and I think one of the reasons is that we got out in front of this idea and tracked our productivity at a global level, not an individual level."

Around the nine-month mark, they began to gather data to measure 4+4's impact and see what changes needed to be made, starting with a simple three-question survey that asked all colleagues at Saul Ewing what their experience of 4+4 was like, what they wanted to keep, and what they wanted to change.

"We had a ton of people respond to the survey," said St. John. "I mean, that doesn't happen anywhere. But the level of engagement in response was remarkable throughout our footprint and gave us a lot of data.

"What came through as common themes were that people really valued flexibility, and the number one thing they valued was the autonomy related to their schedules and their lives," said St. John. "And that autonomy made them feel even more committed to their work because they were able to do it at a location or at a pace that worked for them, with an understanding that we have expectations for the benefit of our clients. That came through loud and clear."

Although the majority of comments were positive, there was some critical feedback related to the fact that 4+4 was strongly encouraged but not required. First, there was a perception that a larger burden of work fell upon people who were in the office. Second, lawyers who weren't in the office either weren't receiving the benefit of mentoring or weren't mentoring others.

St. John took the feedback seriously and engaged me and my team at the Diversity & Flexibility Alliance to help his team address it. "We heard that feedback, and we took that information and engaged Manar to come in and facilitate a session with our executive committee," said St. John. "I felt like it was important to take our executive committee back to what the purpose of the policy was and what we wanted to get out of it. Let's see where we were winning, and let's see where we need to evolve."

In terms of business benefits, St. John has seen several. First, attrition is down, and as a result, clients have benefited from that continuity of service. Also, the survey results revealed a happier, engaged workforce.

"Knowing they can work from anywhere and have the flexibility to do that ensures people don't have to feel chained to a certain location to be able to deliver outstanding service to clients," said St. John.

> *And I think that's been a benefit for folks. I also think flexibility has created an environment where people are able to manage their time differently. Interestingly, we don't hear or read as much anymore about people struggling with prioritization. I truly believe that when people have greater flexibility and autonomy around where they work, it allows them to prioritize in a more meaningful way rather than simply jumping from task to task or reacting. Flexibility requires you to plan. To make flexibility work, you have to know where you are going to work the next day and what you want to accomplish, wherever you're going to be. And I think that helps people prioritize.*

In measuring the impact of flexibility, St. John recognizes the value of hearing directly from the people through survey data, rather than leaders alone. "Leaders are people, too," said St. John. "They have their own teams and have developed their own biases around how it works for them. The survey data ensured we were listening to our people and not just relying upon one's own experience. Because different people work differently. Some teams just work locally, and that experience is very different from working nationally. So getting that data was incredibly valuable as we think about how we're going to evolve 4+4."

Leading Flex Success

As a leader, St. John prioritizes staying connected in the firm's hybrid environment.

"I still get on the road and try to get to all our offices on a Wednesday, because I know I will see most people there. When I do that, I try to do organic listening sessions with folks.

"From a technology standpoint," he continued, "in addition to continuing to use the app as a resource, we've added people to our team focused solely on training our people on how to use technology, such as how to use Microsoft Teams with your team, with your office, and with groups, and how to get comfortable using instant Zoom."

Saul Ewing has also expanded its online resources through an updated intranet that is customizable and personalized for everyone's experience.

When you open up your computer and log on to the system each day, your homepage is our intranet. It starts with a message from me about what's going on at Saul Ewing today, and then identifies a whole bunch of resources, including who was in your office that day, events, and announcements, and then allows you to navigate to anything and everything that you would want to know about the law firm, instead of having to make a call or ask someone. You can access that 24/7, and that has been another way to keep people connected while furthering autonomy.

Through their investment in their firm's intranet, Saul Ewing is leveraging technology to create an instant sense of belonging wherever their people work. They're intentionally welcoming their people into their virtual office space just as they welcome people into their physical office space on Wednesdays.

4+4 has reached its one-year anniversary, and it continues to pay dividends for the firm, its people, and its clients. "We have people who now are saying, 'I never thought I'd be excited to come back to work in the office, but it feels good to come in,'" said St. John. "'I know what I'm doing and what I need to accomplish on the office days, which are things I can't do when I'm working from home. I'm happy about that. And then I plan my week differently for when I'm working virtually.'"

As Saul Ewing continues to gather data on 4+4, they will continue to iterate over time, positioning themselves to continue to lead the future of work.[1]

FOCUSING ON PEOPLE FIRST IS BCU'S SECRET TO SUCCESS

Baxter Credit Union (BCU) is a credit union serving 350,000 members in the United States and Puerto Rico, with over $6 billion in assets, and a decidedly people-focused culture. I recently had a chance to catch up with long-time chief executive officer (CEO) Mike Valentine, and he generously shared BCU's evolution from pre- to post-COVID-19 pandemic which I'll share through the lens of key messages that can help any leader succeed in a flexible, human-centered organization.

Put People First

According to Valentine, his philosophy has always been people-first, as he describes it: "People first, employee first, has been my adage since the beginning of my journey as a CEO. If you put the employee first, everything follows, everything else falls into place."

People have always been central to BCU's culture, and flexibility has always been a part of it. But the COVID-19 era was a pivot point that helped to establish even deeper connections, enhanced practices that support flexibility, and prompted more cultural understanding and improvements—all of which have continued to propel the business forward, maintaining double-digit (13 to 20 percent) growth every year of their forty-two-year history.

Like most leaders, Valentine found the abrupt COVID-19-driven changes difficult at first. Once employees had to leave the office and work from home, he was a self-described "fish out of water" because, as a "people person," he missed seeing everyone in the office. Valentine started scheduling leader chats with his executive leadership to maintain connection. He also continued his version of a coffee chat. He explained,

> *I also wanted to be in touch with several levels down from my executive leaders, so, not being a coffee drinker, I host Dew Chats (named after the drink, Mountain Dew). In these meetings, no members of leadership are there, and we get together maybe ten to fifteen people, a cross-section of the company. Myself and usually our CHRO [chief human resources officer] sit and talk [with the group] for an hour, mainly about life, kids, family, and work (in that order). Toward the end, we get to what's happening [in the company]. What do you like and dislike? What can we do to make*

your jobs easier? It's a way for me to get an ear to what's happening because, in leadership groups, everybody sounds great. But you have to peel the onion back to get to a deeper level of feedback.

During COVID-19, I'll be honest with you, at first I just wanted to see the employees—to see how they're doing, where they are, and to understand what was going on for them. Then it evolved to include what the group is doing, what are their pain points. We continued through COVID-19, and it just escalated. Now I go into the office three or four days per week, and I still do these meetings virtually from my office. I realized I've got to get deeper with employees, especially those I would never have been able to connect with like that before.

Let Your Values Drive Your Culture

Valentine was able to learn a lot from employees with these intentional, well-orchestrated meetings, but he has also proactively shared important messages directly with more employees. As discussed earlier in the book, humanizing culture and implementing flexibility are most successful when driven by values and purpose. One of the issues many organizations face is a gap between values and messages shared by the CEO and how employees receive those messages, many layers below. As Valentine knows, accurately conveying those messages throughout a larger organization requires intention, with a special emphasis on equipping middle managers to do this successfully.

The secret to spreading values throughout an organization is simple, though not easily done. According to Valentine: "It's putting the values forefront and rewarding the values." For BCU, their values include things like *inclusion, collaboration*, and *creating a wow factor*. Valentine and his team share those values in every way they can because they know that embodying these values leads to their success. But how do you ensure managers in the middle carry the same message and walk the same walk? Ensuring effective communication throughout an organization is a challenge. The middle of an organization is often where this communication of values and ideas can break down. In BCU's case, Valentine and his team have developed practices that convey to their management team that living these values is a priority, and they're accountable for doing it.

As a company that values feedback and data, they have many processes in place to gauge how managers are doing overall, like employee net promoter scores (eNPS) that allow employees to rate other departments on their internal service to each other. Since collaboration is a value, if a group isn't providing a high level of service to other groups internally, this feedback can be surfaced and addressed.

Another opportunity to evaluate leaders on their demonstration of shared values is through their talent review process. BCU requires every manager to specify how employees embody inclusion, courage, collaboration, integrity, and *wow*. The information they receive, while subjective, does contribute to ongoing development conversations and opportunities for promotion. On the plus side, rewards are reflected in annual management incentive compensation. This is a fantastic example of putting systems in place to reinforce clear communication, feedback, and accountability within the ranks of middle management. Getting the transmission of values right at this level of an organization is key to building and reinforcing culture in an environment where not every employee works in the same location.

Intentionally Cultivate Communication and Connection

Another evolution to BCU's culture resulted from what Valentine called "unintended consequences," where feedback surfaces that cause changes to someone's leadership style or an organization's practices that hadn't been contemplated until the feedback arose. Valentine experienced several of these crucial moments directly due to improved communication practices the company implemented to work better in a virtual workplace. Valentine described instances of this:

> *We had a goal to reduce our expense ratio from four to three and a half. At first glance, that sounds great. But then you start to hear some things from employees that you didn't realize. Can you really reduce expenses in a way that doesn't affect our employees? Then you have to balance that. In another example, we were discussing one of our core products, an interest-bearing checking account. It's a high-rate product, but we were only paying interest on the first $20,000. After that it goes to a lesser amount. One employee said, okay $20,000 sounds nice if you have it, but what about us down here that might have $1,000 average balance, what will you do for us to reduce fees? It's stuff like that you learn in listening.*

This type of feedback also comes from cultivating a culture of trust and honesty.

BCU had another shift that elevated communication and connection in their post-COVID-19 pandemic hybrid workplace. BCU always operated dozens of remote branch offices, meaning about a third of their total employee population has never worked at the headquarters campus. Considering the experience of those people connecting to a meeting virtually was not top of mind pre-pandemic. As Valentine describes, "Our all-hands meetings were very focused on whoever was in the office on that day. We offered a call-in line, but that was it. Now we do all-hands meetings completely virtual, with live Q&A [question and answer sessions] and post the recorded meeting on our company SharePoint." Valentine and his team learned through COVID-19 that the employees who connected virtually to a meeting that was more of an in-person meeting never felt very included. It's something that changed when everyone was remote that circumstance forced everyone to have the same meeting experience. BCU describes this as "making lemonade from lemons" by enhancing centralized communication in ways they likely wouldn't have if they weren't put in a situation necessitating creativity and finding new ways to connect better with employees.

Immediately following the COVID-19 pandemic, BCU saw a slight increase in turnover, a sign that prompted them to work harder at connection and engagement. As Valentine shared, "It's this new intentional way that you've got to communicate because in a hybrid world, some people feel like they're on an island. Connection has to be core to everything." With effort and intentionality, turnover reverted back down, and their employee engagement scores are as high as ever. According to Gallup's annual Q[12®] survey that measures employee engagement, BCU earned a score of 4.47 out of 5.0. This score made them eligible to apply for the Gallup Exceptional Workplace designation, which they received in 2023.

Keep Evolving

One of the most critical messages Valentine shares is about continually learning, improving, and being open to hearing things that may be difficult but essential to hear. One of BCU's often-repeated adages is "Progress over perfection!" This thinking is in sync with the reiterate stage of the Flex Success Framework.

BCU conducts ongoing employee surveys that give them a view on employee engagement overall, but they get specific issues and ideas through verbatim responses that are just as important. As Valentine says,

> *A score is an indicator, it's what you do with the score that counts. Once we get our engagement scores, we break it into individual groups and go back and ask, what were we doing, what can we*

do to improve things. We look at the highest and lowest scores and ask what's going on there, is it leadership or communication, or both? There are usually fifty or sixty pages of comments. I read every last one probably fifteen times. I rest on each one; maybe I shouldn't because it will make me lose my hair! But it really matters. It's one of those things that says [to employees] you matter to me, I want to hear it, then what do we do to fix it?

It is important to create environments where employees can open up to their leaders even if their questions or feedback might be difficult or unpopular. This can be more challenging in a hybrid environment if you're not intentional about engaging your teams. But it's critical in laying the groundwork for continuing to grow and iterate. Intentionality and a growth mindset can not only mitigate potential pitfalls in a flexible or hybrid environment—or any environment for that matter—but can also lead to breakthroughs and individual and organizational growth.

Another feedback mechanism BCU uses to fuel continual improvement is net promoter score, a score their members (customers) give them based on whether or not they would recommend BCU to others. This metric helps BCU check on their own strategic execution and evaluate if they're getting what they expected. No doubt it is, as BCU maintains a best-in-class net promoter score between seventy-nine and eighty, nearly double that of large national banks.

The ultimate feedback mechanism is growth—do their members stay with BCU, and do member numbers and assets increase? For Valentine and BCU, this directly correlates with how the organization takes care of its people and delivers a purposeful culture that values inclusion, well-being, and flexibility. According to Valentine, "If I take care of you (employees), you take care of the business. If the expectation is that we are creating a culture where everyone embodies the shared values, and if you take care of yourself as an individual, if our teams take care of each other, the business will grow, and we will be a healthy and thriving organization serving our membership."[2]

Saul Ewing and BCU are completely different organizations in unrelated industries, but they share many common values and priorities. They invest in their people first. They fuel their strategies and imbue their workplaces with purpose. They rolled out flexibility initiatives with support and infrastructure that made it successful. They have growth-oriented leadership that emphasizes continual improvement. These organizations exemplify human-centered culture, and their business and people are reaping the rewards.

REFLECTION QUESTIONS

You've read how two successful organizations are putting flexibility and human-centered culture into practice. Would any of their practices, or a modified version of them, translate to your organization? What ways can you apply their lessons learned to your workplace?

10

THE FUTURE OF FLEXIBILITY

I recently had a conversation with the chair of a law firm about the importance of offering gender-neutral leave and ensuring that everyone uses it. He said, "Yes, we give men leave, but I just had somebody in my group who came back early from their leave.

"They're not using it!" he added emphatically. This was the premise for his assertion that men didn't really need parental leave. "Did you ask him why he came back early?" I asked. He said no. To his credit, he went back and asked why the person had returned from leave early. He learned that the employee was interrupted so many times during his leave, working so much as a result, that he figured he might as well go into the office where at least he would get credit for working.

I hear stories like this all the time, and it's important to note because this story shines a light on *the biggest pitfall of flexibility*—a lack of boundaries. Boundaries can make or break the positive impact flexibility can have on engagement, productivity, and importantly, on employee well-being.

These experiences are all too common, and as stated many times throughout this book, employees don't want to work in that kind of workplace anymore. This is why I put such an emphasis in my practice on helping organizations create human-centered cultures. I've looked at workplace culture through the lens of flexibility in this book, but flexibility is one piece of an interconnected whole. In my experience, the future of human-centered workplace culture is at the intersection of flexibility, inclusion, and well-being.

WHAT IS WORKPLACE WELL-BEING?

There are many ways to define well-being. Gallup looks at well-being as a function of how well one is thriving in five universal components of their life—career (do you like what you do every day?), social (do you have meaningful friendships?), financial (are you managing your money well?), physical (do you have energy to get things done?), and community (do you like where you live?).[1] This definition is about individual well-being.

The fact that we spend one third of our lives working makes the importance of the career component of well-being even more profound.[2] If we are doing well in other parts of life—perhaps we have meaningful friendships—but we are struggling with a chronically stressful work environment that interrupts our sleep and affects our mood every day, the workplace component will have an outsized effect on our overall well-being. In fact, Gallup's research into workplace well-being shows that negative work environments can impact more than your own well-being. They say "having a job you hate is worse than being unemployed—and those negative emotions end up at home, impacting relationships with family. If you're not thriving at work, you are unlikely to be thriving at life."[3]

Workplace well-being is different than individual well-being. Workplace well-being includes individual employee's well-being and the collective well-being of the whole organization. It's also distinct in that its solutions include not only how an organization can help an individual improve their own health and well-being, but also organizational solutions that impact one's well-being at work—recognizing that organizations control many of the factors that contribute to well-being (or lack thereof).

With a growing mental health crisis, with burnout at an all-time high, and the strong, proven correlation between employee health and well-being and employee performance,[4] employee well-being needs to be an urgent priority. As *The US Surgeon General's Framework for Workplace Mental Health and Well-Being* states, workplace well-being, "has numerous and cascading impacts for the health of individual workers and their families, organizational productivity, the bottom-line for businesses, and the US economy."[5] It doesn't get much more impactful than that.

On the positive side, the Surgeon General states, "Work is one of the most vital parts of life, powerfully shaping our health, wealth, and well-being. . . At its best, work provides us the ability to support ourselves and our loved ones and can also provide us with a sense of meaning, opportunities for growth, and a community."[6] Through this lens, we see that work has the power to positively impact individuals, organizations, and society as well.

When I'm asked what the next evolution of the flexibility conversation is going to be, the answer is clear. We're not going to be talking as much about how many days a week employees should work in the office. We're not going to be as focused on whether flexibility works—the data is in on that, and it does work! We're going to be talking about how flexibility influences well-being, and how to effectively implement flexibility so that it supports human-centered culture.

Similarly, the conversation about well-being will evolve from a narrow focus on individual strategies to a holistic focus that includes both individual *and* organizational strategies—an approach that is much more impactful for all. Flexibility, inclusion, and well-being are integral to this because they address three key factors that organizations can control when it comes to human-centered culture: boundaries, burnout, and belonging. When leaders address all three of these factors, they can create healthy high-performing organizations. This is a holistic approach to human-centered culture.

BOUNDARIES

Boundaries must be in place for flexibility to support and contribute to well-being. When I ask conference or workshop audiences, "How many of you worked longer and harder than you ever had during the pandemic? How many of you had more work-life conflict?" people would emphatically raise two hands! I would jokingly say, "But why? You had all of that flexibility!" making the point that flexibility is *not* a work-life balance tool without boundaries (as I explained in chapter 3).

First, let's clear up a myth that might get in the way—the myth that boundaries are a sign of weakness or a sign of a lack of commitment. This might be especially prevalent in demanding environments or high-performance cultures. But because you need high performers to perform at their best over time, it becomes more important to have and enforce boundaries. As one law firm partner said to me recently, "I don't mind hard work, I expect it, but it *cannot* happen 24/7, 365 days per year. That is not sustainable."

I've talked with more than a few leaders who are resistant to the idea of flexibility with boundaries. There are those who say that they never had flexibility as they were working their way up and they did just fine, so why focus so much on it now? They might not have had formal flexibility policies as they were coming up, but what they probably did have was boundaries. Before everyone had a cellphone and a laptop, for example, they could go out to dinner or go on vacation and know that they couldn't be interrupted! They actually got real downtime!

Fast forward, these same senior leaders may still be able to go on vacation today without interruption because they have power, something the rest of their employees do not have. If the most senior leaders say they don't want to be disturbed on vacation, most others would not dare to interrupt them. It doesn't work that way for everyone. In fact, just recently, a more junior associate told me that on his latest vacation, he kept getting interrupted by his boss and colleagues. "Didn't you have your out-of-office message on?" I asked. He said, "Having my out-of-office message on is like holding up a napkin to a charging bull! It doesn't work!"

Boundaries are about valuing that work is one aspect of an employee's life. It is seeing your people as humans and not just employees. Organizations can create environments that empower their people to have boundaries around the role that work plays in their lives. Where people feel safe to speak about work-life conflicts without being seen as less committed, reliable, or trustworthy. Without boundaries in place, flexibility can be, and often is, a slippery slope that leads to overwork, stress, frustration, and other negative outcomes.

Lack of boundaries isn't only a pitfall, it's a long-running trend that was exacerbated during COVID-19 with the proliferation of Zoom and other online video platforms. Because workers could hop onto a video call from *anywhere*, they were suddenly expected to do so at *any time* too—at eight o'clock at night, during vacations, and even during parental or bereavement leaves.

My early career was in professional services where we've long glorified long hours in furtherance to the client, celebrating overwork, emphasizing client-first cultures, and applauding those at work sacrificing all. But disregarding boundaries and driving people to burnout is not in service to the client. It is to the detriment of the client.

I say this with urgency because it's happening in so many workplaces and every employee who is chronically overworked is an employee at risk of mental health problems, disengagement, burnout, and ultimately of leaving their job.

Values Mismatch

Lack of boundaries is a major contributor to overwork, which in turn results in stress. Another issue that often accompanies this, or is a result of it, is a misalignment between an employee's personal values and the demands of their workplace.

Since the COVID-19 pandemic, and arguably because of it, many employees struggle with a lack of alignment between what they value and what their workplace offers or allows. COVID-19 changed the workplace for good, and it fundamentally changed our expectations of work. The problem is that organizations aren't all responding in ways that work for employees, and when employees are frustrated, disengaged, or worse, it hurts the organization.

Before the pandemic, people didn't think it was possible for their work lives and personal lives to be in alignment, or to integrate more harmoniously. They thought they had to lead two separate lives. Then the pandemic created more of an alignment. For the first time, organizations were experiencing the same thing that individuals were experiencing. Workers didn't have to hide their personal lives at work anymore. If someone said that they needed to miss a meeting because their caregiver couldn't come in, it was accepted that a toddler might soon be running into view on the Zoom screen. People had lives outside of work that deeply affected them both at home *and* in the workplace, and that was okay. Even leaders who were previously not known for their compassion showed their employees support and empathy. Studies show that since COVID-19, this kind of compassion or empathy has declined.[7]

Now with the pandemic in the rearview mirror, employees feel like organizations want them to go into reverse, to go back into hiding, to come into the office with their personal lives parked safely at home. But people don't want to do that anymore and that's causing tension. People are saying, "Wait a second, I could do it before and now you want me to go backward!"

In a podcast interview for her new book, *Bold Move: A 3-Step Plan to Transform Anxiety into Power*, Harvard psychologist and anxiety researcher Dr. Luana Marques describes this as a "value shift." She explained, "The values that worked before the pandemic no longer fit for most people. We hear people talking about wanting more flexibility in their jobs. . . Why? Because they realized that family mattered and that was being compromised by the way they worked. So they're trying to fit their old values into this post-pandemic life—and they need a realignment."[8] Yes, exactly! And it makes sense that this value conflict contributes to employee's anxiety. It certainly did for me when I was working long hours after having my first son.

BURNOUT

Not surprisingly, a mismatch in values is one of the six causes of burnout according to author and researcher, Dr. Christina Maslach, along with the unsustainable workload, perceived lack of control, insufficient rewards for effort, lack of supportive community, and lack of fairness.[9] As mentioned earlier in the book, burnout is arguably one of the biggest issues facing employee well-being and workplaces now and as we move into the future. Research from a Future Forum Pulse Survey of over 10,000 global workers from 2023 showed that "Burnout is still on the rise globally, with 42 percent of the workforce reporting it—a slight uptick (2 percent rise) from the previous quarter and an all-time high since May 2021 when Future Forum first started measuring employee burnout."[10]

This is a disastrous number as burnout affects organizations and individuals profoundly, negatively, and broadly. In fact, burnout, which the World Health Organization included in its International Classification of Diseases, described as "a syndrome conceptualized as resulting from chronic workplace stress that has not been successfully managed,"[11] is the top challenge to employee engagement according to a recent report from the HR Exchange Network.[12] And as discussed earlier, lack of engagement suppresses performance, engagement, and ultimately profitability.

BELONGING

Another key factor that affects engagement is belonging. Great Place to Work®, the publisher of the "Best Places to Work" lists, defines belonging as "an employee's sense that their uniqueness is accepted and even treasured by their organization and colleagues." Their research also shows that workers who feel a sense of belonging are more likely to look forward to going to work and more likely to stay in their jobs for a long time.[13]

Belonging at work encompasses essential elements such as social support, diversity and inclusion, collaboration and teamwork, and trusted relationships. A sense of social support and inclusion can mitigate one of the biggest social determinants of health—loneliness and isolation. A culture of belonging is also a culture of inclusion. "Organizations that focus on fostering belonging and inclusion also foster a powerful protective force against bias, discrimination, and exclusion in the workplace" according to the US Surgeon General.[14]

Collaboration and teamwork are essential to high level performance, productivity, and innovation. Belonging is core to high functioning teams. A culture of belonging lets people from diverse backgrounds and experiences work together productively. Cultivating belonging allows for diversity of thoughts and ideas, as well as the psychological safety and trust needed to share them. It allows teams to function creatively, and it allows individuals to grow and shine.

According to Vernā Myers, "diversity is being invited to the party. Inclusion is being asked to dance."[15] Tony Bond, chief diversity and innovation officer at

Great Place to Work, built upon this sentiment: "Diversity is being invited to the party, inclusion is being asked to dance, and belonging is dancing like nobody's watching, because that's how free you feel to be yourself."[16] I would add that for this to happen, whoever plans the party, drafts the invitation list, picks the music, and welcomes guests at the door must intentionally cultivate a culture of belonging—in the workplace, the party host is the organization. Intentionally fostering belonging, ensuring boundaries, and preventing burnout are key to cultivating a human-centered culture.

THE NEXT EVOLUTION OF THE HUMAN-CENTERED WORKPLACE

So what can organizations do to humanize their workplace in ways that work for the employees and support their business objectives? Fortunately, plenty! But first they must shift their perspective from individual strategies to organizational strategies, from individual responsibility to shared responsibility, and from a singular view to a holistic view. This shift will enable the most powerful solutions.

In the case of workplace well-being, for example, taking a holistic approach sounds simple or obvious, but at this writing, many organizations aren't doing this. I see lots of organizations providing support for individual physical and mental health issues and for the prevention of the same—including health benefits, gym memberships, mental health and substance abuse support and benefits, healthy food in the cafeteria, yoga at lunchtime, and the list goes on. Some organizations offer more than others. These benefits are all important. But they're not enough on their own.

The onus should not be on the employees alone to take care of their physical or mental health issues, especially when they often result from issues emanating from the workplace. Rather than dealing mostly with downstream effects (which are costly), upstream interventions are much more powerful. In many cases, changing culture or processes organizationally can prevent downstream damage from occurring in the first place. This is a powerful shift that takes strong ownership on the part of organizations.

Recognizing the importance of workplace well-being, and seeing this clearly as an organizational issue, is the only way to address burnout and the effects of the mental health crisis in the workplace. Some companies are doing this. Even countries are doing it! Australia not only expected but demanded organizational ownership of employee well-being when they passed a law that gives companies a legal obligation to assess and mitigate psychosocial hazards in the workplace that contribute to mental health issues and burnout. An article on this issue in *Lawyers Weekly* explained how this issue spiked during and after the COVID-19 pandemic: "a vast combination of things caused a spike in burnout, including an increase in virtual, back-to-back meetings, working-from-home boundaries being 'obliterated', and leaders in particular being called on to manage more mental well-being in the workplace, which is emotionally taxing."[17] Some might say that regulating the workplace is extreme; however, when trying to address problems as big as burnout and the mental health crisis, extreme ownership is called for. It's the only way!

Once organizations take a holistic view of cultivating a people-first workplace, and make the needed investment in it, they will see the powerful impact that these combined strategies will have on individuals, teams, and overall productivity and performance.

ORGANIZATIONAL SOLUTIONS FOR HUMAN-CENTRIC CULTURE

Joe Krzywicki, chief banking officer at American Community Bankers Bank (ACBB), is responsible for revenue-generating functions in his organization, including sales, relationship management, and product development—all very people-driven functions. Krzywicki's job is to bring out the best in his team by focusing on building human-centric culture, including an emphasis on flexibility, autonomy, transparency, intentionality, and accountability.

Like many leaders, Krzywicki has seen a shift since the COVID-19 pandemic to a workforce that expects organizations to deliver this kind of culture. Some leaders are slower to respond, as Krzywicki says, "I think a huge part of the reluctance to [shift to] hybrid and remote work is trust—if I can't see it, I don't know it. There's a little bit of old-school paying your dues, putting in the hours. But I find that hybrid and remote is incredibly efficient. You have to be very intentional around culture and teamwork." Like many companies, ACBB supported some flexibility prior to COVID-19. They had multiple offices and employees who worked virtually. Now flexibility is baked into the culture and Krzywicki believes it will stay. As he says, "I now find that flexibility is required, especially for employees with unique talents. It was always there but less visible for those that had it and unrequested by those afraid to ask. Virtually all my employees have flexible work arrangements based on their unique needs and they cite it as an important factor in their satisfaction."

This kind of cultural change requires intentional shifts, as we've discussed throughout the book. One example of this shift is ACBB's weekly huddles. "Every

Monday morning, for thirty minutes, we get every employee together on [Microsoft] Teams and we just talk. It originated (four years ago) to address a crisis situation with the COVID-19 lockdown and honestly, it might have continued to make sure everyone was working. But it has evolved into something else. We find out what's going on, how people are feeling. Are we all good? What do you need? It's collaborative and gets everyone on the same page." With employees in different parts of the country and multiple offices, making this practice virtual elevated the opportunity to make it purposeful (intentional), include everyone equally (inclusive), and continually get feedback that can help take the business forward (iterative).

Krzywicki's trust-based approach to working with his team members is another example of a practice that supports flexibility, boundaries, and well-being. He described it this way:

> *It starts with trust, and you have it from me 100 percent, unless it's broken. I will assume that you are giving your job 100 percent. We create very clear job expectations that are aligned with company objectives. In one-on-one meetings, we communicate progress toward goals [instead of me requiring a full accounting of your time]. With this kind of discipline in the structure, it is somewhat counterintuitive, but it creates more room for flexibility, more space and freedom for employees to do more.*[18]

Leading with trust and providing employees with autonomy, coupled with accountability and clear communication of expectations, allows managers and their teams to thrive in a flexible environment. This clear communication of job expectations is also highly supportive of boundaries. It can help avoid the common pitfall of employees being asked to do too much work beyond their job description.

Every organization approaches their journey toward a more human-centered culture differently, but those who do it well have many things in common such as putting people first, cultivating trust, supporting flexibility, inclusion, and well-being. To continue your journey, here are ten essentials for cultivating a human-centered culture in your organization.

Alignment of Values and Purpose

Factors such as COVID-19 and the generational shift in the workforce have put a new focus on values and purpose in organizations. More than ever, values matter to employees and a sense of purpose helps drive people to higher levels of productivity and performance. When organizations have high expectations of their employees, those employees with a strong sense of purpose tied to their work and their organization will be more likely to deliver, fueled by their strong sense of purpose, their *why*.

Unfortunately we know what happens when organizations place high demands on employees who do not feel a connection to their organization's values or a sense of purpose in their work—disengagement, lower productivity, and toxic attitudes and behaviors that affect their coworkers, too.

I mentioned earlier in the chapter that a values mismatch is one of the drivers of burnout, and certainly it's a driver of disengagement as well. This leads to negative outcomes for the whole organization. McKinsey & Company published a research report entitled "Help Your Employees Find Purpose—or Watch Them Leave" within which they stated, "Employees expect their jobs to bring significant sense of purpose to their lives. Employers need to help meet this need or be prepared to lose talent to companies that will."[19]

For organizations to prevent this, it's essential that they take their values seriously. They should look not just at their marketing values but at the cultural values that they really stand for and put into practice every day—and make sure these are aligned. Then they should communicate these values and this purpose in meaningful ways to their employees and do so repeatedly. Or as the McKinsey report says, "Reflect, connect, repeat."[20] This is all the more effective when the organization authentically has leaders who lead with compassion and empathy.

Lead with Empathy

During the pandemic, people led with empathy in ways that they never had before. Leaders were suddenly starting meetings with check-ins (e.g., "On a scale of one to ten, how are you doing?") or asking what they could be doing to support their team at work and at home. They empathized, telling employees, "I know things are really rough right now. Let me know how I can help." That shouldn't go away. The brunt of the COVID-19 pandemic may be over, but expressing that you care, or sharing your humanity, is how we humanize the workplace. If empathy has left the building in your organization, bring it back! It must remain strong to promote a positive, human-centered culture that supports flexibility and well-being.

Though some people mistake empathic leadership for soft leadership, it involves many hard-hitting things. One of the most compassionate and empathetic things a leader can do is to make sure their employees don't overwork their way to burnout. The most senior leaders need to make sure managers throughout the organization are enforcing this. Holding managers accountable for leading with empathy is an often-overlooked step. Chief executive officers (CEOs) or managing partners might express a compassionate approach but then allow middle managers to manage however they want, often without empathy. Upward reviews are key here, creating a review and feedback process that allows employees to share feedback about their manager. Another effective tool is the stay interview, mentioned in chapter 8.

Leading with empathy at every level of an organization has the power to impact every element of workplace well-being.

Invest in Career Development

It makes sense to invest in career development as it results in a more competitive, skilled, and better educated workforce. Importantly it also fills fundamental needs for employees. According to a survey from the American Staffing Association, 80 percent of employees say that professional development is an important factor when looking for a new job.[21]

When an organization takes the time and puts resources toward career development, it makes employees feel valued. And according to the American Psychological Association (APA), "employees who feel valued are more likely to report better physical and mental health, [and] higher levels of engagement, satisfaction, and motivation."[22]

Investing in career development can include many things including simple feedback, mentoring and sponsoring, and professional education and training. The same survey from the American Staffing Association shows that only 39 percent of employees say their employer is offering professional development opportunities.[23] Make sure this is happening in your organization, at every level.

This is an investment that pays off across many measures. Importantly career development helps organizations meet their goals, but individually, it helps employees feel more engaged and valued, and it mitigates one of the top causes of work stress, which according to the APA, is "lack of opportunities for growth or advancement."[24]

Manage Workload

As mentioned earlier, work overload, or a chronic mismatch between high demand and low resources, is one of the six triggers of burnout. It's also one of the top causes of work stress according to the APA.[25] This can be a tricky issue to address as overwork can be glorified in some work cultures.

In the professional services industries, most organizations have systems in place to track billed hours. However, the systems are usually set up to flag an employee who doesn't have *enough* work, not employees who have *too much* work. I fully understand the need to have high-performing teams who can work many hours to meet client demand. In many cases, it's understood that individuals should and will work hard. But you do not want them to work too hard for too long. This is when an employee burns out. Ideally leaders and managers work to prevent this. You don't want employees to get to the point of diminishing returns, because that is usually also the point of no return! You don't want to first learn that you have an employee at risk of burnout when they walk into your office and quit.

We all know that many hard-charging or exceedingly committed employees will overwork and not raise their hand when they are starting to burn out. They will just keep working hard. But just because you know they will doesn't mean they should. Allowing overwork hurts the individual and will ultimately hurt the organization.

This is very preventable. Monitoring work hours to make sure employees are not chronically overworking and checking in with them on how they're doing is critically important to retain your most productive workers and help keep them healthy and productive.

Stop Celebrating Overwork and Make Time for Life Outside of Work

On the point of the messages we send as leaders, please stop celebrating overwork. When we start praising an employee in a performance evaluation because they missed their grandmother's funeral to get work done, or missed a friend's wedding to make a client presentation, what message are we sending? That message says that to get ahead, to get a raise or promotion or professional acknowledgement, you must be willing to sacrifice your personal life. Instead the organization or leader should be saying "I'm so sorry that that happened. Let's figure out how to prevent it from happening again. Of course, client and work emergencies happen but what can we do to alleviate the disruption from happening all the time?"

And let's not hold that person up as the hero in meetings or group forums because they did that. That expresses the wrong values. I understand that if people go above and beyond to get work done, you want to thank them. But if it is something that is an ongoing occurrence that is routinely celebrated, it should be stopped. And consider again, if people got their life back during COVID-19, it will be even worse if it's taken away again. I recently had a manager say to me, with tears in his eyes, that during COVID-19 he saw his son walk for the first time. That made him realize there was so much he missed out on that he didn't realize, and he didn't want to go back to missing out on everything.

Once we've stopped celebrating overwork, let's make it fully acceptable to support and celebrate life outside of work. In human-centered work culture, it is not just appropriate, it's essential to support employees' life events. This is part of acknowledging an employee's humanity and expressing that they matter—not just their work lives, but their whole lives matter.

From an organizational standpoint, make sure you are not only giving time off but making sure employees take it. I see plenty of firms that give their employees unlimited vacation but the employee can't take it because they still have to meet their billable hours requirement, or their workload is so heavy that taking a vacation would make their work life unbearable when they return.

Other ways that organizations can support their employees lives outside of work include offering leave or extended time off to support key life milestones, events, or occurrences, such as

- *Parental leave*: Most organizations offer some paid form of leave after the birth or adoption of a child. It's essential to make these gender-neutral without any distinction between primary and secondary designations, meaning both parents should be free to take leave under the same policy.
- *Caregiving leave*: Most people regardless of gender will be a caregiver at some point, whether it's caring for a sick spouse, child, or parent. Offering support for the broader set of caregiving needs goes a long way in supporting employees' lives, and this type of benefit helps to keep people in their jobs.
- *Off-ramping and on-ramping programs*: It's important to support parents before, during, and after the birth or adoption of their child and their parental leave. Off-ramping and on-ramping should have processes that are written and easily available for employees so that they can plan accordingly, and these policies should be automatic— with no permission needed for use. This can be viewed in three steps: communicate, systematize, and support. Communicate resources such as leave policies, flexible work policies, and any other resources such as childcare, support for breastfeeding, and working parent affinity groups. Systematize the work transition processes to ease the stress for new parents. Supervisors should supply a checklist of things the parent needs to provide to make

sure nothing falls through the cracks, such as client information, document descriptions, and any upcoming deadlines. Employers should consider staffing support where needed well in advance. Support parents in this vulnerable time beyond work transition and support. For example, utilize existing mentoring programs to have mentors reach out to employees to see how they can help. Implement a parents affinity group for peer-to-peer support. Consider policies that offer added support such as backup or on-site childcare or childcare subsidies.

- *Bereavement leave*: It's essential to give employees paid time off after the loss of a family member or friend, and most organizations do. In the Alliance's 2022 Law Firm Flexibility Benchmarking Study for example, we see that over 90 percent of respondents offer bereavement leave of around three days for the death of a spouse, child, parent, or relative but only around 15 percent offer this for a friend.[26] Like other leave, the policy should be written, clearly accessible, and offered to everyone. We would suggest allowing bereavement leave for the death of a partner or close friend as well. In addition consider allowing the employee to take extra time or use vacation time if they need more than three days.

- *Sabbaticals*: This form of leave is not as prevalent within professional services organizations and not as standardized as other forms. In the Alliance's 2022 Law Firm Flexibility Benchmarking Study, only 22.1 percent of respondents offer formal programs, the majority of which have tenure requirements. The length of sabbaticals varies greatly.[27] I recommend offering a minimum of four weeks of paid leave (in addition to vacation time) after a specified number of years with the organization. Sabbaticals should be available to everyone within the organization.

Aside from improving policies, leaders and managers must focus on the day-to-day practice of offering their full support to their employees. This means giving them time to mourn a loss without expecting them to turn in a project or respond to emails just days after they celebrate the birth of a child. This also means paving the way and setting processes up to make sure workload and expectations are managed and support is given by the entire team.

Valuing an employee's life outside of work mitigates stress and burnout, shows that you respect boundaries, and contributes to an employee's sense of belonging because it says that you value them as a whole person and as a unique individual who you want to treat well and keep on your team.

Provide Psychological Safety in Teams and Organizations and Create a Culture of Speaking Up

When you set out to build a culture of belonging, it's essential to start by laying a foundation of safety. Consider Abraham Maslow's Hierarchy of Needs. At its base, providing the solidity for everything built upon it, is physiological needs—including mental and physical health. The second level of the hierarchy is safety. This includes safety from threats or factors that put overall physical and mental health at risk. Psychological safety, where individuals feel safe sharing their own needs, thoughts, concerns, and ideas, is essential to this (as discussed in chapter 2). This addresses inclusion and belonging. Feeling safe at work means an employee does not fear bullying, threats, harassment, or discrimination. It means they feel confident that they are being treated fairly and that they are accepted and valued for who they are.

Consider your organization. Are you enabling environments of psychological safety not only organization wide, but within your teams as well? Do members of teams and groups trust one another? Do they have each other's backs in a crisis? Can they do their most creative and innovative work because they are not afraid to share their thoughts with others?

Many leaders would like to think their organization promotes psychological safety. But this is not the case for every organization, or every group, team, or employee within an organization. According to Deloitte's Women @ Work 2023 report, while fewer women reported non-inclusive behaviors at work in 2023 than they did in 2022, it remains that nearly half of women experienced them in the last twelve months—a concerning number. For example, 22 percent of women report being interrupted and talked over in meetings, 20 percent report being given fewer opportunities to speak up compared to male colleagues, and 15 percent report someone else taking credit for their ideas. Women who identify as lesbian, gay, bisexual, or transgender (LGBT) are more likely to have experienced non inclusive behaviors, and women in ethnic minority groups are also more likely to have experienced non-inclusive behaviors.[28]

Given the prevalence of these issues, I think it's important to dive deeper into the topic of creating a culture of speaking up. This is important to all the realms of workplace well-being.

With a culture of openness and trust, employees will not only feel more comfortable reporting non-inclusive behaviors, but also will feel more comfortable coming forward with questions and issues that impact health and well-being they might not otherwise raise. For example, a manager might be giving an employee more work than they can handle. If that employee feels comfortable giving their boss that feedback, it might be easily remedied by offering that employee training or mentoring, or perhaps the distribution of work on the team was unbalanced but could be easily fixed. Without the feeling of safety that allows that employee to come forward, the problem remains, the employee feels stressed, and the problem compounds.

When it comes to preventing burnout and mental health issues, creating a culture where people feel they can openly talk about these issues is critical. And this is not the case in many companies. According to the "Women @ Work 2023" report, "stigma around mental health issues remains. Only a quarter of respondents feel comfortable discussing mental health in the workplace, down significantly from 43 percent in 2022." Another finding in the report showed that among those women who experienced harassment at work, 41 percent did not report it.[29]

The ability to speak up can make or break effective boundaries too. If employees' boundaries are being crossed repeatedly—yet they feel they can talk about it with their manager—this has a much better chance of not snowballing into a bigger issue.

Organizations will be most successful in addressing psychological safety and cultivating a culture of speaking up if senior leaders prioritize this and walk the walk themselves. And when more leaders are speaking up at every level, more people will adopt these practices too. If more leaders talk about the fact that they have a lot on their plate or are planning a vacation, the more it is normalized. By demonstrating their use of boundaries and the acceptance of boundaries with others, more people will feel entitled to do that themselves.

Path for Advancement and Fair Compensation

Closely related to career development and psychological safety are the concepts of fair compensation and advancement. When investing in someone's career, organizations must not stop at mentoring and education, but instead they must go further to properly advance that employee as they develop. I've seen cases in which organizations help an employee develop and the employee becomes more valuable, but they don't promote them and pay them more. This is a necessary part of creating a culture of equity and fairness. If an employee feels they are not being treated fairly, they will quickly disengage or leave.

It's critical to look at pay, advancement, and promotions through the lens of both individual equity and fairness, and organizational equity and fairness. Don't only look at whether an employee deserves more money or a promotion as they advance, but also look across the team and the whole organization to ensure that people are advancing at the same rate and the same pay as their equally skilled peers, making sure there is no systemic bias in the process.

Resources for Individual Well-Being

As mentioned earlier, individual well-being strategies are an important part of the overall solution to workplace well-being. I've seen great progress in this area.

It's hard to quantify how many companies and organizations are currently providing wellness programs to their employees, but research suggests a little over half of companies currently do so. The same research shows that of those companies, 72 percent said that healthcare costs decreased after implementing them, absenteeism decreased by 14 to 19 percent, and the average return on investment (ROI) for dollars spent on wellness programs is six to one.[30]

The specifics of wellness program benefits and offerings vary greatly across companies, but can include general wellness benefits, flu vaccine clinics, smoking cessation programs, substance abuse support programs, stress management programs, rewards for participating in health-promoting activities, and many more. Supporting employee health and wellness is critical for employee retention as it helps to mitigate factors like stress, burnout, and mental health issues that hurt individuals and cause declines in productivity for organizations. Alternately, workforces that are mentally and physically healthy, with safe, human-centered cultures, produce greater quality work, more innovation, and higher productivity and profitability.[31]

Autonomy

Burnout expert Dr. Christina Maslach includes autonomy in her list of factors that address burnout.[32] Why? Because one of the biggest triggers of burnout is the feeling of lack of control—when an employee feels they don't have choice or discretion in how they do their work or when and where they do their work. This leads to a feeling that they are not trusted to make decisions and function as the professionals they were hired to be. It also promotes a lack of flexibility if an employee's work life is micromanaged. Giving employees autonomy is the opposite—it says, I trust you to know how and where to get your job done.

Flexibility (with proper supports and boundaries) as described throughout the book is a big part of promoting autonomy. As the Future Forum Pulse Survey states, "amid spiking burnout, offering employees flexibility fuels company culture and productivity." This survey showed that workers who did not have schedule flexibility reported 4.6 times worse work-related stress and anxiety and 2.6 times worse work-life balance. Further, it indicates that workers who don't feel they have flexibility are 43 percent more likely to say they feel burned out at work than those who are satisfied with their level of flexibility.[33] On the flip side, those workers who had flexibility felt positive about their company culture, felt connected to their company values, and were productive and focused.[34] In chapter 2 and throughout the book, highlights from research overwhelmingly show that flexibility works.

Cultivate Supportive Community

Cultivating positive, supportive community is closely tied to belonging but also provides a mitigating factor to chronic stress, which leads to burnout. Community at work includes those you interact with in an ongoing manner—members of your team, your boss, and even clients or industry colleagues who you have ongoing relationships with. When that community is not supportive, it might include bullying, harassment, non-inclusive behaviors, lack of fairness, and many other toxic behaviors. These are obviously major issues. But when you foster a positive, supportive community, you are providing employees with psychological safety, a sense of equity and inclusion, a feeling that they are cared for and valued, and knowledge that someone is there to help them when they need it. Social connection in this kind of culture leads to higher performing teams, employee engagement, and loyalty.

There are many ways to foster this kind of human-centered culture that are addressed throughout the book. Empathic leadership is key, as is providing trust and psychological safety through meaningful policies and practices that promote diversity, equity, and inclusion, and a zero tolerance toward bullying, harassment, or disrespect.

Social connections also provide much needed support for employees. Many organizations promote this through employee resource groups, or ERGs. As discussed in chapters 7 and 8, these can more specifically support employees based on their individual interests, backgrounds, career stages, or needs.

One additional factor that helps to promote a sense of belonging and community is public recognition. Giving recognition to employees in front of their peers shows them they are valued and allows them to have the collective support from their team for a job well done or a special contribution they made. It also models positive behaviors and human-centered leadership for the rest of the group.

MOVING TOWARD A MORE HUMAN-CENTERED CULTURE IS A JOURNEY

If your organization is like most, you are likely evolving in some of these areas to meet the needs of your workforce and to keep up with our changing times. There isn't an organization that I work with or learn about that isn't in a state of flux and evolution. As we cover in step five of the Flex Success Framework, organizations will ultimately succeed as a result of investing in culture and iterating over time. There is much to be done to continue to move toward more human-centered culture, and many rewards coming to those who make the investment.

REFLECTION QUESTIONS

In developing the future of your organization's culture, which of the ten essential factors feel most important in your workplace? How does your organization support workplace well-being? Where do you shine and where do you need to invest?

CONCLUSIONS

In recent years, we've lived through the COVID-19 pandemic, witnessed the *great resignation*, engaged in the *great reflection*, and observed the impact of quiet quitting. From the dramatic shifts between fully virtual work to strict return-to-office mandates, one thing is abundantly clear: people must always remain at the center of our ever-evolving workplace landscape.

We're due for a shift to the next iteration of making our workplaces work for organizations and people. Ernst & Young Global Limited's (EY) 2023 Work Reimagined Survey predicts that the "next normal" of work will result from a "great rebalancing" when organizations "rebalance workforce realities with what factors contribute most to better outcomes" giving organizations the opportunity to "re-energize their workforce strategy to be technologically evolved yet inherently people-centric, agile, and resilient." EY's research clearly shows that "cultivating trust and having a people-centric leadership model is linked to significantly better organizational outcomes, including perceptions of better culture and productivity."[1] Successful organizations that continue to adapt their approaches and practices to meet the evolving needs of their employees will undoubtedly deliver measurably better results.

Future-ready organizations will keep learning, iterating, and evolving to meet the needs of the workforce and the events of the world. In this quickly changing volatile, uncertain, complex, and ambiguous (VUCA) world, leaders need to shift to an agile mindset that embraces constant evolution.

Joe Krzywicki, chief banking officer at Atlantic Community Bankers Bank (ACBB), has a view of the future that syncs well with this:

> *Agility is critical as external factors like COVID-19, economic conditions, technology, and employee requirements change on a*

*rapid and unpredictable basis. The old-school way of thinking
where employees worked primarily in an office with scheduled
hours, paid their dues, and worked their way up the corporate
ladder just isn't valid anymore. And that's a good thing.
Organizations that succeed will be rooted in strong values and
have cultures that are flexible enough to adapt to changing needs,
both internal and external.*[2]

To build and manage future-ready organizations and to meet the needs of
the current and future workforce, leaders must stay open and agile, continue to
evolve, and intentionally cultivate a shift to human-centered culture.

At this point, you've read this book and understand the five critical steps of
the Flex Success Framework that you need to take to ensure that your flexibility
initiative is well designed and leads to the necessary transformation of your organization's culture. If you follow these steps and embrace these fundamentals you
will not only develop and implement a successful flexible work initiative, but you
will also catalyze a cultural shift, enabling your organization to thrive as technologies and work environments continue to evolve.

As you look to the future, remember that you're working in an ever-changing
and evolving workplace. Resist the urge to return to something in the past—that
is a dangerous pitfall. As Peter Drucker said, "A time of turbulence is a dangerous time, but its greater danger is a temptation to deny reality."[3] Instead embrace
an agile mindset and invest in a human-centered future. Even with the accelerated
impact of technology, people will still remain at the center of your organization;
how you support and lead them will make all the difference in the level of success you attain. Core to this is holistic flexibility.

Echoing the wisdom of Dr. Maya Angelou, "Do the best you can until you
know better. Then when you know better, do better."[4] Today we collectively possess the knowledge, data, and awareness to make positive changes. We carry a
shared responsibility to act upon this knowledge. We have witnessed the trans-
formative power of a well-executed and well-designed flexibility initiative on our
people and our business. The bottom line is that flexibility done right benefits
everyone. It's my hope that going forward, more organizations will embrace flexibility and cultivate people-first cultures, and that the insights, examples, and
research brought together in this book will help organizations evolve and succeed,
with people at their center. It's time to act, lead, and shape a brighter future of
our organizations and the individuals within them.

NOTES

Introduction

1. "Survey: US Employees Prioritize Workplace Flexibility as a Key Component of Compensation," *The Conference Board*, November 7, 2023, https://www.conference-board.org/press/workplace-flexibility.
2. Lisa Belkin, "The Opt-Out Revolution," *The New York Times Magazine*, October 26, 2003, https://www.nytimes.com/2003/10/26/magazine/the-opt-out-revolution.html.
3. Sylvia Ann Hewlett and Carolyn Buck Luce, "Off-Ramps and On-Ramps: Keeping Talented Women on the Road to Success," *Harvard Business Review Magazine*, March 2005, https://hbr.org/2005/03/off-ramps-and-on-ramps-keeping-talented-women-on-the-road-to-success.
4. Mike Valentine, interview with the author, September 5, 2023.
5. Paul Davidson, "More Employers Offer Flexible Hours, but Many Grapple with How to Make It Succeed," *USA TODAY*, October 20, 2019, https://www.usatoday.com/story/money/2019/10/20/flexible-hours-jobs-more-firms-offer-variable-schedules/4020990002/.
6. André Dua, Kweilin Ellingrud, Phil Kirschner, Adrian Kwok, Ryan Luby, Rob Palter, and Sarah Pemberton, "Americans are Embracing Flexible Work—and They Want More of It," McKinsey & Company, June 23, 2022, https://www.mckinsey.com/industries/real-estate/our-insights/americans-are-embracing-flexible-work-and-they-want-more-of-it.
7. Liz Fealy and Roselyn Feinsod, "How Can a Rebalance of Power Help Re-Energize Your Workforce?," *EY*, September 12, 2023, https://www.ey.com/en_gl/workforce/work-reimagined-survey.
8. "Future of Jobs Report 2023," *World Economic Forum*, May 2023, https://www3.weforum.org/docs/WEF_Future_of_Jobs_2023.pdf.
9. David Shaw, "Every person's potential could elevate the future of work," *Accenture*, June 18, 2021, https://www.accenture.com/us-en/blogs/business-functions-blog/every-person-has-potential-how-might-that-elevate-the-future-of-work.

1. The Evolution of Flexibility

1. Martin Nemirow, "Work-Sharing Approaches: Past and Present," *Monthly Labor Review* 107, no. 9 (September 1984), https://www.bls.gov/opub/mlr/1984/09/art6full.pdf.

2. Mary Lou Santovec, "Creating Flexible Work Policies: One Size Does NOT Fit All," *Women in Higher Education* 22, no. 8 (August 2013): 1–2, https://onlinelibrary.wiley.com/doi/10.1002/whe.10483.

3. Vicky Gan, "The Invention of Telecommuting," *Bloomberg*, December 1, 2015, https://www.bloomberg.com/news/articles/2015-12-01/what-telecommuting-looked-like-in-1973.

4. Gan, "The Invention of Telecommuting."

5. Frank W. Schiff, "Working at Home Can Save Gasoline," *The Washington Post*, September 2, 1979, https://www.washingtonpost.com/archive/opinions/1979/09/02/working-at-home-can-save-gasoline/ffa475c7-d1a8-476e-8411-8cb53f1f3470/.

6. Mitra Toossi, "A Century of Change: The US Labor Force, 1950–2050," *Monthly Labor Review* (May 2002): 18, https://www.bls.gov/opub/mlr/2002/05/art2full.pdf.

7. Richard Fry, Carolina Aragão, Kiley Hurst, and Kim Parker, "In a Growing Share of US Marriages, Husbands and Wives Earn About the Same," *Pew Research Center*, April 13, 2023, https://www.pewresearch.org/social-trends/2023/04/13/in-a-growing-share-of-u-s-marriages-husbands-and-wives-earn-about-the-same/.

8. Jennifer Moss, "Beyond Burned Out," *Harvard Business Review*, February 10, 2021, https://hbr.org/2021/02/beyond-burned-out.

9. "Bill Gates's Desert Island Playlist," *BBC News*, January 31, 2016, https://www.bbc.com/news/magazine-35442969.

10. Paul Allen, "Microsoft's Odd Couple," *Vanity Fair*, March 30, 2011, https://www.vanityfair.com/news/2011/05/paul-allen-201105.

11. Michael Blanding, "National Health Costs Could Decrease if Managers Reduce Work Stress," *Harvard Business School Working Knowledge*, January 26, 2015, https://hbswk.hbs.edu/item/national-health-costs-could-decrease-if-managers-reduce-work-stress.

12. Marcel Schwantes, "Bill Gates Said You Must Offer This Perk to Hire the Best Workers," *Inc.*, September 26, 2019, https://www.inc.com/marcel-schwantes/bill-gates-said-you-must-offer-this-perk-in-order-to-hire-best-workers.html.

13. Bill Gates, "5 Things I Wish I Heard at the Graduation I Never Had," *Gates Notes.com*, May 13, 2023, https://www.gatesnotes.com/NAU-Commencement-Speech.

14. "Fortune 100 Best Companies to Work For® 2023," *Great Place To Work®*, 2023, https://www.greatplacetowork.com/best-workplaces/100-best/2023.

15. Genhi Givings Bailey, interview with the author, March 31, 2023.

16. Eve Howard, interview with the author, April 17, 2023.

17. Cathy Benko and Anne Weisberg, "Mass Career Customization: Building the Corporate Lattice Organization," *Deloitte Review* 3 (2008): 50–61, https://www2.deloitte.com/content/dam/insights/us/articles/mass-career-customization-building-the-corporate-lattice-organization/US_deloittereview_MassCareerCustomization_jul08.pdf; Cathleen

Benko and Anne Weisberg, *Mass Career Customization: Aligning the Workplace with Today's Nontraditional Workforce* (Harvard Business School Press, 2007); Cathleen Benko and Molly Anderson, *The Corporate Lattice: Achieving High Performance in the Changing World of Work* (Harvard Business Review Press, 2010).

18. Bailey, interview with the author.
19. Bailey, interview with the author.
20. Patrick Guggenberger, Dana Maor, Michael Park, and Patrick Simon, "The State of Organizations 2023: Ten Shifts Transforming Organizations," *McKinsey & Company*, April 26, 2023, https://www.mckinsey.com/capabilities/people-and-organizational-performance/our-insights/the-state-of-organizations-2023.
21. "Law Firm Flexibility Benchmarking Study 2022," *Diversity & Flexibility Alliance*, 2022.
22. Jennifer Moss, "Beyound Burned Out."
23. Taylor Telford, "Disney Employees Fight Mandate to Work at Offices Four Days a Week," *The Washington Post*, February 16, 2023, https://www.washingtonpost.com/business/2023/02/16/disney-rto-pushback-petition/.
24. Will Daniel, "Disney Employees Are Furious over Bob Iger's Return-to-Office Mandate and More than 2,000 Have Signed a Petition To Fight Back," *Fortune*, February 17, 2023, https://fortune.com/2023/02/17/remote-work-disney-employess-furious-return-to-office-bob-iger-petition/.
25. Nupur Anand and Lananh Nguyen, "Exclusive: JPMorgan Employees Gripe about Dimon's Return-to-Office Edict," *Reuters*, April 27, 2023, https://www.reuters.com/business/finance/jpmorgan-employees-gripe-about-dimons-return-to-office-edict-2023-04-27/.
26. Sridhar Natarajan and Bloomberg, "Goldman Sachs Is Frustrated by Many Workers Failing to Be in the Office 5 Days a Week And Is 'Reminding' Them It's Required," *Fortune*, August 22, 2023, https://fortune.com/2023/08/22/goldman-sachs-return-to-office-rto-five-days-weekly/.
27. Susan Caminiti, "A Message for Male CEOs on Return to Office from a Wall Street Women's Leader," *CNBC*, April 3, 2023, https://www.cnbc.com/2023/04/03/a-message-for-male-ceos-on-return-to-office-from-top-wall-street-woman.html.
28. "Who First Originated the Term VUCA (Volatility, Uncertainty, Complexity, and Ambiguity)?," US Army Heritage and Education Center Find Your Answer, last modified December 6, 2022, https://usawc.libanswers.com/faq/84869.
29. Warren G. Bennis, "Managing the Dream: Leadership in the 21st Century," *Journal of Organizational Change Management* 2, no. 1 (January 1989): 6–10.
30. Bennis, 6–10.
31. Gregory H. Watson, "Cycles of Learning: Observations of Jack Welch," *Six Sigma Forum Magazine* (November 2001): 14–15, https://www.academia.edu/42615938/Cycles_of_Learning_Observations_of_Jack_Welch.
32. The Aspen Institute, "Closing Lunch: In Conversation with Tom Friedman," July 31, 2017, video, 45:14–46:41, https://www.deloitte.com/content/dam/assets-shared/docs/campaigns/2023/dcloitte-2023-genz-millennial-survey.pdf?dlva=12.

33. Krystal Hu, "ChatGPT Sets Record for Fastest-Growing User Base—Analyst Note," *Reuters*, February 2, 2023, https://www.reuters.com/technology/chatgpt-sets-record-fastest-growing-user-base-analyst-note-2023-02-01/.

34. "The Deloitte Global 2023 Gen Z and Millennial Survey," *Deloitte*, July 21, 2023, https://www.deloitte.com/global/en/issues/work/content/genzmillennialsurvey.html.

35. "The Deloitte Global 2023 Gen Z and Millennial Survey," *Deloitte*.

36. "Self-employed, total (% of total employment) (modeled ILO estimate)," The World Bank, accessed September 14, 2023, https://data.worldbank.org/indicator/SL.EMP.SELF.ZS?end=2019&start=1991&view=chart.

37. "Number of Freelancers in the US 2017–2028," *Statista*, September 30, 2022, https://www.statista.com/statistics/921593/gig-economy-number-of-freelancers-us/.

38. André Dua, Kweilin Ellingrud, Bryan Hancock, Ryan Luby, Anu Madgavkar, and Sarah Pemberton, "Freelance, Side Hustles, and Gigs: Many More Americans Have Become Independent Workers," *McKinsey & Company*, August 23, 2022, https://www.mckinsey.com/featured-insights/sustainable-inclusive-growth/future-of-america/freelance-side-hustles-and-gigs-many-more-americans-have-become-independent-workers.

39. "Freelance Forward 2022," *Upwork*, 2022, https://www.upwork.com/research/freelance-forward-2022.

40. Edward Segal, "How And Why The Freelance Workforce Is Setting New Records," *Forbes*, December 13, 2022, https://www.forbes.com/sites/edwardsegal/2022/12/13/how-and-why-the-freelance-workforce-is-setting-new-records/?sh=2996a56f4b18.

41. "Law Firms Competing for Talent in 2022," *Thomson Reuters Institute*, 2022, https://www.thomsonreuters.com/en/reports/law-firms-competing-for-talent-in-2022.html; Karen Sloan, "To Stem Lawyer Attrition, Law Firms Must Look Beyond Cash—Report," *Reuters*, January 11, 2022, https://www.reuters.com/legal/legalindustry/stem-lawyer-attrition-law-firms-must-look-beyond-cash-report-2022-01-11/; Karen Sloan, "Culture, Not Cash, is Key to Lower Turnover at Law Firms—Report," *Reuters*, April 21, 2022, https://www.reuters.com/legal/legalindustry/culture-not-cash-is-key-lower-turnover-law-firms-report-2022-04-21/.

42. André Dua, Kweilin Ellingrud, Phil Kirschner, Adrian Kwok, Ryan Luby, Rob Palter, and Sarah Pemberton, "Americans are Embracing Flexible Work—and They Want More of It," *McKinsey & Company*, June 23, 2022, https://www.mckinsey.com/industries/real-estate/our-insights/americans-are-embracing-flexible-work-and-they-want-more-of-it.

43. "Survey Finds Positive Trends in Law Firm Flexibility, However Bias Continues to Impede Usage," *Diversity & Flexibility Alliance*, March 22, 2017, https://dfalliance.com/survey-trends-law-firm-flexibility/.

44. The Aspen Institute, "In Conversation with Tom Friedman."

45. "Redesigning Work for the Hybrid World: Opportunities for Knowledge Workers," *Gartner*, June 21, 2021, https://www.gartner.com/en/documents/4002776.

46. Otto Scharmer, "As Systems Collapse, People Rise: Seven Faces of an Emerging Global Movement," *Medium*, June 6, 2019, https://medium.com/presencing-institute-blog/as-systems-collapse-people-rise-seven-faces-of-an-emerging-global-movement-204df6f06e27.

2. The Business Case for Flexibility

1. Kim Koopersmith, interview with the author, May 19, 2023.
2. Ellen Ernst Kossek and Jesse S. Michel, "Flexible Work Schedules," *APA Handbook of Industrial and Organizational Psychology* 1 (2011): 535–72, https://doi.org/10.1037/12169-017.
3. "Future Forum Pulse: Leveling the Playing Field in the Hybrid Workplace," *Future Forum*, January 2022, https://futureforum.com/research/leveling-the-playing-field-in-the-hybrid-workplace/.
4. "Survey: Flexible Work Rises as Top Perk," *Zoom*, September 5, 2023, https://explore.zoom.us/en/survey-workers-want-flexible-work/.
5. Holger Reisinger and Dane Fetterer, "Forget Flexibility. Your Employees Want Autonomy," *Harvard Business Review*, October 29, 2021, https://hbr.org/2021/10/forget-flexibility-your-employees-want-autonomy.
6. Jamie Spannhake, "What Motivates Millennials? Ways Law Firms Are Retaining Young Lawyers," *Attorney at Work*, May 28, 2022, https://www.attorneyatwork.com/what-motivates-millennials-retaining-young-lawyers.
7. Roberta D. Liebenberg and Stephanie A. Scharf, "2022 Practice Forward Report: Where Does the Legal Profession Go from Here? Lawyers Tell Us How and Where They Want to Work," *American Bar Association*, 2022, https://www.scribd.com/document/609327549/2022-Practice-Forward-Report.
8. "The US Surgeon General's Framework for Workplace Mental Health and Well-Being," *Office of the US Surgeon General*, 2022, https://www.hhs.gov/sites/default/files/workplace-mental-health-well-being.pdf.
9. "Workplace Burnout Survey," *Deloitte*, https://www2.deloitte.com/us/en/pages/about-deloitte/articles/burnout-survey.html.
10. Kossek and Michel, 535–72.
11. "Women in the Legal Profession," *American Bar Association Profile of the Legal Profession 2022*, 2022, https://www.americanbar.org/content/dam/aba/administrative/news/2022/07/profile-report-2022.pdf.
12. Marc Brodherson, Laura McGee, and Mariana Pires dos Reis, "Women in Law Firms," *McKinsey & Company*, October 2017, https://www.mckinsey.com/~/media/mckinsey/featured%20insights/gender%20equality/women%20in%20law%20firms/women-in-law-firms-final-103017.ashx.
13. Fiona M. Kay, Stacey Alarie, and Jones Adjei, "Leaving Private Practice: How Organizational Context, Time Pressures, and Structural Inflexibilities Shape

Departures from Private Law Practice," *Indiana Journal of Global Legal Studies* 20, no. 2 (January 1, 2013): 1223–60, https://doi.org/10.2979/indjglolegstu.20.2.1223.

14. Alexis Krivkovich, Wei Wei Liu, Hilary Nguyen, Ishanaa Rambachan, Nicole Robinson, Monne Williams, and Lareina Yee, "Women in the Workplace 2022," *McKinsey & Company*, October 18, 2022, https://www.mckinsey.com/~/media/mckinsey/featured%20insights/diversity%20and%20inclusion/women%20in%20the%20workplace%202022/women-in-the-workplace-2022.pdf.

15. Liebenberg and Scharf, "2022 Practice Forward Report."

16. Zakiyyah Salim-Williams, interview with the author, June 16, 2023.

17. "Framework for Workplace Mental Health," *Office of the US Surgeon General*.

18. "The State of Remote Work 2021," *Global Workplace Analytics*, January 6, 2023, https://globalworkplaceanalytics.com/downloads/the-state-of-remote-work-2021; "An Operating Model for the Next Normal: Lessons from Agile Organizations in the Crisis," *McKinsey & Company*, June 25, 2020, https://www.mckinsey.com/capabilities/people-and-organizational-performance/our-insights/an-operating-model-for-the-next-normal-lessons-from-agile-organizations-in-the-crisis.

19. Liebenberg and Scharf, "2022 Practice Forward Report."

20. Genhi Givings Bailey, interview with the author, March 31, 2023.

21. "Amid Spiking Burnout, Workplace Flexibility Fuels Company Culture and Productivity: Winter Snapshot," *Future Forum Pulse*, Winter 2022/2023, https://futureforum.com/wp-content/uploads/2023/02/Future-Forum-Pulse-Report-Winter-2022-2023.pdf.

22. "Law Firms Competing for Talent in 2022," *Thomson Reuters Corporation*, https://www.thomsonreuters.com/en/reports/law-firms-competing-for-talent-in-2022.html; Karen Sloan, "To Stem Lawyer Attrition, Law Firms Must Look beyond Cash—Report," *Reuters*, January 12, 2022, https://www.reuters.com/legal/legalindustry/stem-lawyer-attrition-law-firms-must-look-beyond-cash-report-2022-01-11/; Karen Sloan, "Culture, Not Cash, Is Key to Lower Turnover at Law Firms—Report," *Reuters*, April 21, 2022, https://www.reuters.com/legal/legalindustry/culture-not-cash-is-key-lower-turnover-law-firms-report-2022-04-21/.

23. "Flexibility Fuels Company Culture and Productivity," *Future Forum Pulse*.

24. Prithwiraj (Raj) Choudhury, "Our Work-from-Anywhere Future," *Harvard Business Review*, July 7, 2021, https://hbr.org/2020/11/our-work-from-anywhere-future.

25. Liqun Jiang, Zhiyuan Pan, Yunshi Luo, Ziyan Guo, and Deqiang Kou, "More Flexible and More Innovative: The Impact of Flexible Work Arrangements on the Innovation Behavior of Knowledge Employees," *Frontiers in Psychology* 14 (April 26, 2023), https://doi.org/10.3389/fpsyg.2023.1053242.

26. "re:Work," Google, accessed September 2023, https://rework.withgoogle.com/print/guides/5721312655835136/.

27. Amy C. Edmondson and Mark Mortensen, "What Psychological Safety Looks like in a Hybrid Workplace," *Harvard Business Review*, May 22, 2023, https://hbr.org/2021/04/what-psychological-safety-looks-like-in-a-hybrid-workplace.

28. Michael Bush and Great Place To Work, "The Fortune 100 Best Companies Prove That Caring for Employees and Increasing Productivity Can Go Hand in Hand," *Fortune*, April 4, 2023, https://fortune.com/2023/04/04/the-fortune-100-best-companies-prove-that-caring-for-employees-and-increasing-productivity-can-go-hand-in-hand/.

29. Bush and Great Place To Work, "The Fortune 100 Best Companies."

30. "The Costs and Benefits of Hybrid Work," *Global Workplace Analytics*, October 8, 2021, https://globalworkplaceanalytics.com/resources/costs-benefits.

31. Christine Smith and Kenji Yoshino, "Uncovering Talent: A New Model of Inclusion," *Deloitte*, 2019, https://www2.deloitte.com/content/dam/Deloitte/us/Documents/about-deloitte/us-about-deloitte-uncovering-talent-a-new-model-of-inclusion.pdf.

32. "Leveling the Playing Field in the Hybrid Workplace," *Future Forum Pulse*, January 25, 2022, https://futureforum.com/wp-content/uploads/2022/01/Future-Forum-Pulse-Report-January-2022.pdf.

33. "Flexibility Fuels Company Culture and Productivity," *Future Forum Pulse*.

34. "Flexibility Fuels Company Culture and Productivity," *Future Forum Pulse*.

35. "Leveling the Playing Field," *Future Forum Pulse*.

36. "Women in the Workplace 2022," *McKinsey & Company*

37. Zakiyyah Salim-Williams, "The Power of People: Embracing Inclusion and Building a Successful Hybrid Team," *Diversity & Flexibility Alliance 2022 Annual Conference: Cultivating A Holistic Work Culture: The Power of People, Purpose & Productivity*, November 3, 2022.

38. Vernā Myers, interview with the author, April 13, 2023.

39. Myers, interview with the author.

40. Bailey, interview with the author.

41. Bailey, interview with the author.

42. "How to Improve Employee Engagement in the Workplace," *Gallup*, accessed August 21, 2023, https://www.gallup.com/workplace/285674/improve-employee-engagement-%20workplace.aspx.

43. "How to Improve Employee Engagement," *Gallup*.

44. Daniel H. Pink, *Drive: The Surprising Truth About What Motivates Us* (Penguin, 2011).

45. "State of the Global Workplace Report—2023 Report," *Gallup*, accessed February 2023, https://www.gallup.com/workplace/349484/state-of-the-global-workplace.aspx#ite-506924.

46. "Global Indicator: Hybrid Work," *Gallup*, accessed February 2023, https://www.gallup.com/401384/indicator-hybrid-work.aspx.

47. S. Kumar, S. Sarkar, and B. Chahar, "A Systematic Review of Work-Life Integration and Role of Flexible Work Arrangements," *International Journal of Organizational Analysis* 31, no. 3 (2021): 710–736, https://doi.org/10.1108/IJOA-07-2021 2855.

48. Kossek and Michel, 535–72.

49. Ellen Ernst Kossek, Leslie B. Hammer, Rebecca J. Thompson, and Lisa Buxbaum Burke, "SHRM Foundation's Effective Practice Guidelines Series: Leveraging Workplace Flexibility for Engagement and Productivity," *Society for Human Resource Management*, 2014, https://www.shrm.org/content/dam/en/shrm/topics-tools/tools/toolkits/leveraging-workplace-flexibility.pdf.

50. Sundiatu Dixon-Fyle, Kevin Dolan, Dame Vivian Hunt, and Sara Prince,"Diversity Wins: How Inclusion Matters," *McKinsey & Company*, May 19, 2020, https://www.mckinsey.com/featured-insights/diversity-and-inclusion/diversity-wins-how-inclusion-matters.

51. Aliah D. Wright, "Study: Profits Rise with Flexible Work," *Society for Human Resource Management*, February 16, 2016, https://www.shrm.org/resourcesandtools/hr-topics/technology/pages/study-profits-rise-with-flexible-work.aspx.

52. "The Business Case for Remote Work: For Employers, Employees, the Environment, and Society," *Global Workplace Analytics*, 2021, https://globalworkplaceanalytics.com/wp-content/uploads/edd/2021/01/The-Business-Case-for-Remote-Work-2021-Report-Final-Web-1.pdf.

53. C. L. Dodson, S. Dodson, and L. H. Rosenthal, "The Zooming of Federal Civil Litigation," *Judicature* 104, no. 12 (2020).

54. C. S. Meyer, S. Mukerjee, and A. Sestero, "Work-Family Benefits: Which Ones Maximize Profits?," *Journal of Managerial Issues* (2001): 28–44.

55. Ted Kitterman and Great Place to Work, "The World's Best Workplaces Invest in Well-Being, Flexibility, and Equity," *Fortune*, October 13, 2022, https://fortune.com/2022/10/13/worlds-best-workplaces-2022-dhl-express-us-flexibility/.

56. Ted Kitterman, "5 Ways Workplace Culture Drives Business Profitability," *Great Place to Work*, February 13, 2023, https://www.greatplacetowork.com/resources/blog/5-ways-workplace-culture-drives-business-profitability.

57. G. Dionne and B. Dostie, "New Evidence on the Determinants of Absenteeism Using Linked Employer-Employee Data," *Industrial and Labor Relations Review* 61, no. 1 (2007): 108–20; J. N. Van Ommeren and E. Gutiérrez-i-Puigarnau, "Are Workers with a Long Commute Less Productive? An Empirical Analysis of Absenteeism," *Regional Science and Urban Economics* 41, no. 1 (2011): 1–8.

58. S. Nicholson, M. V. Pauly, D. Polsky, C. Sharda, H. Szrek, and M. L. Berger, "Measuring the Effects of Work Loss on Productivity with Team Production," *Health Economics* 15, no. 2 (2006): 111–23.

59. Ganga Shreedhar, Kate Laffan, and Laura M. Giurge, "Is Remote Work Actually Better for the Environment?," *Harvard Business Review*, March 7, 2022, https://hbr.org/2022/03/is-remote-work-actually-better-for-the-environment.

60. Noam Noked, "The Corporate Social Responsibility Report and Effective Stakeholder Engagement," *The Harvard Law School Forum on Corporate Governance*, December 28, 2013, https://corpgov.law.harvard.edu/2013/12/28/the-corporate-social-responsibility-report-and-effective-stakeholder-engagement/.

61. Kate Lister, "Latest Work-at-Home/Telecommuting/Remote Work Statistics—Global Workplace Analytics," *Global Workplace Analytics*, January 18, 2022, https://globalworkplaceanalytics.com/telecommuting-statistics.
62. Bhushan Sethi, Kristin Rivera, and Marco Amitrano, "CEO Panel Survey: How Business Can Emerge Stronger," *PwC*, 2020, https://www.pwc.com/gx/en/ceo-agenda/ceo-panel-survey-emerge-stronger.pdf.
63. Wright, "Study: Profits Rise with Flexible Work."

3. The Flex Success Framework

1. Getting to Know our Conference Speakers—Barri Rafferty," *Diversity & Flexibility Alliance*, October 2, 2020, https://dfalliance.com/getting-to-know-our-conference-speakers-barri-rafferty/; "Barri Rafferty To Be Honored For Extraordinary Commitment to Flexibility," *Diversity & Flexibility Alliance*, October 21, 2020, https://dfalliance.com/barri-rafferty-to-be-honored/.
2. "Barri Rafferty To Be Honored," *Diversity & Flexibility Alliance*.
3. Marlon Lutfiyya, "The Power of People: Embracing Inclusion and Building a Successful Hybrid Team," *Diversity & Flexibility Alliance 2022 Annual Conference: Cultivating A Holistic Work Culture: The Power of People, Purpose, and Productivity*, November 3, 2022.
4. Nikki Morin and Heather Barrett, "Don't Confuse 'Being in the Office' with 'Culture,'" *Gallup*, July 21, 2023, https://www.gallup.com/workplace/401576/dont-confuse-office-culture.aspx.
5. Morin and Barrett, "Don't Confuse 'Being in the Office' with 'Culture'."
6. "Work Trend Index Annual Report: Great Expectations: Making Hybrid Work Work," *Microsoft*, March 16, 2022, https://www.microsoft.com/en-us/worklab/work-trend-index/great-expectations-making-hybrid-work-work.
7. Kristy Threlkeld, "Employee Burnout Report: COVID-19's Impact and 3 Strategies to Curb It," *Indeed*, March 11, 2021, https://www.indeed.com/lead/preventing-employee-burnout-report.
8. Jacqueline M. Stavros, Lindsey N. Godwin, and David L. Cooperrider, "Appreciative Inquiry: Organization Development and the Strengths Revolution," in *Practicing Organization Development: Leading Transformation and Change*, 4th ed., ed. William J. Rothwell, Jacqueline M. Stavros, and Roland Sullivan (Wiley, 2015), 96.
9. "Future Forum Pulse: Leveling the Playing Field in the Hybrid Workplace," *Future Forum*, January 2022, https://futureforum.com/research/leveling-the-playing-field-in-the-hybrid-workplace/.
10. Roberta D. Liebenberg and Stephanie A. Scharf, "2022 Practice Forward Report: Where Does the Legal Profession Go from Here? Lawyers Tell Us How and Where They Want to Work," *American Bar Association*, 2022, https://www.scribd.com/document/609327549/2022-Practice-Forward-Report.

11. Gleb Tsipursky, "What Is Proximity Bias and How Can Managers Prevent It?" *Harvard Business Review*, October 4, 2022, https://hbr.org/2022/10/what-is-proximity-bias-and-how-can-managers-prevent-it.

12. "Assumed Similarity Bias," Dictionary of Psychology, American Psychological Association, accessed August 2023, https://dictionary.apa.org/assumed-similarity-bias.

13. Damian Barr, "We Are Not All in the Same Boat. We Are All in the Same Storm. Some Are on Super-Yachts, Some Have Just the One Oar," *Damian Barr*, May 30, 2020, https://www.damianbarr.com/latest/https/we-are-not-all-in-the-same-boat.

14. Vernā Myers, interview with the author, April 13, 2023.

15. Myers, interview with the author.

16. Jenn Flynn, interview with the author, May 22, 2023.

17. Larry Page and Sergey Brin, "A Letter from Larry and Sergey," *Google*, December 3, 2019, https://blog.google/alphabet/letter-from-larry-and-sergey/.

4. What Is Flexibility's Purpose?

1. Simon Sinek, *Start with Why: How Great Leaders Inspire Everyone to Take Action* (New York: Portfolio, 2011), 2–7.

2. Jacqueline M. Stavros, Lindsey N. Godwin, and David L. Cooperrider, "Appreciative Inquiry: Organization Development and the Strengths Revolution," in *Practicing Organization Development: Leading Transformation and Change*, 4th ed., ed. William J. Rothwell, Jacqueline M. Stavros, and Roland Sullivan (Wiley, 2015), 105.

3. Edgar H. Schein, "Coming to a New Awareness of Organizational Culture," *Massachusetts Institute of Technology Sloan Management Review*, January 15, 1984, https://sloanreview.mit.edu/article/coming-to-a-new-awareness-of-organizational-culture/.

4. "Organizational Culture," Gallup, accessed August 2023, https://www.gallup.com/workplace/229832/culture.aspx.

5. Schein, "Coming to a New Awareness."

6. "Our Purpose and Values," PwC, accessed August 2023, https://www.pwc.com/us/en/about-us/purpose-and-values.html.

7. "Flex Impact Award," Diversity & Flexibility Alliance, accessed May 2023, https://dfalliance.com/impact/awards/flex-impact/.

8. Kim Koopersmith, interview with the author, May 19, 2023.

9. Susan Neely, interview with the author, April 6, 2023.

10. Jenn Flynn, interview with the author, May 22, 2023.

11. Joe Krzywicki, interview with the author, September 11, 2023.

12. Vicky McKeever, "Goldman Sachs CEO Solomon Calls Working from Home an 'Aberration,'" *CNBC*, February 25, 2021, https://www.cnbc.com/2021/02/25/goldman-sachs-ceo-solomon-calls-working-from-home-an-aberration-.html.

13. Britta Lehn, "Flex Working at SAP," *Systems, Applications & Products in Data Processing*, August 11, 2022, https://blogs.sap.com/2022/08/11/flex-working-at-sap/.

5. Who Do You Want to Be?

1. Peter M. Senge, *The Fifth Discipline* (New York: Currency, 2006), 21.
2. Senge, 283.
3. Nikki Morin and Heather Barrett,"Don't Confuse 'Being in the Office' With 'culture,'" *Gallup*, September 28, 2022, https://www.gallup.com/workplace/401576/dont-confuse-office-culture.aspx.
4. Jenn Flynn, interview with the author, May 22, 2023.
5. Manar Morales and Ivan Misner, "5 Myths about Flexible Work," *Harvard Business Review*, June 3, 2021, https://hbr.org/2021/06/5-myths-about-flexible-work.
6. Vernā Myers, interview with the author, April 13, 2023.
7. Aman Kidwai, "Here Are 3 Types of Meetings That Should Be Face-to-Face—And 6 That Are Better As Emails," *Fortune*, June 29, 2022, https://fortune.com/2022/06/29/types-meetings-require-face-to-face-employees-attend-participation-waste-time/.
8. Flynn, interview with the author.
9. Susan Neely, interview with the author, April 6, 2023.

6. What Flexibility Initiatives Will Support Your Purpose and Principles?

1. "Our Approach to Hybrid Workplace Flexibility," *Microsoft*, accessed August 2023, https://careers.microsoft.com/v2/global/en/flexible-work.
2. Jenn Flynn, interview with the author, May 22, 2023.
3. Ellen Kaye Fleishhacker, "It's Time to Reimagine the Workplace: Companies and Firms Blazing the Trail—Flex Impact Awards," *Diversity & Flexibility Alliance 2021 Annual Conference: Reflect. Reimagine. Recalibrate. Paving the Way to Inclusive Flexibility*, November 3, 2021.
4. Susan Neely, interview with the author, April 6, 2023.
5. Genhi Givings Bailey, interview with the author, March 31, 2023.
6. Jason St. John, "Presentation of the 2022 Flex Leader Award: Leadership Lessons for Cultivating Your Holistic Hybrid Working Culture," *Diversity & Flexibility Alliance 2022 Annual Conference: Cultivating a Holistic Work Culture: The Power of People, Purpose, and Productivity*, November 3, 2022.
7. Lisa Madden, interview with the author, May 12, 2023.
8. "Diversity & Flexibility Alliance to Present Inaugural Flex Impact Awards," *Diversity & Flexibility Alliance*, February 27, 2017, https://dfalliance.com/2017-flex-impact-award-hogan-lovells-winston-strawn/.
9. "Inaugural Flex Impact Awards," *Diversity & Flexibility Alliance*.
10. "PwC and Morgan Lewis to Be Honored for their Innovative and Comprehensive Flexible Working Initiatives," *Diversity & Flexibility Alliance*, October 1, 2019, https://dfalliance.com/pwc-morgan-lewis-honored/.
11. "PwC and Morgan Lewis to Be Honored," *Diversity & Flexibility Alliance*.
12. "PwC and Morgan Lewis to Be Honored," *Diversity & Flexibility Alliance*.

13. "Introducing My+: PwC's $2.4B Investment in Our People Experience," *PwC US*, May 5, 2022, video, https://www.youtube.com/watch?v=1dMrAFQ-p64.
14. "Flex Impact Award—2022 Flex Impact Award Honorees," Diversity & Flexibility Alliance, accessed August 2023, https://dfalliance.com/impact/awards/flex-impact/.
15. Tim Ryan, "Introducing My+, How PwC Is Changing the Way We Work," *PwC*, May 6, 2022, https://www.pwc.com/us/en/about-us/newsroom/press-releases/tim-ryan-on-how-pwc-is-changing-way-we-work.html.
16. "2022 Flex Impact Award Honorees," Diversity & Flexibility Alliance.
17. Flynn, interview with the author.

7. How Will You Integrate Flexibility into Your Culture?

1. Alison King, "From Sage on the Stage to Guide on the Side," *College Teaching*, 41, no. 1 (Winter 1993): 30–35.
2. Heidi K. Gardner, *Smart Collaboration: How Professionals and Their Firms Succeed by Breaking Down Silos* (Harvard Business Review Press, 2017).
3. Keith E. Ferrazzi, "Boost Your Collaboration to Become a Top Remote and Hybrid Working Team," *World Economic Forum*, April 14, 2023, https://www.weforum.org/agenda/2023/04/remote-hybrid-working-collaboration/.
4. Ferrazzi, "Boost Your Collaboration."
5. Ferrazzi, "Boost Your Collaboration."
6. Gardner, *Smart Collaboration*.
7. Grace Speights, interview with the author, April 25, 2023.
8. Vipula Gandhi, "Innovative Insights: Cultivating People, Purpose, and Productivity in the Hybrid Workplace," *Diversity & Flexibility Alliance 2022 Annual Conference: Cultivating A Holistic Work Culture: The Power of People, Purpose, and Productivity*, November 3, 2022.
9. Ellen Kaye Fleishhacker, "It's Time to Reimagine the Workplace: Companies and Firms Blazing the Trail—Flex Impact Awards," *Diversity & Flexibility Alliance 2021 Annual Conference: Reflect. Reimagine. Recalibrate. Paving the Way to Inclusive Flexibility*, November 3, 2021.
10. Work Trend Index Special Report:"Hybrid Work Is Just Work. Are We Doing It Wrong?," *Microsoft*, September 22, 2022, https://www.microsoft.com/en-us/worklab/work-trend-index/hybrid-work-is-just-work.
11. "How to Get More Done with Fewer Meetings," *Dropbox*, accessed April 25, 2023, https://experience.dropbox.com/resources/get-more-done-with-fewer-meetings.
12. Sylvia Ann Hewlett, *Executive Presence: The Missing Link Between Merit and Success* (Harper Business, 2014).
13. Eve Howard, interview with the author, April 17, 2023.
14. Speights, interview with the author.
15. Speights, interview with the author.
16. Nancy Laben, interview with the author, April 11, 2023.
17. Kim Koopersmith, interview with the author, May 19, 2023.
18. Laben, interview with the author.

19. Speights, interview with the author.
20. Jami McKeon, "Secrets to Success: Reflecting on Strategies for Advancing More Women to Leadership," *Diversity & Flexibility Alliance 2021 Annual Conference: Reflect. Reimagine. Recalibrate. Paving the Way to Inclusive Flexibility,* November 3, 2021.
21. Koopersmith, interview with the author.
22. Work Trend Index Annual Report:"Great Expectations: Making Hybrid Work Work," *Microsoft,* March 16, 2022, https://www.microsoft.com/en-us/worklab/work-trend-index/great-expectations-making-hybrid-work-work/.
23. Daniel Friedland, MD, *Leading Well from Within: A Neuroscience and Mindfulness-Based Framework for Conscious Leadership* (SuperSmartHealth, 2016): 53.
24. Austin Suellentrop and E. Beth Bauman, "How Influential Is a Good Manager?," *Gallup,* November 11, 2022, https://www.gallup.com/cliftonstrengths/en/350423/influential-good-manager.aspx.
25. Laben, interview with the author.

8. How Will You Measure, Monitor, and Iterate Over Time?

1. Gleb Tsipursky, "How to Measure the Success of Your Hybrid Work Model," *Medium,* March 11, 2023, https://medium.datadriveninvestor.com/how-to-measure-the-success-of-your-hybrid-work-model-51b01ea58284.
2. "Executives Feel the Strain of Leading in the 'New Normal,'" *Future Forum Pulse,* Fall 2022, https://futureforum.com/wp-content/uploads/2022/10/Future-Forum-Pulse-Report-Fall-2022.pdf.
3. Grace Speights, interview with the author, April 25, 2023.
4. Jami McKeon, "Secrets to Success: Reflecting on Strategies for Advancing More Women to Leadership," *Diversity & Flexibility Alliance 2021 Annual Conference: Reflect. Reimagine. Recalibrate. Paving the Way to Inclusive Flexibility,* November 3, 2021.
5. "Work Trend Index Special Report: Hybrid Work Is Just Work. Are We Doing It Wrong?" *Microsoft,* September 22, 2022, https://www.microsoft.com/en-us/worklab/work-trend-index/hybrid-work-is-just-work.
6. "Hybrid Work Is Just Work," *Microsoft.*
7. Amy Richman, Arlene Johnson, and Karen Noble, "Business Impacts of Flexibility: An Imperative for Expansion," *Corporate Voices for Working Families,* February 2011, https://www.canada.ca/content/dam/canada/employment-social-development/migration/documents/PDFS/BusinessImpactsofFlexibility_March2011.pdf.
8. Richman, Johnson, and Noble, "Business Impacts of Flexibility."
9. Richman, Johnson, and Noble, "Business Impacts of Flexibility."
10. Jami McKeon, "Advancing More Women to Leadership."
11. Simon Sinek, *Start with Why: How Great Leaders Inspire Everyone to Take Action* (New York: Portfolio, 2011), 2–7.
12. "Law Firm Flexibility Benchmarking Study 2022," *Diversity & Flexibility Alliance,* 2022.

13. Don Smith, "2022 Flexibility Benchmarking Summit," *Diversity & Flexibility Alliance 2022 Flexibility Benchmarking Summit*, April 4, 2023.

9. Putting the Flex Success Framework into Practice

1. Jason St. John, interview with the author, April 20, 2023.
2. Mike Valentine, interview with the author, September 5, 2023.

10. The Future of Flexibility

1. "What Is Employee Well-Being? And Why Does It Matter?," *Gallup*, accessed September 2023, https://www.gallup.com/workplace/404105/importance-of-employee-well-being.aspx.aspx.
2. "One Third of Your Life Is Spent at Work," *Gettysburg College*, accessed September 2023, https://www.gettysburg.edu/news/stories?id=79db7b34-630c-4f49-ad32-4ab9ea48e72b.
3. "State of the Global Workplace Report—2023 Report," Gallup, accessed February 2023, https://www.gallup.com/workplace/349484/state-of-the-global-workplace.aspx#ite-506924.
4. Colleen Reilly, "Well-Being Positively Impacts Firm Performance," *Forbes*, June 9, 2020, https://www.forbes.com/sites/colleenreilly/2020/06/09/wellbeing-positively-impacts-firm-performance/.
5. "The US Surgeon General's Framework for Workplace Mental Health and Well-Being," *Office of the US Surgeon General*, 2022, https://www.hhs.gov/sites/default/files/workplace-mental-health-well-being.pdf.
6. "Framework for Workplace Mental Health," *Office of the US Surgeon General*.
7. Amy J. Wilson, "Our Workplaces Are Not Okay: New State of Workplace Empathy Report," *LinkedIn*, May 19, 2023, https://www.linkedin.com/pulse/our-workplaces-okay-new-state-workplace-empathy-amy-j-wilson-frsa/.
8. "Turn Anxiety Into Power: A 3-Step Process to Master Your Emotions From a Harvard Psychologist with Dr. Luana Marques," *The Mel Robbins Podcast*, July 20, 2023, https://www.melrobbins.com/podcasts/episode-85.
9. "Speaking of Psychology: Why We're Burned Out and What to Do about It, with Christina Maslach, PhD," *American Psychological Association (APA)*, July 2021, https://www.apa.org/news/podcasts/speaking-of-psychology/burnout.
10. "Amid Spiking Burnout, Workplace Flexibility Fuels Company Culture and Productivity: Winter Snapshot," *Future Forum Pulse*, Winter 2022/2023, https://futureforum.com/wp-content/uploads/2023/02/Future-Forum-Pulse-Report-Winter-2022-2023.pdf.
11. "Burn-Out an 'Occupational Phenomenon': International Classification of Diseases," *World Health Organization*, May 28, 2019, https://www.who.int/news/item/28-05-2019-burn-out-an-occupational-phenomenon-international-classification-of-diseases.

12. Francesca Di Meglio, "Burnout: Biggest Threat to Employee Engagement," *Human Resources Exchange Network*, April 5, 2023, https://www.hrexchangenetwork.com/employee-engagement/articles/the-biggest-threat-to-employee-engagement-is-burnout.

13. Tony Bond, "Belonging in the Workplace: What Does It Mean and Why Does It Matter?," *Great Place to Work*, June 16, 2022, https://www.greatplacetowork.com/resources/blog/belonging-in-the-workplace-what-does-it-mean-and-why-does-it-matter.

14. "Framework for Workplace Mental Health," *Office of the US Surgeon General*.

15. Laura Sherbin and Ripa Rashid, "Diversity Doesn't Stick Without Inclusion," *Harvard Business Review*, February 1, 2017, https://hbr.org/2017/02/diversity-doesnt-stick-without-inclusion.

16. Bond, "Belonging in the Workplace."

17. Lauren Croft, "Employee Wellbeing Is Now a 'Positive Legal Obligation'—and One that Needs to Be Met," *Lawyers Weekly*, March 27, 2023, https://www.lawyersweekly.com.au/biglaw/36978-employee-well-being-is-now-a-positive-legal-obligation-and-one-that-needs-to-be-met.

18. Joe Krzywicki, interview with the author, September 11, 2023.

19. Naina Dhingra, Andrew Samo, Bill Schaninger, and Matt Schrimper, "Help Your Employees Find Purpose—or Watch Them Leave," *McKinsey & Company*, April 5, 2021, https://www.mckinsey.com/capabilities/people-and-organizational-performance/our-insights/help-your-employees-find-purpose-or-watch-them-leave.

20. Dhingra, Samo, Schaninger, and Schrimper, "Help Your Employees Find Purpose."

21. "Below Expectations: Employers Not Meeting Training Expectations of Workers," *American Staffing Association*, January 20, 2022, https://americanstaffing.net/posts/2022/01/20/employers-not-meeting-training-expectations-of-workers/.

22. "APA Survey Finds Feeling Valued at Work Linked to Well-Being and Performance," *APA*, 2012, https://www.apa.org/news/press/releases/2012/03/well-being.

23. "Below Expectations," *American Staffing Association*.

24. "Feeling Valued at Work Linked to Well-Being," *APA*.

25. "Feeling Valued at Work Linked to Well-Being," *APA*.

26. "Law Firm Flexibility Benchmarking Study 2022," *Diversity & Flexibility Alliance*, 2022.

27. "Law Firm Flexibility Benchmarking Study 2022," *Diversity & Flexibility Alliance*.

28. "Women @ Work 2023: A Global Outlook," *Deloitte*, 2023, https://www.deloitte.com/global/en/issues/work/content/women-at-work-global-outlook-2023.html.

29. "Women @ Work 2023," *Deloitte*.

30. Abby McCain, "22 Telling Employee Wellness Statistics [2023]: How Many Companies Have Wellness Programs," *Zippia*, November 14, 2022, https://www.zippia.com/advice/employee-wellness-statistics/.

31. Reilly, "Well-Being Positively Impacts Firm Performance."

32. "Speaking of Psychology," *APA*.

33. "Flexibility Fuels Company Culture and Productivity," *Future Forum Pulse.*
34. "Flexibility Fuels Company Culture and Productivity," *Future Forum Pulse.*

Conclusions

1. Liz Fealy and Roselyn Feinsod, "How Can a Rebalance of Power Help Re-Energize Your Workforce?," *EY*, September 12, 2023, https://www.ey.com/en_gl/workforce/work-reimagined-survey.
2. Joe Krzywicki, interview with the author, September 11, 2023.
3. Peter Drucker, *Managing in Turbulent Times*, (New York: Harper & Row, 1980), x.
4. "21 of Maya Angelou's Best Quotes to Inspire," *Harper's Bazaar*, May 22, 2017, https://www.harpersbazaar.com/culture/features/a9874244/best-maya-angelou-quotes/.

INDEX

state of flexibility committee 105
The State of Organizations 2023 7
State of the Global Workplace 2023 29
static vs. dynamic 46
Statista 10
Stay Firms vs. Go Firms 11, 23
stay interviews 154, 191
stigma against flexibility. *See* bias against
    flexibility
St. John, Jason 96, 165–74
strength preservation 76–77, 80–81. *See*
    also non-negotiables
stress 19–20, 184, 197
structure 78
successes, celebrating 163
support 6
Surgeon General 19, 22, 182, 186
surveys 58, 149, 153–54, 172, 178–79
sustainability xiv
  commuting 2, 31
systems 70
Systems, Applications & Products in Data
    Processing (SAP) 70

T

talent vii. *See also* mentoring;
    professional deveopment;
    recruitment; retention
task force 170–71
Teams. *See* Microsoft Teams
technology 202
  acceleration 9
  app 171
  applications xv
  artificial intelligence xiii, 9
  automation xiii
  development xii–xiii, 2–3
  flexibility applications 106–8
  intranet 174
  resources 59, 70, 106–8, 174
  training 106–8, 174
*The Telecommunications–Transportation
    Tradeoff* 2
telecommuting 2–4. *See also* virtual work
Teller, Eric (Astro) 9
tenure requirement 102

Thomson Reuters Institute 11, 23
Thomson West 19
time policies. *See* flexible time policies
town hall 115
training 131, 171, 191
  leadership 117, 118, 123, 162, 166
  technology 106–7, 174
travel viii, 170, 174
true-up policy 104
turnover. *See* retention
*2022 Practice Forward Report: Where
    Does the Legal Profession Go
    from Here?* 19, 22, 42
*2022 Report on the State of the Legal
    Market* 11, 23

U

unconscious bias 34, 36, 42, 152
  assumed similarity bias 43–45
  confirmation bias 45, 138–39
  groupthink 159
  proximity bias 42, 138
  rosy retrospection 159
underlying assumptions 54
Upwork 10
US Army War College 8
US Surgeon General 19, 22, 182, 186
*The US Surgeon General's Framework
    for Workplace Mental Health and
    Well-Being* 19, 182

V

vagueness vs. flexibility 37
Valentine, Mike x, 175–79
value shift 185
Vanity Fair 4
virtual gatherings 25
virtual work 165–67, 188
  concerns xiii
  COVID-19, and x–xii, 6–7, 13–14, 15
  flexibility and xiii–xiv
  history 2–3
  personal experience ix
  productivity 22, 140
  technology 9, 15
  transition vii, 201

ABOUT THE AUTHOR

Manar Sweillam Morales is a national thought leader and visionary on building human-centered workplace cultures at the intersection of diversity, flexibility, and well-being. As the founder and CEO of the Diversity & Flexibility Alliance, Manar is on a mission to empower organizations to unlock their full potential by creating inclusive environments, implementing effective flexible work strategies, and prioritizing holistic employee well-being.

For nearly 20 years, Manar has been collaborating with leading organizations to drive meaningful culture change and business results. Through the Alliance's cutting-edge research, strategic advisory services, and vibrant peer network, Manar and her team provide practical, customizable solutions that help members attract and retain diverse talent, enhance engagement and innovation, and navigate the ever-changing world of work with agility and purpose.

A sought-after speaker, author, and trusted advisor, Manar's thought leadership and impact have been widely recognized. She is a recipient of the 2023 President's Lifetime Achievement Award and a member of the President's Council of Cornell Women and the International Women's Forum. Her work has been featured in major publications including *Harvard Business Review* and *Fast Company*. As a passionate advocate for inclusion, flexibility, and well-being, Manar is committed to creating a future where every individual can thrive and every organization can reach its full potential.